Index to the Superior Court Records

of

Sonoma County, California

Volume 1:
1880–1889

Sonoma County
Genealogical Society, Inc.

HERITAGE BOOKS
2017

HERITAGE BOOKS

AN IMPRINT OF HERITAGE BOOKS, INC.

Books, CDs, and more—Worldwide

For our listing of thousands of titles see our website
at
www.HeritageBooks.com

Published 2017 by
HERITAGE BOOKS, INC.
Publishing Division
5810 Ruatan Street
Berwyn Heights, Md. 20740

International Standard Book Number
Paperbound: 978-0-7884-5756-2

Contents

Index to the Superior Court Records
of Sonoma County, California, 1880–1889

In 2014, the Friends of Santa Rosa Libraries funded a project to convert the microfilm images of the existing Sonoma County Superior Court record indices to digital images. Volunteers from the Sonoma County Genealogical Society (SCGS) transcribed the records of the General Plaintiff Index, volume 2, and the General Defendant Index, volume 2, from these digital images to produce the first rough draft of an index in late 2016. Volunteers also abstracted information from eight volumes of original Sonoma County Superior Court Registers of Actions (volumes 1–8) for the same time period capturing each suit's cause, when noted, Register of Actions volume and page number reference(s), and action date. The action date is the date of the first action in each suit as recorded in the Registers of Actions. For civil suits, this is usually the date the initial complaint was filed, and for criminal suits, it is usually the date the information or indictment was filed. For suits that were transferred or appealed to the Superior Court, it is usually the date the suit's transcript and papers from the lower Court were filed.

A total of 2337 Sonoma County Superior Court suits for the years 1880 through 1889 are indexed in this publication. The suits are numbered 1 to 2326 with 11 suits using non-integers (316½, 317½, 551½, 732½, 859½, 1053½, 1186½, 1425½, 1516½, 1759½, and 2023½). Both civil and criminal cases are included.

Microfilm copies of the original Sonoma County Superior Court suit papers are available at the Archived Records Office of the Sonoma County Superior Court in Santa Rosa. Some original Sonoma County Superior Court suit papers are available at the California State Archives in Sacramento, but the majority of the original papers were destroyed after microfilming.

Superior Courts Established by the 1879 California State Constitution
The delegates of the second California State Constitutional Convention of 1878–1879 produced a second California State Constitution that was adopted in Convention at Sacramento on 3 March 1879 and ratified by a vote of the People of the State of California on 7 May 1879.[1] Article XXII, section 3 of this Constitution abolished all courts then existing, including the District and County Courts, except for the Justices' and Police Courts, and Article VI, section 1 established a new judicial department composed of a Supreme Court, Superior Courts, Justices of the Peace, and such inferior Courts as the Legislature may establish in any incorporated city or town, or city and county. All records, books, papers, and proceedings from the abolished Courts were to be transferred to the new Courts on 1 January 1880. Article VI, section 6 directed that two Superior Court judges were to be elected for Sonoma County.

---

[1] *The Statutes of California Passed at the Twenty-Third Session of the Legislature, 1880, began on Monday, January Fifth, and Ended on Friday, April Sixteenth, One Thousand Eight Hundred and Eighty* (Sacramento: State Office, J. D. Young, Supt. State Printing, 1880), xxiii–xlv; digital images, *California State Assembly Office of the Chief Clerk* (http://clerk.assembly.ca.gov : accessed 11 May 2015).

Superior Court Jurisdiction

Article VI, section 5 of the 1879 California State Constitution defined the jurisdiction of the newly established Superior Courts:

> The Superior Court shall have original jurisdiction in all cases in equity, and in all cases at law which involve the title or possession of real property, or the legality of any tax, impost, assessment, toll, or municipal fine, and in all other cases in which the demand, exclusive of interest, or the value of the property in controversy, amounts to three hundred dollars, and in all criminal cases amounting to felony, and cases of misdemeanor not otherwise provided for; of actions of forcible entry and detainer; of proceedings in insolvency; of actions to prevent or abate a nuisance; of all matters of probate; of divorce and for annulment of marriage; and of all such special cases and proceedings as are not otherwise provided for. And said Court shall have the power of naturalization, and to issue papers therefor. They shall have appellate jurisdiction in such cases arising in Justices' and other inferior Courts in their respective counties as may be prescribed by law. They shall always be open (legal holidays and non-judicial days excepted), and their process shall extend to all parts of the State; *provided*, that all actions for the recovery of the possession of, quieting the title to, or for the enforcement of liens upon real estate, shall be commenced in the county in which the real estate, or any part thereof affected by such action or actions, is situated. Said Courts, and their Judges, shall have power to issue writs of mandamus, certiorari, prohibition, quo warranto, and habeas corpus, on petition by or on behalf of any person in actual custody in their respective counties. Injunctions and writs of prohibition may be issued and served on legal holidays and non-judicial days.[2]

Sonoma County Superior Court's First Meeting

The Superior Court of Sonoma County convened for the first time on 5 January 1880 with Judges Jackson Temple and John G. Pressley *in banc*.[3] After presenting their commissions and oaths of office, the two judges divided the business of the Court into two departments. Department 1 presided over by Judge Temple was apportioned all business appertaining to the administration of the estates of deceased persons' estates, guardianships of minors and incompetent persons, all criminal proceedings, and all appellate jurisdiction of the Superior Court, while Department 2 presided over by Judge Pressley was apportioned all other business of the Court.

---

[2] *The Statutes of California Passed at the Twenty-Third Session of the Legislature, 1880, began on Monday, January Fifth, and Ended on Friday, April Sixteenth, One Thousand Eight Hundred and Eighty*, xxxi.

[3] Sonoma County, California, Superior Court, Department 1, Minutes Book A: 1–5, minutes of the proceedings of the Court, 5 January 1880; Sonoma County Archives, Santa Rosa.

How to Use This Index

The researcher should first locate the name of the person or entity in the first section of this publication, a comprehensive name index of Sonoma County Superior Court suits numbered 1 to 2326. To the right of each name in this section are two columns that give the Sonoma County Superior Court suit number to which the person or entity is party, either as plaintiff or defendant. The researcher should then locate the desired suit number in the second section of this publication. Each entry in the second section lists the suit number, plaintiffs and defendants in the suit, the cause of the suit, the Register of Actions volume and page reference(s), and action date.

The researcher should then examine the appropriate Register of Actions volume and page(s) to determine what actions were taken in the suit and when each occurred. These Registers of Actions are housed at the Sonoma County Archives. Microfilm copies of the original suit court papers can be viewed at the Archived Records Office of the Sonoma County Superior Court in Santa Rosa. Other avenues of research include examining the Superior Court Minute Books housed at the Sonoma County Archives during the time frame in which the suit was in process or scanning the local newspapers of the period such as the *Sonoma Democrat*, the *Santa Rosa Daily Democrat*, the *Petaluma Journal and Argus*, the *Healdsburg Enterprise*, and the *Russian River Flag* during that same time frame for information on the suit. Occasionally enlightening, sometimes humorous accounts of court proceedings can be found there.

The names in the index are those generally given in the Registers of Actions for each suit. Spelling in the 19th century was not standardized, and names are spelled a multiple of ways even within each suit. The researcher is advised to look for all possible variations of the name for which they are searching in the index. The handwriting in the original Superior Court indices, Registers of Actions, and court papers varied, but was generally quite good. The transcribers did their best; however, errors may have occurred. Fictitious names such as John Doe and Richard Roe are not indexed in this publication.

Abbreviations/Latin terms/Marks

-	a hyphen after a surname, such as Adams, -, indicates that the forename of the person was not given in the records.
ad litem	a Latin term meaning "for the suit," "for the purposes of the suit," or "pending the suit." A guardian *ad litem* is a guardian appointed to prosecute or defend a suit on behalf of a party incapacitated by infancy or otherwise.[4]
Adm.	administrator/administratrix
Adms.	Administrators
aka	also known as
Bro./Bros.	brother/brothers
Co.	company or county
dba	does business as
dec'd	deceased
Est.	estate
et al.	an abbreviation of either the Latin term *et alius* meaning "and another" or *et alii* meaning "and others."[5]
et als.	sometimes written as the plural of et al.[6]
ex officio	a Latin term meaning "from office," "by virtue of the office," or "without any other warrant or appointment than that resulting from the holding of a particular office." Powers may be exercised by an officer which are not specifically conferred upon him, but are necessarily implied in his office; these are *ex officio*.[7]
ex rel.	an abbreviation of the Latin term *ex relatione* meaning "upon relation or information." Legal proceedings which are instituted by the attorney general or other proper person in the name and behalf of the state, but on the information and at the instigation of an individual who has a private interest in the matter, are said to be taken "on the relation" (ex rel.) of such person, who is called the relator.[8]
Pub.	Public

---

[4] Henry Campbell Black, *A Dictionary of Law Containing Definitions of the Terms and Phrases of American and English Jurisprudence, Ancient and Modern* (St. Paul, Minnesota: West Publishing Co., 1891), 33.

[5] Black, *A Dictionary of Law*, 438.

[6] Black, *A Dictionary of Law*, 438.

[7] Black, *A Dictionary of Law*, 445.

[8] Black, *A Dictionary of Law*, 447.

Law Terms

Assumpsit: an action for the recovery of damages by reason of the breach or non-performance of a simple contract, either express or implied, and whether made orally or in writing.[9]

Attachment: the act or process of taking, apprehending, or seizing persons or property, by virtue of a writ, summons, or other judicial order, and bringing the same into the custody of the law. Used either for the purpose of bringing a person before the court, of acquiring jurisdiction over the property seized, to compel an appearance, to furnish security for debt or costs, or to arrest a fund in the hands of a third person who may become liable to pay it over.[10]

Certiorari: a type of writ issued by a superior court directing an inferior court to send up to the former some pending proceeding, or all the record and proceedings in a cause before verdict, with its certificate to the correctness and completeness of the record, for review or trial; or it may serve to bring up the record of a case already terminated below, if the inferior court is one not of record, or in cases where the procedure is not according to the course of the common law.[11]

Detainer: the act or the juridical fact of withholding from a person lawfully entitled the possession of land or goods, or the restraint of a man's personal liberty against his will. In practice, it is a writ or instrument issued or made by a competent officer, authorizing the keeper of a prison to keep in his custody a person therein named.[12]

Ejectment: the common-law term for civil action to recover the possession of or title to land. Originally, an ejectment was concerned with the recovery of possession of land, for example, against a defaulting tenant or a trespasser, who did not have or no longer had any right to remain there.[13]

Grand larceny: is larceny committed in either of the following cases: 1.) When the property taken is of a value exceeding fifty dollars, 2.) When the property is taken from the person of another, and 3.) When the property taken is a bicycle, horse, mare, gelding, cow, steer, bull, calf, mule, jack, or jenny.[14]

---

[9] *Wikisource* (https://en.wikisource.org), "1911 Encyclopaedia Britannica/Assumpsit," rev. 20:52, 13 November 2013.

[10] Black, *A Dictionary of Law*, 102.

[11] Black, *A Dictionary of Law*, 187.

[12] Black, *A Dictionary of Law*, 361.

[13] *Wikipedia* (https://en.wikipedia.org), "Ejectment," rev. 13:26, 11 May 2015.

[14] James H. Deering, editor, Walter S. Brann, and R. M. Sims, *The Penal Code of California. Enacted in 1872; As Amended up to and Including 1905, with Statutory History and Citation Digest up to and Including Volume 147, California Reports* (San Francisco: Bancroft-Whitney Company, 1906), 192; digital images, *Google Books* (http://books.google.com : accessed 13 January 2017).

Habeas corpus: the name given to a variety of writs having for their object to bring a party before a court or judge. In common usage, and whenever the words are used alone, they are understood to mean the *habeas corpus ad subjiciendum*, a writ directed to the person detaining another, and commanding him to produce the body of the prisoner, or person detained, with the day and cause of his caption and detention, to do, submit to, and receive whatsoever the judge or court awarding the writ shall consider in that behalf.[15]

Larceny: the felonious stealing, taking, carrying, leading, or driving away the personal property of another.[16]

Mandamus: a type of writ which issues from a court of superior jurisdiction and is directed to a private or municipal corporation, or any of its officers, or to an executive, administrative, or judicial officer, or to an inferior court, commanding the performance of a particular act therein specified, and belonging to his or their public, official, or ministerial duty, or directing the restoration of the complainant to rights or privileges of which he has been illegally deprived.[17]

Petit larceny: is larceny committed that is not grand larceny.[18]

Quiet title: a lawsuit to establish a party's title to real property, or personal property having a title, against anyone and everyone, and thus "quiet" any challenges or claims to the title.[19]

Replevin or claim and delivery: a lawsuit that enables a person to get back personal property taken wrongfully or unlawfully, pending a final determination by a court of law, and get compensation for resulting losses.[20]

Sole trader: in 1852 the California legislature passed an Act giving married women the right to carry on and transact business under their own name and on their own account as sole traders.[21]

Trover: a form of lawsuit in common-law countries for recovery of damages for wrongful taking of personal property. Trover belongs to a series of remedies for such wrongful taking, its distinctive feature being recovery only for the value of whatever was taken, not for the recovery of the property itself (see replevin).[22]

---

[15] Black, *A Dictionary of Law*, 554.

[16] Deering, Brann, and Sims, *The Penal Code of California*, 191.

[17] Black, *A Dictionary of Law*, 748.

[18] Deering, Brann, and Sims, *The Penal Code of California*, 192.

[19] *Wikipedia* (https://en.wikipedia.org), "Quiet title," rev. 17:48, 12 July 2016.

[20] *Wikipedia* (https://en.wikipedia.org), "Replevin," rev. 05:39, 13 October 2016.

[21] *The Statutes of California, Passed at the Third Session of the Legislature, Begun on the Fifth of January, 1852, and Ended on the Fourth Day of May, 1852, at the Cities of Vallejo and Sacramento* (San Francisco: G. K. Fitch & Co. and V. E. Geiger & Co., State Printers, 1852), 101–102, Chapter XLII, "An Act to Authorize Married Women to Transact Business in Their Own Name as Sole Traders"; digital images, *California State Assembly Office of the Chief Clerk* (http://clerk.assembly.ca.gov : accessed 13 January 2017).

[22] *Wikipedia* (https://en.wikipedia.org), "Trover," rev. 18:00, 5 June 2016.

Jackson Temple (served 1880–1886)

Jackson Temple
Courtesy of the Supreme Court of California

On 20 May 1879 the Sonoma County Democratic party nominated Jackson Temple and J. G. Pressley as Sonoma County Superior Court judges.[23] Both men were elected by large majorities on 3 September 1879 for five-year terms over G. A. Johnson and J. B. Southard of the New Constitution party.[24] Sonoma County voters again elected Temple and Pressley on 4 November 1884 as Sonoma County Superior Court judges for six-year terms over their Republican opponents J. A. Barham and J. J. Henderson.[25] Two years later on 2 November 1886 California voters chose Jackson Temple as an associate justice of the California Supreme Court to fill out the unexpired term of E. M. Ross who had resigned. Judge Temple was the only Democrat on the State ticket who was elected, receiving "nearly 61,000 votes—the largest vote cast for any State candidate."[26] Governor Stoneman commissioned Judge Temple for this position on 13

---

[23] "Sonoma County Democrats—Another Arrest in Connection with the Murder of Paul Rieger," *Sacramento (California) Daily Record-Union*, 21 May 1879, p. 1, col. 5; digital image, *California Digital Newspaper Collection* (http://cdnc.ucr.edu : accessed 4 October 2015).

[24] "Official Vote of Sonoma County," *The Sonoma Democrat (Santa Rosa, California)*, 13 September 1879, p. 8, cols. 2–3; digital image, *California Digital Newspaper Collection* (http://cdnc.ucr.edu : accessed 10 December 2016).

[25] "Official Vote of Sonoma County," *The Sonoma Democrat (Santa Rosa, California)*, 15 November 1884, p. 2, cols. 4–5; digital image, *California Digital Newspaper Collection* (http://cdnc.ucr.edu : accessed 10 December 2016).

[26] "Latest Election Returns," *Daily Republican (Santa Rosa, California)*, 10 November 1886, p. 2, col. 1; microfilm, Sonoma County History and Genealogy Library, Santa Rosa. According to the official election returns, Temple received 108,655 votes while the Republican Noble Hamilton received 83,837, a majority of 24,818 votes. It does appear, however, that Judge Temple did receive more votes than any other State candidate. See "The Official Count," *Sacramento (California) Daily Record-Union*, 9 December 1886, p. 3, col. 2; digital image, *California Digital Newspaper Collection* (http://cdnc.ucr.edu : accessed 1 December 2016).

December 1886.[27] Judge Temple resigned as a Sonoma County Superior Court judge four days later.[28]

Jackson Temple was born on 11 August 1827 in Heath, Franklin County, Massachusetts, the son of David and Rosamond (Nims) Temple.[29] He died on 25 December 1902 in San Francisco, California and is buried in Santa Rosa Rural Cemetery, Santa Rosa, Sonoma County, California (Western Half Circle, plot 9).[30]

John Gotea Pressley (served 1880–1890)

John Gotea Pressley
Image Courtesy of the Williamsburgh Historical Museum

The Sonoma County Democratic party nominated J. G. Pressley as a Sonoma County Superior Court judge on 20 May 1879.[31] Sonoma County voters elected him by a large majority for a five-year term on 3 September 1879 over G. A. Johnson and J. B. Southard of the New Constitution party.[32] Judge Pressley was elected again on 4 November 1884 as a Sonoma County Superior Court judge for a six-year term over his Republican opponents J. A. Barham and J. J.

---

[27] Entry for Jackson Temple as a Justice of the Supreme Court, 13 December 1886; F3680-4, Executive Records, p. 47; Secretary of State Records, California State Archives, Sacramento.

[28] Hon. Jackson Temple to Governor George Stoneman, resignation letter, 17 December 1886; F3672:1368, Loose Documents; Resignations, Deaths, and Leaves of Absence, 1849-1959; Secretary of State Records, California State Archives, Sacramento.

[29] *Vital Records of Heath, Massachusetts to the Year 1850* (Boston: New England Historic Genealogical Society, 1915), 61.

[30] "Justice Jackson Temple Dies at McNutt Hospital," *The San Francisco (California) Call*, 27 December 1902, p. 4, cols. 1–3; digital image, *California Digital Newspaper Collection* (http://cdnc.ucr.edu : accessed 25 March 2015) and *Find A Grave*, database with images (http://www.findagrave.com : accessed 5 October 2015), memorial 29634580, Jackson Temple (1827–1902), Santa Rosa Rural Cemetery, Santa Rosa, Sonoma County, California; gravestone photograph by Jean Rhoades. His gravestone gives his death date as 24 December 1901.

[31] "Sonoma County Democrats—Another Arrest in Connection with the Murder of Paul Rieger," *Sacramento (California) Daily Record-Union*, 21 May 1879, p. 1, col. 5; digital image, *California Digital Newspaper Collection* (http://cdnc.ucr.edu : accessed 4 October 2015).

[32] "Official Vote of Sonoma County," *The Sonoma Democrat (Santa Rosa, California)*, 13 September 1879, p. 8, cols. 2–3; digital image, *California Digital Newspaper Collection* (http://cdnc.ucr.edu : accessed 10 December 2016).

Henderson.[33] He did not run again for Sonoma County Superior Court judge in the 1890 election.

John Gotea Pressley was born on 24 May 1833 in Williamsburg District, South Carolina, the son of John B. and Sarah (Gotea) Pressley.[34] He died of heart disease on 5 July 1895 while camping near Fort Ross, Sonoma County, California and is buried in Santa Rosa Rural Cemetery (Western Half Circle, plots E and F).[35]

Thomas Rutledge (served 1886–1888)

Thomas Rutledge
Image from the Santa Rosa Republican newspaper[36]

Governor Stoneman commissioned Thomas Rutledge as a Sonoma County Superior Court judge on 20 December 1886 upon the resignation of Jackson Temple.[37] Judge Rutledge rendered his first decision from the Sonoma County Superior Court bench on 23 December 1886 in the case of Cooper vs. Bishop.[38] Article VI, section 6 of the 1879 California State Constitution stipulated that a judge appointed to fill a Superior Court judge vacancy was to only serve until the next general election. At that time, a judge would be elected to fill out the rest of the original

[33] "Official Vote of Sonoma County," *The Sonoma Democrat (Santa Rosa, California)*, 15 November 1884, p. 2, cols. 4–5; digital image, *California Digital Newspaper Collection* (http://cdnc.ucr.edu : accessed 10 December 2016).

[34] *An Illustrated History of Sonoma County. Containing a History of the County of Sonoma from the Earliest Period of its Occupancy to the Present Time, together with Glimpses of its Prospective Future; with profuse Illustrations of its Beautiful Scenery, Full-Page Portraits of some of its most Eminent Men, and Biographical Mention of Many of its Pioneers and also of Prominent Citizens of To-day* (Chicago: The Lewis Publishing Company, 1889), 580.

[35] Sonoma County, California, Register of Deaths, 40: 103, John Gotea Pressley, 5 July 1895; Sonoma County Archives, Santa Rosa and *Find A Grave*, database with images (http://www.findagrave.com : accessed 3 November 2016), memorial 16777037, LTC John Gotea Pressley (1833–1895), Santa Rosa Rural Cemetery, Santa Rosa, Sonoma County, California; gravestone photograph by G.Photographer.

[36] "Good Man Laid to his Final Rest," *Santa Rosa (California) Republican*, 16 November 1904, p. 3, cols. 3–4; microfilm, Sonoma County History and Genealogy Library, Santa Rosa.

[37] Entry for Thomas Rutledge as a Superior Court Judge, 20 December 1886; F3680-5, Executive Records, p. 127; Secretary of State Records, California State Archives, Sacramento.

[38] "Judge Rutledge's First Decision," *Daily Republican (Santa Rosa, California)*, 23 December 1886, p. 3, col. 1; microfilm, Sonoma County History and Genealogy Library, Santa Rosa.

unexpired term.[39] Consequently, Rutledge, a Democrat, ran against S. K. Dougherty, a Republican, in the general election of 6 November 1888, but lost to him by 44 votes, thus ending his tenure as a Sonoma County Superior Court judge.[40]

Thomas Rutledge was born on 21 November 1834 in Ireland, the son of Patrick and Mary Rutledge.[41] He arrived in New York City from Dublin, Ireland along with his parents, three brothers, and a sister on 25 July 1848 aboard the Ship *Juno*.[42] He came to Santa Rosa in 1877 via Wisconsin and Minnesota.[43] Judge Rutledge died of chronic Bright's disease on 14 November 1904 in Sonoma County, California and is buried in Santa Rosa Rural Cemetery (Western Half Circle, plot J).[44]

Samuel Kimmel Dougherty (served 1888–1902)

Samuel Kimmel Dougherty
Image from the Illustrated Atlas of Sonoma County, California[45]

Governor Waterman commissioned S. K. Dougherty as a Sonoma County Superior Court judge on 27 November 1888 to fill out the remaining unexpired term of Jackson Temple ending in

---

[39] *The Statutes of California Passed at the Twenty-Third Session of the Legislature, 1880, began on Monday, January Fifth, and Ended on Friday, April Sixteenth, One Thousand Eight Hundred and Eighty*, xxxi.

[40] "Official Vote of Sonoma County for 1888," *The Sonoma County Tribune (Healdsburg, California)*, 17 November 1888, p. 4, cols. 3–5; digital image, *California Digital Newspaper Collection* (http://cdnc.ucr.edu : accessed 10 December 2016).

[41] *Find A Grave*, database with images (http://www.findagrave.com : accessed 3 November 2016), memorial 29603765, Thomas Rutledge (1834–1904), Santa Rosa Rural Cemetery, Santa Rosa, Sonoma County, California; gravestone photograph by Tracy H.

[42] "New York, Passenger Lists, 1820–1957," database and images, *Ancestry.com* (http://www.ancestry.com : accessed 30 November 2016), manifest, Ship *Juno*, 25 July 1848, penned p. 4, line 51, Thomas Rutladge [sic], age 13; citing National Archives microfilm publication M237, roll 74.

[43] *An Illustrated History of Sonoma County*, 690.

[44] Sonoma County, California, Register of Deaths, 43: 120, Thomas Rutledge, 14 November 1904; Sonoma County Archives, Santa Rosa and *Find A Grave*, memorial 29603765, Thomas Rutledge (1834–1904), Santa Rosa Rural Cemetery, Santa Rosa, Sonoma County, California; gravestone photograph by Tracy H.

[45] *Illustrated Atlas of Sonoma County, California Compiled and Published from Personal Examinations, Official Records and Actual Surveys* (Santa Rosa, California: Reynolds & Proctor, [1898]), 2.

January 1891 after Judge Dougherty defeated Thomas Rutledge in the 6 November 1888 general election.[46] Two years later on 4 November 1890 Sonoma County voters elected Judge Dougherty for a full six-year term as a Sonoma County Superior Court judge.[47] Governor Waterman commissioned him on 15 December 1890.[48] Voters again elected Judge Dougherty for another six-year term on 3 November 1896, and he served as a Sonoma County Superior Court judge through 1902.[49]

Samuel Kimmel Dougherty was born on 2 July 1851 in Berrien Springs, Berrien County, Michigan, the son of William and Julia Ann (Kimmel) Dougherty.[50] He died of tuberculous meningitis on 13 October 1916 in Santa Rosa, Sonoma County, California and is buried in Cypress Hill Memorial Park, Petaluma, Sonoma County, California.[51]

[46] Entry for S. K. Dougherty as a Sonoma County Superior Court Judge, 27 November 1888; F3680-4, Executive Records, p. 245; Secretary of State Records, California State Archives, Sacramento.

[47] "Local News," *Santa Rosa (California) Daily Democrat*, 15 November 1890, p. 1, cols. 2–3; digital image, *California Digital Newspaper Collection* (http://cdnc.ucr.edu : accessed 10 December 2016).

[48] Entry for S. K. Dougherty as a Sonoma County Superior Court Judge, 15 December 1890; F3680-4, Executive Records, p. 245; Secretary of State Records, California State Archives, Sacramento.

[49] "The Vote of Sonoma County, California, as Canvassed by the Board of Supervisors—Election Held November 3, 1896," *The Sonoma Democrat (Santa Rosa, California)*, 14 November 1896, p. 6, cols. 3–7; microfilm, Sonoma County History and Genealogy Library, Santa Rosa.

[50] Oscar T. Shuck, editor, *History of the Bench and Bar of California Being Biographies of Many Remarkable Men, a Store of Humorous and Pathetic Recollections, Accounts of Important Legislation and Extraordinary Cases, Comprehending the Judicial History of the State* (Los Angeles, California: The Commercial Printing House, 1901), 691; digital images, *Google Books* (http://books.google.com : accessed 31 October 2016).

[51] City of Santa Rosa, Sonoma County, California, Record of Deaths, 1906–1924, 60: 41, Samuel Kimmel Dougherty, 13 October 1916; Sonoma County Archives, Santa Rosa and *Find A Grave*, database with images (http://www.findagrave.com : accessed 3 November 2016), memorial 73805330, Samuel K. Dougherty (1851–1916), Cypress Hill Memorial Park, Petaluma, Sonoma County, California; gravestone photograph by Colletta.

Records Utilized in the Assembly of this Publication

1. General Index, Plaintiffs, volume 2, Superior Court, Sonoma County, housed at the Sonoma County Archives, Santa Rosa (Sonoma County Archives accession # 2566). This volume is also available on microfilm and microfiche at the Archived Records Office of the Sonoma County Superior Court as "Civil Index, Superior Court, A–Z, Plaintiffs, 1878-1894."

2. General Index, Defendants, volume 2, Superior Court, Sonoma County, housed at the Sonoma County Archives, Santa Rosa (Sonoma County Archives accession # 2567). This volume is also available on microfilm and microfiche at the Archived Records Office of the Sonoma County Superior Court as "Civil Index, Superior Court, A–Z, Defendants, 1878-1894."

3. Register of Actions, Superior Court, Sonoma County, volumes 1 through 8, housed at the Sonoma County Archives, Santa Rosa. These volumes contain a listing of actions in each of the Superior Court civil and criminal suits and the court fees associated with each suit.

a. Volume 1, suit numbers 1 to 228, 1 January 1880 to 20 September 1880, 648 stamped pages, pages 1, 26–31, and 648 are blank, plaintiff and defendant indices, Sonoma County Archives accession # 1651.

b. Volume 2, suit numbers 229 to 525, 21 June 1880 to 5 December 1881, 648 stamped pages, pages 1 and 644–648 are blank, plaintiff and defendant indices, Sonoma County Archives accession # 1646.

c. Volume 3, suit numbers 526 to 859, 13 December 1881 to 28 May 1883, 368 stamped pages, stamped only on left-hand page, page 367 is missing, page 368 is blank, plaintiff and defendant indices, Sonoma County Archives accession # 1728.

d. Volume 4, suit numbers 860 to 1186½, 2 June 1883 to 14 February 1885, 370 stamped pages, pages 368–369 are missing, pages 363, 367, and 370 are blank, plaintiff and defendant indices, Sonoma County Archives accession # 1724.

e. Volume 5, suit numbers 1187 to 1513, 16 February 1885 to 22 June 1886, 370 stamped pages, pages 156 and 359–370 are blank, plaintiff and defendant indices, Sonoma County Archives accession # 1770.

f. Volume 6, suit numbers 1514 to 1865, 26 June 1886 to 27 December 1887, 380 stamped pages, pages 378–379 are missing, page 380 is blank, plaintiff and defendant indices, Sonoma County Archives accession # 1638.

g. Volume 7, suit numbers 1866 to 2240, 3 January 1888 to 23 September 1889, 384 stamped pages, plaintiff and defendant indices, Sonoma County Archives accession # 1601.

h. Volume 8, suit numbers 2241 to 2418½, 25 September 1889 to 28 May 1890, 189 stamped pages, pages 183–189 are blank, plaintiff and defendant indices, Sonoma County Archives accession # 1775.

Further Reading

Blume, William Wirt. "California Courts in Historical Perspective." *Hastings Law Journal* 22 (No. 1, November, 1970): 121–195.

Rose, Christine. *Courthouse Research for Family Historians: Your Guide to Genealogical Treasures.* San Jose, California: CR Publications, 2004.

Black, Henry Campbell. *A Dictionary of Law Containing Definitions of the Terms and Phrases of American and English Jurisprudence, Ancient and Modern*. 1st edition. St. Paul, Minnesota: West Publishing Co., 1891.

Digital images of California Statutes at *California State Assembly Office of the Chief Clerk* (http://clerk.assembly.ca.gov).

Acknowledgments

Project Coordinator
Steven Lovejoy

Abstractors
Shirley Flick
Joe Panaro
Steven Lovejoy

Person/Entity	Plaintiff Suit #	Defendant Suit #
A. F. Pauli & Co.	1687	
Abbot, J. M.		344
Abbott, George C.		358
Abbott, J. M.		358
Abraham, Casper	1514	
Ackerman, O. B.	377	
Adams, H. D. R.		2180
Adams, Hiram		992
Adams, James		358
Adams, John		2180
Adams, Joshua	1564	1690
Adamson, Belle		1004
Adamson, Isaac Newton	1004	
Adamson, M.		358
Adkins, W. S.		358
Adkisson, Joseph		226
Adler, David	1403	1138
Advent Church		358
African Methodist Episcopal Church of Petaluma, Trustees of	1355	
Ager, J. E.		358
Agnew, Letha Jane	1206	
Agster, John		724
Ahn, Mah		1016
Aiken Bros.		890
Aiken, H. S.		1832
Aiken, Henry		890
Aiken, Robert		358
Aiken, William		890
Aikin, Henry		1018
Aikin, Martha	1348	
Aikin, Matthew		1348
Aikin, William		1018
Aitken, Jane		181
Akers, Stephen	156	
Akin, Mat		1516
Albee, A. B.		1548
Alderson, Annie	602	
Alderson, H. E.		602
Alemany, Joseph S.		358

1

Person/Entity	Plaintiff Suit #	Defendant Suit #
Alescander, John		358
Alexander, Charles		1751
Alexander, Henry		1192
Alexander, Lawrence		1350, 1751
Alexander, Mary A.		1524
Alexander, Peter		441
Alexander, Thomas	2233	
Alexander, William		2190
Algreen, John		2011
Algren, Annie	1544	
Algren, John	1544	
Allen, Achilles		585
Allen, Ann W.		830
Allen, Ault	585	
Allen, B. B.	830	
Allen, C. H.		358
Allen, Elizabeth	1049	
Allen, Flora		358
Allen, George		1400
Allen, Henry		358
Allen, J.		1449
Allen, John	1857	1812
Allen, O. B.		1305
Allen, O. S.		358
Allen, Otis		358
Allen, R. B.		358
Allen, Robert	152	
Allen, S. I.	1298	
Allen, W. T.		1383, 1384, 1385, 1751
Alley, -	150	
Alley, Bowen & Co.	150	
Allman & Queen		631
Allman, George		631
Allman, John	631	
Allsopp, John F.	1009	
Alvarado, Joaquin		121
Amerman, H. J.	444	
Ames, C. G.		358
Ames, Charles G.	193	2261

Person/Entity	Plaintiff Suit #	Defendant Suit #
Ames, Charles S.		2030
Ames, George		2030
Ames, Isabella		2030
Ames, John F.		2030
Ames, Lucy	191	
Ames, Mary Ann	94	2030
Ames, Mary E.		1825
Ammon, L.		358
Anderson, Andrew		882
Anderson, Elizabeth	2081	
Anderson, John	1724	1513
Anderson, Mary A.	2315	
Anderson, Stewart		358
Anderson, W. H.		358
Anderson, W. L.		191, 358
Andrew (an Indian)	2317	
Andrews, James		358
Angel, B. M.		358
Anthony, John		358
Antonio, José		733
Antram, Mary	2298	
Appleton, Eliza	432	
Appleton, H.	432, 703	
Archambeau, Charles		509
Archambeau, Peter T.	970	
Archer, A. C.	1739	
Aredeau, J.	1137	
Arizona Lumber Company	1989	
Armstrong & Brown		1629, 1658
Armstrong, Catharine M.		2229
Armstrong, Eleanor		358
Armstrong, J. B.	723	1629, 1658, 1661, 2229
Armstrong, James B.		358
Armstrong, Lizzie		358, 2229
Armstrong, S.	167	358
Armstrong, Sheldon		2225
Arnold, G. W.		358
Arnold, George J.		358
Arnold, Peter		358

Person/Entity	Plaintiff Suit #	Defendant Suit #
Arnold, William		1067, 1080
Ashcraft, R. (Mrs.)		358
Ashley, C.	1486	
Ashley, William T.	422	
Ashurst, John H.	2118	
Atkins, Nancy J.	615	
Atkins, Nancy T.		426
Atkins, W. G.		615
Atkins, William G.	426	
Atterbury, William B.	207	
Atwater, H. H.	775	
Aulich, Charles G.		1282
Aulich, Mary J.		1282
Auradon, J.	2016	
Austin, Catherine		486
Austin, Charles		2245
Austin, M. A.		486
Austin, Percy	346	
Austin, Rosie		2245
Author, William C.		358
Ayers, David	2106	
Ayers, William		1461, 1538, 1547
Aylett, Alice D.		1369
Ayres, William		709, 712, 945
B. Linville & Son	13	
Bacigalupo, John		1676
Bacigalupo, Louis		1676
Bacigalupo, Luigi		1676
Bacigalupo, Natale		1676
Bacigalupo, Rosa		1676
Badger, Carrie E.	2185	
Badger, D.		358
Badger, H. L.	2284	
Badger, J.		358
Baggett, N. P.		2048
Bail, Adolph		1553
Bailey, M. C.		617
Bailey, Robert		1256
Bailey, S. N.	2093	

Person/Entity	Plaintiff Suit #	Defendant Suit #
Bailhache, John N.	242	162, 243, 655, 1234
Bailhache, Josephine	246, 574, 755	162, 655, 1234
Bailiff, J.		1846
Bailiff, John	1809	1600
Baker & Hamilton		844
Baker, Albert		68
Baker, Clara	2124	
Baker, Henry		358
Baker, Joseph		1701
Baker, Livingston L.		844
Baker, Theodore		2124
Baker, William		358
Baldwin, J. T.		1759½
Baldwin, John T.	1862	
Ballard & Hall		361
Ballard, -		361
Ballard, Carrie		358
Ballman, F. H.		214
Ballon, J. A.		358
Bancheri, Bartolmeo		2277
Bancroft, A. L.		217
Bane, D. C.		358, 1351
Banguess, Eliza M.	589	
Banguess, Lafayette		589
Bank of California	236	
Bank of Healdsburg	61, 162, 210, 243, 321, 1091, 1184, 1234, 1917, 2027, 2080, 2094, 2152, 2154, 2183, 2234	1469
Bank of Sonoma County	283, 284, 420, 479, 1033, 1076, 1191, 1690, 1790, 1818, 2312	358, 994, 1644, 1656, 2156
Bank of Tomales	650	
Bank of Ukiah	664, 665	
Baptist Church		358
Bard, Samuel	286	358
Barker, C. A.	2002	
Barker, John		1469, 2154
Barnes, -		1898

Person/Entity	Plaintiff Suit #	Defendant Suit #
Barnes, Aaron	3, 19, 227, 259, 584, 622, 986, 1435, 2098	94, 358
Barnes, E. H.	505, 2210	218, 1751
Barnes, Ella M. T.		2117
Barnes, H. L.	2218	1858, 1859, 1860, 1870, 1905, 2167
Barnes, John J.	2117	
Barnes, R. (Mrs.)		358
Barnes, Sallie J.		2218
Barnett, Alexander	575	
Barnett, C.		358
Barnett, J. D.	2066	
Baron, A.	1500	
Barron de Luzarraga, Antonia Maria Georgina		1009
Barron, Dolores		1009
Barron, Eustaquio Francisco		1009
Barron, Francisco Carlos		1009
Barron, Guillermo		1009
Barron, William		987
Barry, E. W.		1255
Barry, John		1439
Barry, John P.	1381	
Barry, Julia	93, 507	594, 1893
Barry, Margaret		1381
Barry, Nancy G.		1255
Barry, W. L.		1255
Barry, William D.		1255
Barsocchini, Antonio		86
Bartlett, Mary J.	1319	
Bartlett, T. G.		358
Barton, Emily J.		1506
Barton, Francis A.		1506
Basone, Ellen	1715	
Basone, Louis		1715
Bassett, Elinor	423	
Bassett, James A.		333
Bassi, Allesia	553	
Bassi, Vincenza	523	
Baters, Tom		1700

Person/Entity	Plaintiff Suit #	Defendant Suit #
Bates, George E.	2181	
Bauer, J. W.	1277	
Baumgarten, Joseph	1697	
Baxter & Green	1870, 2175	1905, 2170, 2171
Baxter, Ellen Louise	44	34
Baxter, T. P.	1870	2170, 2171
Baxter, Thomas P.	2175	
Bayler, Karolina	670	
Bazoni, Louis	1708, 1840	1240
Bazzoni, Ellen	1112	
Bazzoni, Louis		1112
Beall, J. B.		358
Beam, Jere		358
Bean, M. (Mrs.)		358
Bean, P. C.		358
Beardein, James M.		551
Beardein, Martha E.	551	
Beatty, John C.		440
Beauregard, Joseph		358
Beaver, Belle		494, 527
Beaver, Henry	1537	1300
Beaver, J. L.	494, 527	
Beckner, Lillie Ethel	2090	
Beckner, Mary M.		1299
Beckner, W. S.	1299	425
Beckner, William S.	610	
Beeson, Isaac R.	1497	
Beeson, William S.	1678	157, 1617
Beets, Louisa	1206	
Beggs, Thomas J.	161	
Behmer, Dan		1797, 1807
Bell, Charles		1387, 2264
Bell, Henry		2253
Bell, J. S.		1208
Bell, Robert E.		358
Bell, Robert W.		19
Bell, S. S.		1905
Benbow, E. M.	1321	
Benetti, John Paul		1423

Person/Entity	Plaintiff Suit #	Defendant Suit #
Benham, A. M.	295	
Benham, J.		358
Benham, Lucius T.	1036	
Benham, Raymond S.	1036	
Benjamin, A.		1107, 1749
Benjamin, A. M.		745
Benjamin, George		1751
Bennet, John		2072, 2073
Bennett, N.		136
Benson, Josiah H.	1924	
Bentley, Henry		358
Benton, Lucina M. (Mrs.)		358
Berger, Agusta		839
Berger, Caroline		839
Berger, Edith		839
Berger, Isaac		839
Berger, Jennette		839
Berger, Lewis		839
Berger, M.	95, 726	839
Berger, Mary A.		839
Berger, Rachel		839
Berka, F.	1859, 1860	1905
Berka, John		358, 526
Berman, Jacob		720
Bermel, Ernestine	1307	1735
Bermel, J. G.	1307	1735
Bermel, Pauline		1735
Berner, Robert		1978
Bernhard & Son	1837	
Bernhard, I.		1924
Bernhard, Isaac	815, 1837	
Bernhard, Jacob	1837	
Berringer, William	2159	
Berry & Place Machine Co.	1357	
Bertolo, Paolo		671
Besagno, Benditto		1399
Bethel, Chester		358
Bew, George		358
Biaggi, D.		77

Person/Entity	Plaintiff Suit #	Defendant Suit #
Bianchi, C. D.	1284	
Bicigalupi, John		1676
Bicigalupi, Louis		1676
Bicigalupi, Natola		1676
Bicigalupi, Rosi		1676
Big Bottom Mill Company of Guerneville		2229
Big Bottom Rail Road Company	1677	
Bihler, W.		1817
Bihler, William	186, 448, 2252	119, 128, 370, 673, 1113, 1441, 1531, 2202
Billings, John		253, 254
Bishop, John J.		1458
Bishop, Martha	859	1458
Bishop, Mary		2293
Bishop, T. C.	1365, 1388	1191, 1260, 1369, 1581, 1612, 1625, 1841, 1855, 2029, 2293
Bither, M. F.		358
Black, -		1095
Black, Allie		1095
Black, Bill		338
Black, Emma F. C.	1805	
Black, Fannie B.		1632
Black, H. S.		1633
Black, James		100
Black, Joseph	876	
Black, Richard	668	
Black, Whisky		358
Black, William		338
Blackburn, C.		775
Blackinton, Emmet		562
Blair, Alexander		358
Blair, T. N.		358
Blakeley, Eugene		850
Blakeley, John A.		850
Blakeley, Unity		850
Blakely, Martin L.		850
Blazer, John S.		1469
Bledsoe, A. C.		1751

Person/Entity	Plaintiff Suit #	Defendant Suit #
Bledsoe, Linn	1247	1751
Bledsoe, Sally		1751
Bledsoe, Sophie		1751
Bliss, Alexander	1812	
Bliss, Ellen Louise	1812	
Bliss, W. D.	1812	319, 941
Bliven, James I.	1375	
Bloch, George, Jr.		2214
Bloch, Lora A.	2214	
Blomfield, H.		1544
Bloom & Cohen	168, 180	
Bloom, Jonas	168, 180	586, 612, 926
Bloomer, Elizabeth	1892	
Bloomer, William	1892	
Bloomfield Masonic Hall Association	135	
Bloomington, L. J.	378, 796	
Blume, Julius	1667, 1876	
Boardman, H. J.		251
Bocock, James E.		358
Bodfish, William C.		358
Body, Mark	626	
Boelcher, Fred		358
Bogart, Charles H.		1639
Bogart, Julia		358
Bogart, Julia R.	1639	
Boggs, Alabama		593
Boggs, G. M.		125
Boggs, George W.		178, 358, 593
Bohan, Miles	882	
Bohen, Miles		847
Bohlin, Frank A.	1789	
Bolden, S.		107, 108, 109, 110
Bolden, Samuel	490	
Bollman, F. H.	117	
Bond, Albert		1714
Bond, Edward W.		305
Bond, George		1714
Bond, J. F.		850
Bond, Lewis Butler		20

Person/Entity	Plaintiff Suit #	Defendant Suit #
Bond, Mary E.		358
Bond, Mary Elizabeth		20
Bond, Thomas I.		20
Bond, William Hammet		20
Bonham, M.		358
Bonnetti, Caterina	598	
Bonnetti, Claudina	599	
Bonnetti, Filomena	600	
Booth, Jesse		358
Boothby, B. F.		1546
Boothby, Caroline	1546	
Boreland, L.	1208, 1211	
Boreland, R. A. (Mrs.)	1208	
Boroner, J.		358
Bosqui, William A.		353
Bostwick, N. W.		218
Bosworth, Albert	2172	
Bosworth, C. M.	2172	
Bosworth, Clemena D.	2172	
Bosworth, Fannie L.	2172	
Bosworth, James O., Jr.	2172	
Bosworth, Lillian V.		2172
Bosworth, Lucinda W.	2172	
Bosworth, Viola	2172	
Botto, Giovanni		2277
Botts, C. T.		1369
Bouton, A.		1751
Bowen, -	150	
Bowen, J. J.	1092	
Bowles, J. M.	2209	
Bowman, J. C.		711, 2207
Bowman, J. H.		304
Bowman, John	1323	
Bowman, John H.	292	
Bowman, Zilpha	1323	
Boyce, A. J.		1448
Boyce, J. F.		171, 235, 358, 436, 737, 2156
Boyce, John F.		213

Person/Entity	Plaintiff Suit #	Defendant Suit #
Boyce, M. A.		171
Boyce, Martha A.		436, 737, 2156
Boyd, William		827
Boyer, Elizabeth		209
Boyes, A. C.	2092	
Boyes, H. E.	1523, 2092	
Boyes, John B.		392
Boyes, Polly H.	392	
Boylan, John		358
Boylan, Mary		770
Boylan, Terrence		770
Boyle, Owen		887
Boyson, P. N.		358
Bradbury, John Q.		153
Bradford, A. C.	628	
Bradford, L. W. (Mrs.)		634
Bradlee, S. H.		358
Bradley, Mrs.		1884
Bradshaw, F. (Mrs.)		358
Bradwick, Albert		913
Bradwick, Mary Roe		913
Brainard, H. P.		59, 921
Braman, J. J.		2084
Branch, George B.	2091	
Branch, Louise J.		2091
Brand, Howard		358
Brander, F.		1865
Brandon, William		889
Brannan, James		358, 975
Branthaver, Daniel		358
Bray, E. J.		989
Bray, L. J.	989	
Bray, M. E.		866
Bray, Reuben	866	
Breen, James H.		1945
Breen, Mary E.	1945	
Brickwedel, Henry	619	
Briggs, E.		358
Briggs, George S.		202

Person/Entity	Plaintiff Suit #	Defendant Suit #
Briggs, J. T.		1374, 1434, 1592, 1726
Briggs, Jennie		358
Brimigian, S.		39, 40
Briscoe, John	213	
Brittain, M. A.		358
Brizzalaar, Louis		1152
Brookfield, Arthur C.		818
Brookfield, Mary R.	818	
Brooks, E. L.	454	
Brooks, Emma S.		879, 917
Brooks, Ernest K.		879, 917
Brooks, Frederick A.		879, 917
Brooks, Henry C.	879, 917	
Brooks, Nancy E.	1206	
Brooks, Rebecca		2063
Brooks, S.		775
Brooks, Silas		2063
Brooks, Thomas J.		879, 917
Brotherton, T. W.	751, 812	
Brotherton, T. Woodly	812	
Brotherton, Woodley	751, 779	
Brown & LeBarron	74	
Brown, A. A.		358
Brown, A. T. C.		358
Brown, Albert		1629, 1658, 1661, 2229
Brown, Alfred		358
Brown, B. W.		1121
Brown, Catherine A.	1344	
Brown, E.		2108, 2109
Brown, H. C.		2077, 2115
Brown, H. E.		253, 254
Brown, H. K.		218, 1236
Brown, Hannah	1197	
Brown, J. H.		1703
Brown, James		1162
Brown, James H.	74	
Brown, John	287	235, 358, 584
Brown, John A.		358
Brown, Martha Ann	939	

Person/Entity	Plaintiff Suit #	Defendant Suit #
Brown, Mary		823
Brown, Mary B.		338
Brown, Mary F.		358
Brown, O. W., Jr.		1773
Brown, Olivia M.	939	
Brown, R. B.		1367
Brown, Samuel	264	
Brown, T. H.		358
Brown, Victoria A.		209
Brown, W. B.	1830	1249
Brown, W. L.	1697	
Brown, William		619, 2151
Brown, William M.		1344
Brown, William S.	1193	1940
Brumfield, Byrd		944
Brumfield, Charles	1628	
Brumfield, George	1628	
Brumfield, George P.	1705	
Brumfield, Priscilla		1095
Brumfield, Summers		1628, 1705
Brush, G. M.	1418	560, 860
Brush, J. H.	2205	2188
Brush, W. T.		304
Brush, William T.	1457	
Bruyere, Louis	2285	
Bryan, Anne E.		1353
Bryan, C. L.	1104	
Bryan, E. (Mrs.)		2209
Bryan, Elizabeth	1353	377, 1837, 1924
Bryan, F. J.		2209
Bryan, Frederick J.		1353, 1924
Bryan, John L.		1353
Bryan, Joseph P.		1353
Bryan, Kate		1924
Bryan, Kate A.		1353
Bryan, Rosina		1353
Bryan, Thomas	1353	1353
Bryan, Thomas J.		377
Bryan, Thomas W.		1353, 1924

Person/Entity	Plaintiff Suit #	Defendant Suit #
Bryan, William F.		1353
Bryant, John		1753, 1784
Bryant, William		656
Bryant, William J.	605, 607	358
Buck, John		358
Buckland, C. J.		1803, 2188
Buckland, L. H.		358
Buell, A. W.		358
Bulotti, V.	1961	
Bumpus, C. H.	2274	
Buna, George		1989
Bunster, Arthur		1637
Burbank, R.		358
Burchfield, James R.		99, 299
Burchfield, Sarah	99, 299	
Burckhalter, A.	367	
Burdell, Mary A.	659	
Burger, C. H.		358, 2029
Burger, G. W.		358
Burgtorf, C. W.	1277	1169
Burgtorff, C. W.	288	
Burk, Julius		1750
Burke, George P.	1351	
Burke, J. H.		1261
Burkhalter, Agnes		358
Burling, George W.	1974	
Burnes, Thomas		1751
Burnett, George		358
Burnett, Matt	1293	1478
Burnetti, Peter		1423
Burney, E. (Mrs.)		1699
Burnham, Edward C.		1740
Burnham, J. W.	2169	
Burnpus, C.		358
Burns, John Doe		2267
Burns, Jud		2267
Burris, David	915	358
Burris, Elizabeth	1020, 2190	
Burris, Jessie	2190	

Person/Entity	Plaintiff Suit #	Defendant Suit #
Burris, John F.	2314, 2232	2081, 2234
Burris, L. W.	510	767
Burris, William	1020, 2190	
Burrough, Alfred	1125	1286, 1312
Burroughs, Alfred		1274
Burrus, G. W.	430, 962	
Burt, Russell		886
Buscelle, James R.	1817	
Bush, David		676
Bush, James	701	
Bush, Louis		358
Bushrell, William E.		358
Busman, A.	1218	
Buss, Henry		358
Bussman, Anton	1327	
Butcher, Squire		1542, 1631
Butler, Ben		358
Butler, James		2126
Butler, Joanna L.	351	
Butner, Joseph		2053, 2054
Butterly, F. S.		25
Button, I. V.	2202	
Buzzell, Albert A.		208
Buzzell, Lucinda	208	
Byington, H. W.		358
Byington, Walter	1962	
Byrne, Bridget	380	
Byrne, H.		358
Byrne, Joseph	2007	
Byrne, M.	1432	380, 928
Byrne, Mary		358
Byrne, Thomas	1952	
Byxbee, John F.		174
C. Michili & Co.		410
Cacello, J. G.		1452
Cadden, Catherine		2000
Cadden, John		541, 774
Cadden, Thomas	2000	2000
Cadet, N. P.		358

Person/Entity	Plaintiff Suit #	Defendant Suit #
Cadwell, J. A.	1778	
Cady, Gail		2017, 2018
Cady, M. K.		2017, 2018
Calanchini, Giacomina		636
Calder, A. E.		67
Calderwood, A.		358
Caldwell & Schmidli	1475	
Caldwell, Amanda J.	412, 519	
Caldwell, F. M.	318, 1231	358, 412, 519
Caldwell, George O.	1475	
Caldwell, Mary L.		1231
Caldwell, R. G.		358
Calf, P. G.		358
California Farmers Mutual Fire Insurance Association	1088	
California Savings & Loan Society	181, 268	
Calkins, J. A.		1179
Call, G. W.	2097	
Callaghan, Walter		900
Callagher, P.		358
Callahan, Daniel T.		899, 942
Callaway, David B.		1337
Callaway, Sarah	1337	
Callender, J. A.		1118
Calpella Gravel Mining Co.		1119
Camm, William		1486, 1547, 1563
Campbell, Barbara		1772
Campbell, Eliza Ann	1926	
Campbell, George S.		1723
Campbell, H.		358
Campbell, J. T.	618	358
Campbell, J. W.		358
Campbell, James		1538
Campbell, Jo H.		358
Campbell, John T.	385, 439	
Campbell, Joseph		1547, 1563
Campbell, Joseph H.	768, 792, 1399, 1926	
Campbell, S. A. (Mrs.)	1723	
Candido, José		833
Canepa, D.	1003	

Person/Entity	Plaintiff Suit #	Defendant Suit #
Canepa, G.	1003, 1057	
Canepa, L.	1003, 1057	
Canfield, Sally Ann		1828
Canfield, W. D.		1828
Cannan, S. W.	2138	
Cannon, B. H.	1955	
Cannon, Charles H.		1955
Cannon, J. C.		1087
Cannon, J. P.		1505, 1567
Cannon, James		57
Cannon, Mattie A.	1206	
Cannon, N. (Mrs.)		358
Cannon, R. B.		1936
Cannon, R. D.	1834	
Cant, George C.		358
Capell, B. B.		708
Carey, Joseph		639
Carey, Margaret		639
Carithers, D. N.		358
Carles, James H.	1522	
Carleton, Charles	1671, 1692	
Carlton, A.		358
Carlton, Fannie		2067
Carlton, Lulu		2067
Carlton, Rachel E.		2067
Carmichael, Archibald		2233
Carmichael, J. T.		2154, 2233
Carmolly, M. W.		358
Carothers, Thomas L.		290
Carpenter, Alice		1990
Carpenter, Alice M.		1990
Carpenter, Calvin D.		1828
Carpenter, George		623, 624
Carpenter, L. F.	1627	1990
Carpenter, S. E.		1990
Carr, Frances A. Watts Hensworth	38	
Carr, H. D.		358
Carr, J. D.	1830	
Carr, James		38, 1920

Person/Entity	Plaintiff Suit #	Defendant Suit #
Carr, Jesse D.		151
Carr, Mary E.		1998
Carr, Pat		358
Carr, Sam		253, 254
Carrie, J. A.		1576, 1690, 1881
Carrie, Joseph A.	1746	
Carriger, A. B.		395
Carriger, Nicholas	1063, 1195	
Carriger, Sophronia J.	395	
Carrillo, Andrew	1550	
Carrillo, F.	1405	
Carrillo, Frank		1407, 2196
Carrillo, Frank J.		925
Carrillo, Joaquin		688
Carrillo, Julio		358, 411
Carrillo, Mary	688	
Carrillo, Mary Ettie	925	
Carrington, C. N.	2246	
Carroll, James H.	1201	
Carroll, Mary Alice	2146	
Carroll, P.	1652	
Carroll, Patrick		2146
Carroll, R. T.	143, 173	
Carter, A. E.	1062	
Carter, E. D.		358
Carter, J. W.		358
Carter, L.		358, 973
Carter, Lander		1048, 1093
Carter, Mary		1178
Carter, Mary Frances		973, 1048, 1093
Carter, R. W.		1178
Carter, W. W.		358
Carty, Charles		1734
Caruthers, T. C.		256
Casarotti, M.	1889	
Casassa, D.	2013	
Casassa, Domenico	1619, 1906	1954
Case, A. B.	60, 388, 1338, 1747	1794, 1933
Case, A. L.	556	

Person/Entity	Plaintiff Suit #	Defendant Suit #
Case, A. S. (Mrs.)		358
Case, Adelaide L.	860	
Case, W. P.		675, 778
Caseres, Cero		682
Caseres, Cyrus		266
Casey, J.		1113
Casey, L. J.	1588, 2025	1881
Casey, Matt		323
Cash, J. F.		1702
Cassassi, D.		1910
Cassels, Everard L.		344
Cassidy, J. W.	745	
Cassidy, Martin		350
Castagnetto, Bartolomeo	1676	
Castens, Henry		348
Castro, Victor		411
Caughey, Robert		664
Cavagnaro, Giovanni		1619
Cavanagh, John	127	
Center, John		338
Central California Land Exchange		1892
Cereghino, A.	787, 918, 919	
Cerini, John	827	2075
Chalfant, E.		1637
Chamberlain, David	735, 1079, 1507, 1896	358
Chamberlain, David C.	1281	
Chamberlin, C.		358
Chamblin, J. L.	1007	
Chandler, H.		358
Chandler, W. R.		1929
Chapman, I. N.		59
Chapman, William S.	686	474
Charles, G. W.		559
Charles, George W.		1185
Charles, J. M.		646
Charles, Vernetta	1185	
Charlie (a Chinaman)		643
Charron, Francis	691	
Chart, Obed		1206

Person/Entity	Plaintiff Suit #	Defendant Suit #
Chase, Misses		358
Chauvet, J.	1866	
Cheape, George C.	1914	
Cheeney, Jonathan		1397
Cheney, D.	328	
Cheney, R. J.	329	
Cheney, Thomas	568	1519
Cheney, Thomas H.	568	1519
Childers, Arnold		272
Childers, Jo		358
Childers, Spencer		383
Chinn, Lewis		358
Chisholm, Annie C.	2275	
Chisholm, Duncan R.		90
Chisholm, William		2275
Chopard, Louis	1567	
Christian Church		358
Christie, J. B.	311	
Christieson, James B.	1728	
Chung, Ah		324, 540
Claassen, J. P.		1941
Claassen, Jens P.		1082
Clanton, D. C.	1409	
Clanton, D. F.		358
Clanton, David C.	1684, 1685	
Clanton, Thomas D.		358
Clark, A.		358, 1887
Clark, A. E.	2269	
Clark, A. N.		2016
Clark, Almer		1014
Clark, Ann J.		554
Clark, B.		358
Clark, D. C.		358
Clark, David		358, 2189
Clark, George C.		1014
Clark, Ida F.	1014	
Clark, J. L.		358
Clark, J. T.		2217
Clark, James		1842

Person/Entity	Plaintiff Suit #	Defendant Suit #
Clark, James P.	151, 524, 897	235, 358
Clark, James, Jr.		2217
Clark, James, Sr.		2217
Clark, John		554
Clark, M. C.		1301
Clark, R.		1765
Clark, W. H.		2217
Clark, William		2199
Clarke, Charlotte F.		1769, 1815
Clarke, J.		1769
Clarke, J. T.		1594
Clarke, James		1594
Clarke, James, Jr.		1594
Clarke, Jeremiah		1815, 1947
Clarke, W. H.		1594
Clarkson, P. M.	2128	
Claussen, George	376	
Clay, C. C.	224	
Clay, Charles C.	869	
Clayburgh, Celia	1815	
Clayburgh, Simon	1815	
Clayton, J. L. A.		358
Cleary, Bridget		1965
Cleary, John		1621
Cleary, Michael	1965	
Cleary, Mike	1787	
Cleary, Thomas J.	244	
Clewe, F.	1206	
Clover, Amanda	531, 1922	
Cloverdale Banking & Commercial Company	1560, 1561	1690, 1746
Cloverdale, Town of	1616, 2025	304
Cluff & DeWitt	2	
Cluff, William B.	1, 2	
Cnopias, John		23
Cnopias, Lewis		23
Coburn, W. R.		1747
Cocke, W. E.		289, 358
Cocke, W. T.	289	
Cockrell, -		358

Person/Entity	Plaintiff Suit #	Defendant Suit #
Cockrell, Roharma		358
Cockrill, Daniel	409	
Cockrill, T. G.	12	
Coe, Cornelius		1351
Coen, James	1637	
Coffey, Henry	1508, 2310	1914
Coffey, William		68
Coffman, J. T.		2183, 2229
Cogill, C. W.	68	
Cohen, A. S.	2215	
Cohen, Abraham	1250	
Cohen, Samuel	168, 180	
Cohn, S.	1107, 1160, 1279, 1289, 1636, 1646, 1682, 1749	
Colburn, W. R.		60
Cole, Charles		1539
Cole, H.		358
Cole, M. A.	1026	
Coleman, A.		559
Coleman, James	359	337
Coleman, John W.		223
Coleman, W. P.		1081
Colgan, E. P.	1848	1642, 1876, 1883, 1890, 1911, 1932, 2042, 2058, 2096, 2155, 2324
Coli, Michael		1971
Collean, Dan	132	
Collier, S.		358
Collins, F. M.	393, 1973	
Collins, Frank		71
Collins, George H.		275
Collins, Jane		181
Collins, John		1246
Colson, John		1645
Colson, Louisa	1620, 1645	
Colson, Nicholas		1620, 1645
Colston, Daniel		358
Colton, Ellen M.	905	
Colusa, Lake & Mendocino Telegraph Co.		398

Person/Entity	Plaintiff Suit #	Defendant Suit #
Colvin, Mary A.	374	
Colvin, W. J.		374
Colwell, Charles Y.		1919
Comfort, John		358
Compton, James		358
Comstock, A.		358
Comstock, B. F.	648	
Comstock, L. N.		648
Congelton, George	979	
Congleton, Agnes L.	1745	
Congleton, George W.		1745
Congrove, Jonathan		1248
Congrove, Lucy A.	1248	
Coniff, Bridget		1076
Coniff, John		1076
Conklin, Annie	1253	1489
Conklin, Charles		1253, 1489
Connell, John	2074, 2260	
Conner, E. P.		1006
Conner, John		930
Connolly, M. W.	984, 1683	
Connor, E. P.		2212
Conon, Peter		358
Conrad, C.		358
Conrad, Charles	149	29, 295, 1428
Conrad, Henry		358
Conrad, Jane	1428	
Conway, John M.		1997, 2065
Conzelman, Gottlieb	1075	
Conzelman, William E.	1075	
Coogen, Bridget	947	
Cook, Algernon M.		357
Cook, Andrew		358
Cook, Ann E.	1206	
Cook, Charles	912	73
Cook, G. E.		338
Cook, I. F.		378
Cook, Irving B.		357
Cook, Isaac		357

Person/Entity	Plaintiff Suit #	Defendant Suit #
Cook, Israel		1095, 1339
Cook, Israel (Mrs.)		1095
Cook, Johanna		73
Cook, Kate W.		357
Cook, Sarah Ann	413	
Coolbroth, Hattie	1872	
Coolbroth, S. W.	1872	
Coolbroth, Samuel		992
Coolbroth, Samuel W.	308	358
Cooley, Charles H.		1699
Cooley, Mary A.	2069	
Coomes, Albert M.		1605
Coomes, Edmund	1605, 1638	
Coon, James	900	
Coon, Mary	900	
Coon, R. W.	542	
Cooper, Annie O.		2158
Cooper, B. M.		1520
Cooper, Betsy M.		565
Cooper, F. M.		2158
Cooper, George W.		437
Cooper, H. H.	1296, 1552	565
Cooper, Hattie H.	437	
Cooper, Henry H.		1520
Cooper, J.		1025
Cooper, J. D.		358
Cooper, Jennette		1772
Cooper, John D.	1911	
Cooper, John R.		1772
Cooper, John S.		1772
Cooper, Lewis S.	2180	358
Cooper, Rhoda		358
Cooper, S. R.	1094	
Cooper, S. V.	1612	
Cooper, Sidney R.	1079	917
Cooper, Sydney R.		358
Cooper, Thomas S.		1772
Cooper, W. W.		358
Cooper, William		358

Person/Entity	Plaintiff Suit #	Defendant Suit #
Cooper, William McK.	1079	
Cope, James		442
Copland, C. F.		358
Copsey, D. M.	1301	
Corbaley, Melvin S.		1097, 1102
Corbaley, Richard		13
Corder, P.		290
Corliss, A.	433	
Corliss, Albert		71
Cornelius, George H. H.	597	
Cornett, Agnes	658	
Cornett, George		658
Corrippo, Peter		456
Cottle, J. W.		2193, 2203
Coughran, Wiley		956
Coulter, S. F.		358
Cox, C. B.	1345	358
Cox, Charles B.	960	
Cox, Fathy	240	
Cox, J. C.		834, 983
Cox, Jesse C.		1000
Cox, Jordan		240
Cox, W. E.		711
Craig, O. W.		978
Craig, Oliver W.		2223
Cralle, L. J.		1443, 1636, 1935
Crane, E. T.		358, 977, 1292
Crane, J. H.		775
Crane, T. J.		358
Crawford, S. G.	834	
Creelman, F.		1341
Creelman, L.	1341	
Creighton, Thomas	1136	358
Crewdson, A. L.	777	
Crewdson, George F.		777
Crigler, Laura A.	1494	
Crigler, Lloyd A.		1494
Crilly, Nicholas	201	
Crisp, John B.	943	

Person/Entity	Plaintiff Suit #	Defendant Suit #
Crist, George F.		279
Crocker, Charles		905
Cronin, P.	1010, 1040, 1992, 1993	
Cronin, Patrick	1412, 1734, 2195	
Crook, Hiram	765	
Crook, Ida		765
Cropley & Son	2130	2155, 2324
Cropley, H. M.	2130	2155, 2324
Cropley, William	2130	2155, 2324
Crosby, James	637	
Crose, J. M.	485	
Crowley, C.		358
Crowley, Cornelius		1043
Crump, R. W.		358
Crystal, B. F.		358
Cumberland Presbyterian Church of Santa Rosa	704	
Cummings, Anna M.	887	
Cummings, Catherine		887
Cummings, Michael		887
Cummings, Thomas		887
Cummins, Linia A.	1206	
Cuneo, A.		787
Cunningham, John	2076	
Cunningham, Susanah		2076
Current, Martha E.	550	
Current, Thomas D.		550
Curry, J. H.		358
Curtis, Catharine	2305	
Curtis, Ellen M.		463
Curtis, J. D.	1368	
Curtis, James		238
Curtis, Lousia C.	238	
Curtis, Richard H.	1362	2305
Curtiss, Francis E.		1172
Curtiss, Maria Louise	1172	
Cutter, James H.	337	
Cuttler, Mary F.		358
Dabner, Anton	2057	
Dahlman, W.	303	

Person/Entity	Plaintiff Suit #	Defendant Suit #
Daly, Edward	2168	
Daly, Fannie N.	1326	
Daly, James R.		1500
Daly, Thomas B.		1326
Dana, George S.		190
Dana, Mary E.		190
Daniels, Charles M.		1641
Daniels, Elmon	559	
Daniels, Henry	983, 1000	
Darden, John		26
Darden, M. C.		358
Dardin, George		358
Dardis, Andrew	221	215, 286, 358
Dardis, Lawrence		286
Darrow, Addie		557
Darrow, William H.	557	
Darwin, A. M.		358
Dassel, Helen	1511	
Dassel, W. H.		1511
Davidson, Alex T.		1228
Davidson, Alexander T.		1698
Davidson, J. E.		338
Davidson, James	400, 1277	
Davidson, Sarah J.	1228, 1698	
Davies, S. W.		358
Davis, -	2085	
Davis, C. L. (Mrs.)		1262
Davis, E. L.		871
Davis, E. W.	2184	
Davis, Ed W.		358
Davis, G. W.	2184	358
Davis, George A.	170	
Davis, Giles		335
Davis, Ira	816	
Davis, Jennie		2079
Davis, John B.		358
Davis, Josias		358
Davis, Levi		317½
Davis, M.	1830	

Person/Entity	Plaintiff Suit #	Defendant Suit #
Davis, Mary L.		358
Davis, Milo S.		358
Davis, Preston		2066
Davis, T. L.		1262
Davis, W. R.		358
Davis, W. W.		986
Davis, William R.	2184	
Davison, N. R.		358
Davisson, D. D.		524
Daw, A. W.	1721	
Dawson, H. C.		1257, 1477
Day, A. L.	826, 1200	
Day, Edwin		1873
Day, Edwin S.		358
De Coe, Thomas C.		2261
De Forest, Margaret	1503	2325
De Forest, W. F.	1503	
De Forest, William F.		2325
De Turk, I.		582
De Turk, Isaac		358
De Vincenzi, Giovanni	1672	
Deal & Davis	2085	
Deal, -	2085	
Dearborn, M. S.		526
Decker, H.	1461	945
Decker, Henry		1928, 1977
Decker, Peter E.		1774, 1775, 1776, 1777
Decker, Phoebe M.	1977	1928, 2297
Decoe, T. C.		1128
Deeds, Adam E.		642
Dei, Ella Wooten		1630
Dei, G. Ph.		1630
Delaney, James		719
Delanoy, Fred. N.		2087
Delanoy, Mary Frances		2087
Deller, C. W.		417
Delzell, David H.	789	
Delzell, Milton A.	789	
Delzell, William R.	789	

Person/Entity	Plaintiff Suit #	Defendant Suit #
DeMartin, Charles		1345
Demartini, Frank		1240
Demartini, Mary		1241
Demetz, Annie J.	1948	
Demetz, Henry	113	1948
Dempsey, Patrick	857	
DeNise, R. C.	1346, 1347	
Denk, Frank	685	
Denman, E.	1041, 1050, 1461	582, 945, 1644, 1656
Denman, Ezekiel	352, 434, 435	
Denny, Carrie	1663, 2145	
Denny, John P.		1663, 2145
DeTurk, Isaac		1902
Deveraux, E. W.		2159
Devine, Michael		190
Devoto, David	1782	
DeWitt, Mortimer	2	
DeWolf, Maria E.	1119	
Dey, Ella Wooten		1630
Dey, G. P.		1630
Dianda, D.	1610	
Dias, A. H. L.	1256	
Dias, Alzina G.		1256
Dias, I. L.		1256
Dias, Rosa	1256	
Dibble, P. K.		358
Dibble, P. K. (Mrs.)		358
Dick (an Indian)		1983
Dickinson, C.		245
Dickson, John	1376	
Dickson, William M.	1843	
Dill, Henry		358
Dillan, James		2099
Dillan, M. C.		2099
Dillon, Annie		358
Dillon, M. C.		1964
Dillon, Margaret G.	1964	
Dimmick, F. M.		358, 869, 971
Dingley, C. L.	448	

Person/Entity	Plaintiff Suit #	Defendant Suit #
Dinussi, Antonio		1060
Dinwiddie, J. L.	1174, 1237, 2038	120, 127, 185, 214, 286, 383, 400, 452, 471, 560, 567, 574, 579, 580, 582, 618
Dinwiddie, James L.		4, 63, 74, 76, 95, 339
Dittemore, Flavilla	908	
Dixon & Fairfax		334
Dixon, E. F.		1457
Dixon, G. L.		358
Dixon, James		334
Dixon, Samuel		358
Dobbins, Thomas		294
Dobbs, Frank		358
Dodge, A. C.	875	
Dodge, Leonard	1273	
Dodge, S. F.		875
Dodson, Elizabeth		939
Doe, Henry		1273, 1351
Doe, Kimball & Co.	1084	
Doe, L. B.		1219
Doe, Loring B.	1084	
Doherty, John W.		223
Dolan, Peter		969, 1207
Dolce, C.		1147
Dollar, John M.		2299
Domica, Luigi	1619	
Donahoe, Peter	1480	
Donahue, Annie	1480, 2303	
Donahue, James	1720	
Donahue, James M.	1480, 2303	2176, 2307
Donahue, Peter		563, 1157
Donahue, Thomas	1164	1163
Donegan, Joseph	1912	
Donken, Joseph F.		358
Donnelly, Frank		910, 920
Donohoe, J. H.	1699	
Donohue, Thomas		1163
Donovan, B.		885

Person/Entity	Plaintiff Suit #	Defendant Suit #
Donovan, B. O.		358
Donovan, Bart		2196
Dont, Joseph		358
Dooley, John C.		668
Dooly, E.	349	
Dorman, James		1109, 2208
Dorman, Jane	1109, 2208	
Dortmond, Henry	2121	1174
Doss, J. W.		2012
Doss, Joel A.	1252	
Doss, John R.		2012
Doss, May Bell		1252
Dougherty & Parsons		996
Dougherty, Ben G.	996	
Dougherty, John	727	996
Dougherty, S. K.		1933
Douglass, W. A.		1079
Dow, George W.		1751
Dowling, Thomas		358
Down, Samuel		358
Downes, Vernon		358
Downing, M. J. (Mrs.)		358
Downing, Mary F.	943	
Downs, Vernon	189	1395
Doyle, M.	1832	709, 712, 1731, 1877
Dozier, E. C.		358
Drake, R. S.	1177	1143
Drane, John H.		358
Drees, Ernest E.		2186
Drees, Gustav A.	2186	
Drees, H. A.	2186	
Drees, Johanna H. L.		2186
Drees, W. E.	2186	
Dresel, Julius		1206
Drice, Manuel		9
Driscoll, Hannah		750
Driscoll, John		750
Drummond, Donald		245
Drummond, E. W.	2282	2290, 2318, 2319

Person/Entity	Plaintiff Suit #	Defendant Suit #
Drummond, Erastus W.		2306
Drummond, Harriet E.	2306	
Drummond, Harriet Elizabeth		2290
Drummond, John H.		2304
Drummond, Milly A.	1206	
Dryden, C. C.		1823
Duard, W.		358
Duck, Black		358
Duck, Charles		358
Duck, Ong Tai		1442
Ducker, Sarah	2063	
Ducker, William	706	
Dudley, Charles		1679
Dudley, Nellie	1679	
Duff, Bella		358
Duffey, Thomas		115
Duffy, Hugh		358
Duffy, Mary		185
Duffy, Mary E.	1958	
Duffy, Thomas	118	185, 358, 1958
Duggan, M. (Mrs.)		358
Dunbar, M. A. (Mrs.)		358
Duncan & Ludwig		52
Duncan Mills Lumber Company		2299
Duncan, -		52
Duncan, Ada M.	1733	
Duncan, Alexander		174
Duncan, E. H.	349	
Duncan, F. L.		1733
Duncan, Florence B.		138, 1340, 2156
Duncan, J. P.		272, 358
Duncan, James P.		83, 788
Duncan, R. H.		127
Duncan, S. M., Jr.		1340, 2156
Duncan, Samuel M.		138
Duncans Mills Land & Lumber Company	70, 2299	174
Dunkley, Joseph		358
Dunpsy, A.		358
Durand, Victor		616

Person/Entity	Plaintiff Suit #	Defendant Suit #
Durham, Thomas S.	211	
Durie, Frankie E.		1990
Durkee, L. O.		1179
Durkee, William		358
Dutton, W.		358
Dutton, Warren	176	1656
Duval, Lucy		1838
Duval, O.		148
E. & K. Shone		143, 173
Eagan, George	1280	
Eames, Margaret		1711
Earl, E. T.		358
East, N. H.		358
East, South J.		358
Easter, George W.		2070
Eastland, Joseph G.		223
Eaton, A. J.		479
Eaton, I. F.		479
Eaton, James		358
Ebers, Abbie A.	1760	
Ebers, Henry F.		1760
Ebner, Charles		90
Eckburn, A.		358
Eddy, Frank J.		358
Edelman, G. W.	1277	150, 1538, 1547, 1563
Eden, Edward	1348	
Edgerton, H.		358
Edgerton, Henry		744
Edouard, Carl L.		344
Edwards, Ben	1875	1693
Edwards, Benjamin	764	1153
Edwards, Helen R.	1153	
Edwards, James	126, 613	
Edwards, John L.	2067	
Edwards, W. P.		2262, 2278
Egan, George L.		1462
Elder, Jane		358
Eldred, Nancy E.	2043	
Eldridge, Oliver		358

Person/Entity	Plaintiff Suit #	Defendant Suit #
Eldridge, William		2238
Eleason, W. A.		358
Elias, Philip		358
Elkins, I. B.		825
Elks, E.		358
Ella, Mrs.	1019	
Ellard, Thomas		358
Elliott, H. C.		358
Elliott, John		1699
Elliott, N. J.	1853	1780
Ellis, A. M. (Mrs.)		1699
Ellis, E. G.		2229
Ellis, L. G.		2094
Ellis, M. A.		358
Ellis, Mary		1606
Ellis, William		1430
Ellis, Wilson R.		1685
Ellison, Charles E.	1074	
Ellison, John B.	1422	
Ellison, L. M.		200
Ellison, Rodman B.	1422	
Ellison, William P.	1422	
Ellsworth & Son	1791	
Ellsworth, H. L.	1791	
Ellsworth, L.		775
Ellsworth, L. G.	1791	
Ellsworth, Lee		1338
Elphick, Anna M.		2064
Elphick, Thomas		2206
Elphick, Thomas A.	2064	
Elwell, Charles S.	743	
Ely, A. P.	2109	
Ely, M. C. (Mrs.)		358
Emerson, Henry	72	
Emerson, J. P.		321
Emerson, N. S.		321
Emerson, P. N.		1122
Emerson, S. R.		1122
Emmerson, J. P.		59

Person/Entity	Plaintiff Suit #	Defendant Suit #
Engelhart, F.		117
Engelhart, Mary		117
England, Barton		358
Englehardt, F.		2215
Englehart, Fred	366	
Englehart, James		970
English, John F.	1386	
Enos, J. S.		427
Enos, Susie		427
Enterprise Planing Mill & Building Company	2109	
Episcopal Church		358
Epperson, J.	968	
Ereleth, James A.		358
Erickson, Conrad	1077	
Escandon y Barron, Carlota		1009
Escandon y Barron, Eustaquio		1009
Escandon y Barron, Guadalupe		1009
Escandon y Barron, Manuel		1009
Escandon y Barron, Maria		1009
Escandon y Barron, Pablo		1009
Espey, J. H.		386
Espey, John	632	1287
Espey, John H.	558	
Esser, H.		1025
Estep, Joseph H.		1444
Estep, S. R. (Mrs.)		358
Estep, Sarah R.		1444
Etheridge, Parmily L.		1401
F. Korbel & Bros.	164, 546	
Faessler, R.		2257
Faessler, Robert	1469	
Fagas, Joseph F.	769	
Fagas, Joseph F. (Mrs.)	769	
Faggiano, J. B.		1635
Fahey, William		358
Fairbanks, Frank		1847
Fairbanks, H. F.		1045
Fairbanks, H. T.	775, 813	241, 709, 712
Fairbanks, J. K.	957	

Person/Entity	Plaintiff Suit #	Defendant Suit #
Fairbanks, Levina	1847	
Fairbanks, Mary		1847
Fairfax, Ada		334
Falietti, Luigi	1709	
Fanning, George C.		358
Farmer, C. C.		358, 1460, 1526, 1771, 1864, 2251
Farmer, Charles R.	1864	1460, 1526, 2261
Farmer, Charles Rollins		1771
Farmer, E. T.		358
Farmer, Elijah T.		1460, 1526
Farmer, Elizabeth	1206	
Farmer, Frances May	2251	1460, 1526, 2251
Farmer, Francis May		1771, 1864, 2261
Farmer, Henry T.		2261
Farmer, Henry Thomas	2251	1460, 1526, 1771, 1864, 2251
Farmer, J. A.	125	358
Farmer, John H.		358
Farmer, Lillie Bell		1460, 1864, 2251, 2261
Farmer, Lillie Belle		1526, 1771
Farmer, Rebecca W.		2261
Farmer, Rebekah W.		1460, 1526, 1771
Farmers & Mechanics Bank	154	
Farmers & Mechanics Bank of Healdsburg	218, 1022, 1171, 1482, 1524, 1737, 1741, 1751, 2033	
Farquar, C. S.	2211, 2297	
Farrell, Martin	776	
Farrell, Thomas		358
Farrell, William	1050, 1461	
Fatherston, James		358
Faught, John H.	1123	2308
Faught, Willis		2131
Faulkner, M.		1388
Favor, John	1339	
Favour, John	1735, 2084	
Fay, E. (Mrs.)		358
Fay, Julius A.		327
Fay, Sarah L.	327	

Person/Entity	Plaintiff Suit #	Defendant Suit #
Fay, William J.		358
Feder, Good		358
Feehan, William		306
Feeley, Peter J.		358
Feldmeyer, B. W.		1978
Fell, Erastus	241	
Fen, Carrie		1480
Fenn, John		1565
Fenn, Richard		1565
Fensier, O. B.		358
Fenton, James		358
Ferera, Louis		1083
Ferguson, E. C.		235
Ferguson, James		140
Fernandez, Bernardo	1804	
Ferrari, Innocenti	1611	
Feusier, Louis	262	
Fichett, C. A.		358
Fick, Fred		358
Field, Black		358
Field, W. A.		152
Filcher, J. T.		358
Finch, H. P.	245	
Finch, R.		1923
Finch, Ziba		1923
Fine, A.		358
Fine, Emily		1376
Fine, Emsley	293	1973
Fine, J. M.	1277	1033
Fine, Joff	66, 394, 595, 746, 786	748, 848, 936
Finlaw, William		358
Finley, Cynthia J.	2271	2050
Finley, Henry M.	2050	2271
Finley, John		345
Finley, W. A.		358
Fiori, Joseph	456	
Fiori, Juditha	456	
First Baptist Church of Healdsburg	2323	
First National Gold Bank of Petaluma	285	

Person/Entity	Plaintiff Suit #	Defendant Suit #
First Presbyterian Church of Fulton	1132	
First Presbyterian Church of Petaluma	1070, 1472	
Fish, F. B.		69
Fish, F. L.		2108, 2109
Fish, Francis L.		2258
Fisher, A. L.		358
Fisher, Ebenezer	1257	
Fisher, Eugene		2272
Fisher, Godfrey	1697	
Fisher, H. J.		358
Fisher, Mollie	2272	
Fitch, John B.	802	
Fitch, Joseph	85	85
Fitch, Libbie		802
Fitch, Mary A.		1020
Fitch, Wallace B.		1020
Fitzgerald, A.		80
Fitzgerald, A. L.		358
Fitzpatrick, A.		326
Fitzpatrick, Andrew	1829	
Fix, J. K.	2235	
Fix, Mary R. J.	2235	
Flack, John	316	205
Flagg, Julia		358
Fletcher, Andrew	649	
Fletcher, D. E.	2114	2135
Fletcher, Duncan	649	
Flint, Eugene		1772
Flint, Purdy		1772
Flippin, J. F.		358
Florence, M.		1311
Flynn, M. S.		358
Fogaerty, Michael	2326	
Fogerty, John		1495
Fogerty, Michael		1495
Folks, John		1127
Fong, Ah	1681	
Fook, Ah		237
Foppiano, Gaitano		1345

Person/Entity	Plaintiff Suit #	Defendant Suit #
Forbes, Alexander		620, 1009
Forbes, Ellen		1009
Ford, B. F.		358
Ford, M.		2259
Foreman, John	342	
Forget, Frank		1400
Forsyth, B.		358
Forsyth, C.		358
Forsyth, Caroline	898	
Forsyth, J. H.	2224	
Forsyth, Rebecca A.	1008	
Forsyth, Robert	1203	
Forsyth, W. B.		2224
Forsyth, William H.		358, 710
Forsythe, W.		591
Forsythe, William		686
Foster, D. A.	651	
Foster, Henry C.		1320
Foster, John F.	356	
Foster, Joseph		776, 1492
Foster, Margaret C.	909	
Foster, Margaret Porteous	1320	
Fountian, Minervia A.	1106	
Fountian, Thomas T.		1106
Fowler, Annie C.	2158	
Fowler, Henry R.		2038
Fowler, J.		1477
Fowler, Jane Doe		1477
Fowler, John H.	477	
Fowler, Mary Jane	1046	
Fowler, Susan M.	1206	
Fox, John Doe		2261
Fox, John T.	1140	
Fox, Lucretia T.	1949	
Fox, Sarah Angeline		1460, 1526, 1771, 1864, 2251, 2261
Foy, Ah	458	
Foy, George J.		358
Frahm, Frank		10

Person/Entity	Plaintiff Suit #	Defendant Suit #
Frame, David		415
Franchi, C.	782, 884	
Francisco, D.		1683
Frank Bros.	1291	
Frank, Frederick A.	1291	
Frank, George P.	1291	
Franklin, D. B.		358, 1099
Franklin, J. C.		358
Franklin, Winnie		1099
Franks, C.		1361
Fraser, A.		161
Fraser, Thomas A.	69	
Fraser, William		2299
Frasier, A. H.		196
Frasier, M. J.		1743
Frazee, D. C.		1898
Frazee, C. D.		358, 1870, 1905
Frazee, C. DeWitt		1858, 1859, 1860
Frazer, D. R.		358
Frazer, G. W.		1913
Frazier, A. H.		572
Frazier, Alexander		1739
Frazier, E. H.		669
Frazier, F.		358
Frazier, James		669
Frazier, Mary A.	899	1351
Fredericks, George	1490	
Free, Thomas H.		1725
Freeborn, James		223
Freehill, Thomas	1402	
Freeman, George		338
Freeman, W. D.		1256
Frehe, H. F.		1170
Frehe, Louis	194	1170
Frehe, Michael		880
French, Charles F.	1071	
French, Ellen M.	1431	
French, George	1415	
French, John H.	1643	

Person/Entity	Plaintiff Suit #	Defendant Suit #
French, William L.		1431
Frey, Joseph		1950
Friedell, George		1117
Friedlander, M.		95
Frisbie, Anatilde		482
Frisbie, Felicita		482
Frisbie, Levi C.		655
Fritch, John	2207	
Fritsch, J. R.		58
Fritsch, John	58, 793, 1923	582, 711, 1338
Fritsch, Walter	793	
Frost, C. W.		189, 358, 638, 1392
Frounson, Peter	621	
Fruetts, Martha		358
Frunz, N.		2252
Fulkerson, John		2221
Fulkerson, Rachel A.	2221	
Fulkerson, Richard	282	358, 582
Fulkerson, T. S.		358
Fuller, O. P.		358
Fuller, V. R.	67	
Fulton, James		358
Fulton, Mary		358
Fulton, Ritta		358
Fung, Lui		453
Furbee, T. J.	2109	1803
Furguson, E. C.		358
Furguson, H. (Mrs.)		358
Furguson, W. C.		358
Furlong, James	1952	
Furner, George		2302
Fussard, L.		358
Fyfe, David K.		1180
Fyfe, Julia C.	1180	
Gabell, M. A. (Mrs.)		358
Gaber, Mary Jane		1528
Gaberel, G. W.	893	891
Gaberel, Mattie		891
Gaffeny, Miles	2241	

Person/Entity	Plaintiff Suit #	Defendant Suit #
Gaffney, Miles	1158	
Gaffnie, Annie		472
Gaffnie, John		472, 760
Gage, Emma		1584
Gage, J. S.	1584	
Gaillard, Josephine	924	
Gain, Ah		758
Galagher, John		1829
Gale, Otis	1674	358
Gallagher, John D.		677
Gallo, Carlo		358
Galvin, M. J. C.	1273	2298
Gambetta, G.		1790
Gamble, A.		358
Gamble, A. W.		154
Gamble, Abram		2144
Gamble, George F.		358
Gamble, John	583	789
Gamble, Mary C.		2144
Garber, John		358
Garbonni, F.		1451
Garddard, James O.		358
Gardella, C. L.	1313, 1954	1309, 1345, 1906, 2013
Gardella, Catarina		2013
Gardella, Caterina	1954	
Gardella, Caterna		1906
Gardella, Catherine	1619	
Gardella, Lorenzo	545	1906
Gardener, August		358
Gardner, B. B.		358
Gardner, Clement		1939, 2269, 2314
Gardner, H.		1939
Gardner, John W.	900, 2030	
Gardner, L. B.		358
Garfield, J. A.		358
Garnett, A. G.		1130
Garnier, Jean Baptiste Emile	2120	
Gater, J. E	1528	
Gater, John E.		1173

Person/Entity	Plaintiff Suit #	Defendant Suit #
Gauger, Bertha	946	
Gauger, William		946
Gaunce, George		253, 254
Gauntz, George		253, 254
Gautier, E. V.		1201
Gautier, Edouard		1201
Gautier, Eudoxie	900	
Gautier, Julienne		1201
Gautier, Lambert		1201
Gautier, Leonidas		358, 1201
Gautier, Leonore		1201
Gautier, Leopold		1201
Gautier, Marguerite		1201
Gautier, Marie		1201
Gaver, A. P.	1703	
Gaver, Andrew P.		43
Gawne, John		2190
Geary, E. B.		358
Geary, T. J.		1479
Geary, Thomas J.		1816
Geer, C. V.		1732
Gelman, R. H.		342
Genazzi, Annie A.	2309	
Genazzi, J.		667
Genazzi, Louis		2309
Genesi, Louis		2102
Gentzel, G.		358
Gentzell, G.		1450
German, William W.	1366	
Geurkink, B. W.	646, 709	
Gianella, L.	572	
Gibb, Daniel		620
Gibb, Thomas Murray		620
Gibb, William		620
Gibbs, Frank H.		65
Gibbs, J. D.	1536	
Gibbs, Sarah A.	65	
Gibbs, William H.	100	
Gibney, George		487

Person/Entity	Plaintiff Suit #	Defendant Suit #
Gibney, Martha C.	487	
Gibson, Ann Eliza		1767
Gibson, Emma		1861
Gibson, Jane Doe		1266
Gibson, John		1266, 1272, 1767
Gifford, J.	386	
Gilbert, T. A.	639	
Gilbride, R.		175
Giles, Grant		1836
Gilfoyle, John		1597
Gill, Fannie E.	1061	
Gill, George Q.		1045
Gill, Marvin		1061
Gillespie, H.		358, 721
Gillespie, Lizzie	2261	
Gillespie, William M.	2261	
Gillett, E. F.	870	864, 865
Gillman, L. J.		358
Gillooly, J. P.		358
Gilmore, James		358
Ginella, L.	196	
Ging, Wong Loo		758
Giovannini, D.		473, 625
Giovannini, Daniel	53	
Giovannini, Daniele		1827
Giovannini, J.	654	
Gipson, John	932	
Girard, Mrs.		358
Gird, H. S.		1988
Gird, Henry S.		1985
Givens, R. R.		1917
Gladden, W. N.		1751
Glass, Margaret		609
Glass, Philip	609	
Glass, Phillip	569	556, 609
Gleason, C. S.		358
Gleason, P. H.		1752
Gleason, Patrick		2270
Gleason, Patrick H.	1808	

Person/Entity	Plaintiff Suit #	Defendant Suit #
Glenn, Robert	611, 647, 2177	532, 820, 842, 2098
Gliddon, William		1537
Gliddon, William A.		1300
Glover, Charles	373	
Glynn, E. (Mrs.)		224
Glynn, Ellen	1793	1800
Glynn, F. B.	526, 1839, 2280	1155, 1905
Glynn, F. J. B.		358
Gobbi, Paul		122
Gobbi, Peter	681	
Gobie, John		2112, 2113
Goby, E.		358
Goddard, Daniel		180
Goess, G. A.		1519
Goetting, -		358
Goetzelman, John		1881
Goetzleman, John		1699
Goforth, A.		358
Goforth, Joseph A.		358
Goheen, Gray		1065, 1066
Gold, Peter		358
Goldfish, -	753	
Goldfish, B.	178, 306, 1107, 1160, 1279, 1289, 1646, 1682, 1749	358
Goldfish, Wilson & Co.	1160, 1289, 1646, 1682, 1749	
Goldstein, H.	934	
Goldstein, Henry	1642, 1654	
Gomez, John F.		358
Good, J.		358
Good, Walter C.	2044, 2051	
Goodfellow, W. S.		1272
Goodman, George R.	761	
Goodman, James		2131
Goodman, L. S.	1952	
Goodrich, James H.		2098
Goodwin, Mary E.		137
Gordon, Charles		358

Person/Entity	Plaintiff Suit #	Defendant Suit #
Gore, A. J.		1453
Gore, J. F.		358
Goss, Caroline		358
Gossage, Jerome B.	1828	
Gossage, Rachel A.	1828	
Gottig, Lawrence		1574
Gould, George F.		1085
Gounsky, Fanny	2147	
Gounsky, J.		2147
Gow, Ah		1535
Gow, Ong	1364	
Grace Church of Petaluma	896	
Gradwohl, M.		66
Graeff, John M.		1487
Graham, A.		358
Graham, Albert W.	2322	1415
Graham, J. P.	2283	2274, 2276, 2280
Graham, Joseph M.		1437
Graham, Mary Isabel	1437	
Grangers Business Association	157, 708, 1027	1171
Grangers Business Association of Healdsburg	1183	
Grant, John D.		137
Grater, Henry		2265
Graves, George W.		1324
Graves, W. S.	1167	
Gray, Elizabeth		1826
Gray, J. W.	82	
Gray, James		358
Green, Julia B.	2313	
Green, Morris		1591
Green, P. F.		2171
Green, Paul F.	1870, 2175	2170
Green, Thomas W.		2313
Green, William S.	2014, 2170	2257
Greenberg, Max		185
Greer, Jane E.	1230	
Gregg, Isaac		358
Gregory, Joseph	1361	
Gregory, T. J.	1220	

Person/Entity	Plaintiff Suit #	Defendant Suit #
Gregory, Thomas		1226
Greiner, Frederick	913	
Greiss, George		410
Grider, Theodore		885
Griess, Catherine		609, 1174
Griess, George		609, 1174, 1396, 1580
Griest, Agnes		1095
Griest, Artie		1095
Griest, Eliza		1095
Griest, Peter		1095, 1339
Grieves, Samuel H.		1485
Griffin, Ida S.	1058	
Griffin, Perry L.		1058
Griffin, Rose	586	
Griffin, William	2109	
Griffith, A. (Mrs.)		561
Griffith, Albert		561
Griffith, C. C.	100	
Griffith, G.	955	
Griggs, J. H.		358
Grimes, John	1397	
Grissim, Lizzie V.	1098, 1229	
Grissim, W. H.	2293	1098
Grissim, William H.		1229
Grobb, Henry		98
Grogan, A. B.	1352	
Groom, M. W.		1732
Groshong, Celia		139, 1034
Groshong, H. F.		1034
Gross, Thomas		358
Grosse, Guy E.		344, 358, 1915
Grove, C.		545
Grove, C. C.		1297
Grove, David		998, 1297
Grove, Elmira	998, 1297	
Grove, L. G.		1297
Grove, S. L.		1297
Grove, W. H.		1297
Grove, William H.		8

Person/Entity	Plaintiff Suit #	Defendant Suit #
Grover Bros.	41	
Grover, B. P.	41	
Grover, J.	41	
Groves, Catherine (Mrs.)		358
Gruenberg, Max	115	
Gruenhagen, W.		358
Guerne & Ludwig	182	163, 164, 165, 166, 168, 169, 170
Guerne & Murphy	700, 1629, 1658	546, 1677
Guerne, A. L.	728, 791	
Guerne, George E.	182, 570, 700, 1629, 1658, 1661	163, 164, 165, 166, 167, 168, 169, 170, 179, 363, 546, 1677, 2192, 2203
Guerne, Murphy & Ludwig		179
Guerra, Giuseppe	577	
Guglielmetti, P. C.	843	
Guidotti, F.		1466
Guilfoyle, Frank		1707
Gummer, James		1791
Gundlach, Jacob		685
Gunn, J. H.		751, 779, 812
Gurnett, A. G.		1186½, 1805
Gutermute, H. S.	2302	
Gwinn, John E.	1538, 1547, 1563	1998
Haas Bros.	475	
Haas, C. H.	475	
Haas, Herman		734, 1543
Haas, K.	475	
Haas, Rosa	1543	
Haas, William	475	
Haehl, Conrad	1714	1583, 1789
Haering, Frederick	199	
Haering, Helen		199
Hager, George D.	956, 958	
Haggard, Ida Mabel		883
Haggard, Vianna		883
Hagmeyer, Gottlieb		1699
Hahman, Charlotte		2181
Hahman, Clara		2181

Person/Entity	Plaintiff Suit #	Defendant Suit #
Hahman, F. G.		358
Hahman, Feodore Gustave		2181
Hahman, Henrietta A.		2181
Hahman, Henry G.		2181
Hahman, Martha		2181
Hahman, Paul		2181
Hahman, Paulina		2181
Haigh, Edwin	247	
Haigh, John B.	247	
Haigh, Mary	247	
Haight, George W.		3
Haight, Robert		1534
Hailman, P. (Mrs.)		358
Halbertson, M.		358
Hale, Elias		2244
Hale, Henry M.		156
Hale, Joseph		290
Hall, -		361
Hall, A. B.	1607	
Hall, A. W.		290
Hall, Albert A.		493
Hall, Alice C.		1243
Hall, Amelia A.		209
Hall, C. T.		15
Hall, Carrie E.		1894
Hall, Clarence C.	1243	
Hall, E. G.	1756, 2141	2094, 2183, 2229
Hall, Effie E.		1607
Hall, Frank		1217
Hall, George		1894
Hall, Henry		409, 520, 629, 826
Hall, Henry G.		2049
Hall, Isaac R.		1533
Hall, J. E.	1902, 1904, 1976, 2028	
Hall, L. B.		358
Hall, L. J.	1633	358, 1985, 1988
Hall, O. M.	1902, 1904, 1976	
Hall, Olive Edna	1902, 1904, 1976	
Hall, R. H.		2183

Person/Entity	Plaintiff Suit #	Defendant Suit #
Hall, Winnie Wright	1902, 1904, 1976	
Hallinan, James S.		750
Ham, E. D.	97	358
Hamilton, Ed R.		1081
Hamilton, Emmor		1751
Hamilton, James P.	2148	1425, 1650
Hamilton, John Doe		689
Hamilton, Robert M.		844
Hamlet, John		356
Hamlin, A.		358
Hamlin, Charles H.		358
Hamlin, N. C.	972	
Hamlin, T. T.	1479	
Hammel, H. H.	1277	228
Hammell, H.	245	
Hammond, A. C.		1392
Handy, Philo	1802	
Haney, Ella J.		1045
Hanify, John R.	1630	
Hannath, C. J.		358
Hanneth, Charles J.	1587	
Hanscomb, E. B.		358
Hansen, A.		2056
Hansen, C.		358
Hansen, Henry		2165
Hansen, Joaquin		231, 270, 630
Hansen, Sarah	2165	
Hansen, Susie	2056	
Hanson, Carl		358
Hanson, Charles		275
Happy, Abe	1285	
Happy, John	682	
Haraszthy, Attila		2068
Haraszthy, Augustin		2068
Haraszthy, Elenora		2068
Haraszthy, Mariano J.		2068
Haraszthy, Natalia		2068
Harbin, William		2182
Harbrough, M. E. (Mrs.)		358

Person/Entity	Plaintiff Suit #	Defendant Suit #
Hard, David T.	1800	1793, 1825
Hard, Estella A.		1793, 1825
Hard, Estelle A.	1800	
Harden, Bridget F.	1111	
Harden, William H.		1111
Harder, William		358
Hardesty, Catherine A.		1636
Hardesty, Charles W.		1636
Hardesty, J.		358
Hardin, J. A.	1830	
Hardin, James A.		358
Hardin, William Jefferson		1277
Harding, Edwin H.		1727
Harding, Reka		1727
Hardt, Augusta		1911
Hardt, Henry W.		1911
Hardt, Henry William	1824	1782
Hardy, George		358
Hardy, J. P.		358
Hare, Richard		358
Hargis, L. D.		358
Harlan, J. J.	1078	
Harlow, James	450, 629	
Harman, F. V.		358
Harman, S. H.		1000
Harmon, E. N.		2097
Harmon, John B.	292	
Harned, J. A. M.		373
Harper, Frank		358
Harris, A. I.	1657	
Harris, Granville		1772
Harris, Henry R.	1206	
Harris, J. C.		358
Harris, Jacob		2029, 2048
Harris, L. S. J.		1089
Harris, R. A.	1089	
Harris, Richard		93, 2005
Harris, Sarah E.		1772
Harris, T. M.	2259	101

Person/Entity	Plaintiff Suit #	Defendant Suit #
Harris, Thomas L.		346
Harris, Thomas M.		225, 1512
Harris, Thomas S.		1399
Harris, Timothy		358
Harrison, A.		2303
Harrold, James		358
Hart, J.		358
Hart, William H. H.		358
Hartman, Adolph		1821
Hartman, Alice Maud		1821
Hartman, Bertha		1821
Hartman, Frederick		1821
Hartman, Hattie		2122
Hartman, Jane Doe		1519
Hartman, Jennie H.		1821
Hartman, John Doe		2181
Hartman, Maggie V.		1821
Hartman, Mary Roe		2181
Hartman, Robert Charles		1821
Hartman, W. D.		2122
Harvey, Albert		338
Harvey, Keturah J.		1063
Hasbrouck, A.	245	
Hasbrouck, A. A.	140	
Hasbrouck, Augustus		1319
Hasbrouck, H. B. H.	1277	
Haser, Theodore		358
Haskell, Emma A.	1204	
Haskell, G. W.		933
Haskell, James		358
Haskell, William B.	2249	
Haskins & Cadwell	1778	
Haskins, Mary		1742
Haskins, Robert		1742
Haskins, T. J.	1778	
Hassett, A.		1221
Hassett, Aaron		210, 415, 1751
Hassett, Ella		2273, 2288
Hassett, J. D.	489	

Person/Entity	Plaintiff Suit #	Defendant Suit #
Hassett, J. T.	2273, 2288	
Hassett, John D.		175, 538, 1037, 1852
Hassett, Sarah E.		1852
Hastings, Alice	1178	
Hastings, Edith	1178	
Hatch, C. P.		775
Hatch, J. H.		2198
Hatfield, Alice M.		1389
Hatfield, Amanda	707	
Hattimer & Matzger		358
Hattimer, -		358
Hatton, Charles B.	203	
Haubrick, Peter	1420	
Haw, Jack Wah		2139
Hawkins, D. S.		2034
Hawkins, Joseph	175	
Hawkins, L. J.	1477, 2034	
Hawley, George T.		1402
Hawley, Marcus C.	399	
Hayden, James		45, 358
Hayes, Emma		106
Hayes, G. H.		106
Hayes, Mary T.	116, 742	
Hayes, R. K. (Mrs.)		358
Hayes, Thomas	116	742
Hays, Mary T.	1168	
Hayward, D. L.		358
Head, R.		510
Head, William		626
Heald, J. G.		1699
Heald, J. T.		358
Heald, Rachel		1690
Heald, T. T.	503	
Healdsburg College	1260	
Healdsburg Institute	96	
Healdsburg Lodge, No. 64, I. O. O. F., Trustees of	608	
Healey, Julia H.	1569	
Heath, Adaline J.	640	
Heath, Barbara M.	1035	

Person/Entity	Plaintiff Suit #	Defendant Suit #
Heath, George A.		640
Heath, Henry A.		1035
Hechheimer, Lee		1033
Hecker, Henry	1053½	
Hecker, Peter	1053½	
Hedges, N. M.		775, 1538, 1547, 1563
Hedges, W. H.		1135, 1618, 1799
Hedges, William H.		1667
Heeser, August	1916	
Heeser, Augustus		933
Heeser, William		933, 1916
Heffelfinger, Laura		415
Heffelfinger, W. J.	841	415
Heffron, A. H.	1314	1322
Heffron, Sarah		1322
Hefner, Philip	317, 699, 1377	
Hegler, Gerhard	348	
Heidom, H.		358
Heilbron, Adolph	1815	
Heilbron, August	1815	
Heisel, Ellen	935	
Heisel, Paul		358, 725, 927, 935
Heiser, Robert	169	
Helen, Lady	1054	
Helman, H. H.		1934
Helman, William		1934
Helmke, Arabella		275
Helmke, Frederick		275
Hembree, Albert		763
Hemenway, M. L.		1373, 1719
Hen, Mary		1480
Hencken, Martin	619	
Henderson, Charles		2257
Henderson, H. W.	1540	
Henderson, James W.	92	
Henderson, Mary		1540
Henderson, Sarah E.		92
Henderson, W. (Mrs.)		358
Hendrickson, A.	1559	

Person/Entity	Plaintiff Suit #	Defendant Suit #
Hendy, George		933
Henley, Barclay	744	285, 358
Henley, Harriett		358
Henley, Patrick	6	
Henninger, Joseph G.		1286
Henry & Peterson		293
Henry Brickwedel & Co.	619	
Henry, A.		945
Henry, John		293, 399, 470
Henry, William		338
Henshaw, W. P.	1505	
Herman, J. F		897
Herman, Rudolph		190
Hermann, Barbory		1583
Hermann, M.		452
Herrmann & Co.	1258	
Herrmann, Siegmund	1258	
Hershberger, Charles		139, 1034
Hershberger, Emily		139, 1034
Hershberger, Frank		139, 1034
Hershberger, Jeremiah		139, 1034
Hershey, D. N.	1830	
Hervey, N. B.		358
Hervey, N. B. (Mrs.)		358
Hettich, Christ	484	
Hettich, Christian	184	
Hettrich, Charles		1697
Hewett, Jane		358
Hewitt, Chassuel F.		2219
Hewitt, Emma	2219	
Hewitt, H. T.		358, 1043
Hewlett, Frederick		1338
Hickey, Morris		709, 712
Hicks, E. S.	1586	
Hicks, Edmund S.		1609
Hicks, Etta M.		1609
Hicks, G. M.		2093
Hicks, J. O.		358
Hicks, M. C.	661	

Person/Entity	Plaintiff Suit #	Defendant Suit #
Hicok, C. C.		420
Hicok, J. J.		420
Higgins, Alfred, Sr.		912
Hildburgh Bros.	317½	475
Hildburgh, D.	317½	
Hildburgh, D. H.		475
Hildburgh, L.	317½	475
Hill, A. B.		102, 103, 111, 112, 195
Hill, Amanda E.	831	
Hill, James M.	391	
Hill, John W.		831
Hill, Louisa	1206	
Hill, Louise J.	195	
Hill, Sarah		391
Hill, William	375, 411, 1121, 1520, 1932, 2070	352, 358, 582
Hill, William B.	1675	
Hill, William McPherson		1866
Hiller, A.		358
Hinckley, George E.		3, 259
Hinckley, Mary R.		259
Hinds, H. B.		37
Hinds, Julia	37	
Hindson, Frank		1317
Hinkle, Dr.		358
Hinkston, Green		381
Hinkston, Greenbury	1816	1957
Hinkston, John		1156, 1816
Hinkston, John G.		1144, 1360
Hinkston, Joseph	1957	
Hinshaw, W. P.	1087	
Hinz & Landt	1810	
Hinz, A.	1810	
Hinz, August C.	865	
Hirschler, Ed.		1935
Hitchcock, Hollis	122, 538, 612, 667, 926, 2075	1091, 1184, 1585, 2027
Hixon, William H.		1514
Hoadley, J. F., Jr.		1881

Person/Entity	Plaintiff Suit #	Defendant Suit #
Hoag, Charles		450
Hoag, David		450
Hoag, J. W.		14
Hoag, James W.		948
Hoag, O. H.		302, 358, 1345, 1368, 1505, 1512, 1744, 2104, 2213
Hoas, John		358
Hobart, Mary A.	1632	1805
Hobbs, Caroline	1517, 1568	
Hobbs, Elijah Moses		1517, 1568
Hobson, A. D.	1221	
Hodgson, David R.	2067	
Hodgson, R.		358
Hoe, Ah	1681	
Hoen, B.		358, 1166
Hoen, Bertha		2181, 2253
Hoen, Berthold	1694	1075, 2181, 2253
Hoen, Carl A.		2181
Hoen, Carl Anderson		2253
Hoen, Ernest		1075
Hoen, Ernest M.		2181
Hoen, Ernest Martin		2253
Hoen, Mary		1075
Hoen, Mary A.	1694	
Hoen, Mary Anderson		2181, 2253
Hoen, Mary E.		2181
Hoen, Mary Elizabeth		2253
Hoffer, Charles		358
Hoffer, Charles A.		2043
Hoffman, C.		358
Hoffman, K. W.	1303	
Hofler, V. F.	1134	
Hofler, W. W.		1134
Hogan, Alice		1032
Hogan, Alice F.	2104	
Hogan, Thomas	1032	
Hohnan, J. H.		358
Holcomb, L. D.		404, 405

Person/Entity	Plaintiff Suit #	Defendant Suit #
Holden, E. S.	2259	
Holland, Mrs.		358
Hollister, Mary		358
Holloway, Lester	1359	
Holly & Magoon	245	
Holly, S. B.	245, 512	
Holm, Jacob F.		1412
Holm, John P.		1412
Holman, Francis C.	2292	
Holman, Josephine		358
Holmes, H. P.		2055
Holmes, C. H.		358
Holmes, Calvin H.		414
Holmes, Edward	1838	
Holmes, Frederick A.		1838
Holmes, H. T.		358
Holmes, Henderson P.		220, 1515, 2008, 2301
Holmes, John W.		1222
Holmes, Lydia N.		1222
Holmes, Rebecca M.		2008, 2301
Holmes, William		1838
Holst, Peter	2129	
Holt, W. A. S.	2108	358
Home Mutual Insurance Company of California		1394
Homer, James L.	12	
Hong, Ah	1981	
Honriet, L.	1006	
Hood, Alfred		338
Hood, E. E.		358
Hood, Eliza A.		716
Hood, Eliza Ann	177, 1336	
Hood, George	1587	358
Hood, George, Sr.		2148
Hood, T. B.		358
Hood, William	177	338, 1336
Hook, G. A.		338
Hooper, George F.		713, 1519
Hooten, M. V.	263	239
Hope, Valentine	472	

Person/Entity	Plaintiff Suit #	Defendant Suit #
Hopkins, Mary	185	358
Hopkins, Moses	2253	
Hopkins, Peter		1551
Hopkins, S. J	858, 1458, 1823, 1894	690
Hopper, Ellen S.		1140
Hopper, Isaiah D.		1140
Hopper, M. F.		1297
Hopper, Thomas	1419, 1515, 2001, 2008, 2301	358, 1467, 1813
Hornick, John	1855	
Hoskins, T. D.	1585	2048
Hosler, William H.	1599	
Hotchkiss, W. J.	1373	2203
Hottimer, J.		358
Houchins, Lucinda J.	1206	
Houne, H. C.		358
Houser, S. R.		448, 1094, 1150, 1151, 1304, 1331, 1332
Houser, Sylvester R.		1149
Hovenden, Thomas		1637
Hovey, Ada A.		1181
Hovey, Theodore	1181	
Howard, Mary C.		660
Howe, Abbie E.	722, 1047	
Howe, Ann Frances		581, 898
Howe, C. W.		152, 722
Howe, Charles W.		1047
Howe, Edwin A.		581, 898
Howe, Elijah	581	
Howe, Henry		1198
Howell, Albina		900
Howell, Eleanor M.		1748
Howell, John G.		61
Howell, L. V.		900
Howell, L. V., Jr.		900
Howell, Margaret		900
Howell, Morris		1748
Hoyt, Austin		191
Hubbell, Phoebe E.		2030

Person/Entity	Plaintiff Suit #	Defendant Suit #
Hubsch, A. J.		966, 980
Hudoff, C. D.		743
Hudoff, Theresa		743
Hudson, Alvin P.		1306, 1770
Hudson, Bettie		1306, 1770
Hudson, Elizabeth	716	358
Hudson, J.		1411
Hudson, John N.	1518	
Hudson, Lena		1306, 1770
Hudson, Mattie		1770
Hudson, Mattie F.		1306
Hudson, W. T.	1411	
Hughes, R.	644	
Hughes, Roland		675, 697, 778
Hugues, Ernest	502	
Humbolt Savings & Loan Society		1767
Humphries, Charles	1050	2187
Hunt, Manasah	839	
Hunt, Mannassah		752
Hunter, R. E.		155
Hunter, Robert E.		515
Hunter, Sarah A.	515	
Huntington, C. A.		301
Huntington, C. P.		905
Huntington, Rosanna	301	
Hurney, J. F.	1189	
Hussey, Edward	1493	
Hutchings, Martha E.	1761	
Hutchings, Mary H.	1182	
Hutchings, Thomas		1182
Hutchings, Thomas R.		1761
Hutchinson, Henry		543
Hutchinson, S.		358
Hutchinson, Samuel	396, 1194	
Hutoff, H.		358
Hutton, C. E.		775
Hutton, Charles E.	341	59
Hyde, -	224	
Hyde, P.		358

Person/Entity	Plaintiff Suit #	Defendant Suit #
Hyde, Patrick		1997
I. & A. M. Cook		357
Ijo, James		358
Immel, August		358
Independent Order of Odd Fellows Lodge		358
Inderstroth, Theodore	1369	
Infanger, Anton		1527
Ingham, A. H.	414, 2023½	358, 2015
Ingham, Andrew H.	900, 1012	
Ingham, Malinda J.		1012
Ingham, V.		358
Inghram, John M.		1674
Inghram, Mary E.		1674
Ingle, John		358
Ingram, I. J.		2031
Ingram, S. D.	1820	
Ink, W. P.		217, 267
Insurance Company of North America		790
Irons, Amos A.		358
Irvine, Henry P.		358
Irwin, Alfred	1526	
Irwin, George W.		358
Irwin, N. C.		1051
Irwin, Thomas N.	850	
Isaac, Morris		358
Isbell, William		292
Israel, Jacob		358
Israel, John		358
Isson, Robert		358
Italian Swiss Agricultural Colony	1596	
Itin, John	1444	358
Ivancovich, George	1794	
Iverson, Niles		290
Ives, George R.		358
J. Baumgarten & Co.	1697	
J. L. Sanderson & Co.		1518
J. Mather & Co.	169	
Jack, William		358
Jacks, Roberta		358

Person/Entity	Plaintiff Suit #	Defendant Suit #
Jackson, A.		1137
Jackson, Alden		358
Jackson, Andrew		358
Jackson, E. N. B.		11, 267, 358
Jackson, Evaline	11	267
Jackson, Frances F.	939	
Jackson, Frank	939	
Jackson, John B.		1372
Jackson, Mary		358
Jackson, Sherry	939	
Jackson, Timothy L.	939	
Jacobi, John		340, 1078
Jacobs, Brit	1549	
Jacobs, G. H.		210, 1751
Jacobs, George H.		418
Jacobs, Louis		358
Jacobs, M.	1686	
Jacques, J. F.		48, 358, 1456
Jacques, T.		358
Jaffe, L.		2138
James Clark & Sons		1842
Jamieson, J. H.		358
Jamison, Anne Jane	1994, 1999	
Jamison, William Jacob		1999
Janssen, F. A.	1470	
Jason Springer & Co.	1236	
Jasper, G. A.	2316	
Jenkins, Eliza	888	
Jenkins, Mary		823
Jenkins, Rebecca		823
Jenkins, W. J.		154
Jenkins, Wesley		823
Jennings, T.		358
Jenny, George		358
Jensen, Ole Chris		79
Jensen, Peter		358
Jesson, Samuel		53
Jewell, A.	555	
Jewell, J. R.		953

Person/Entity	Plaintiff Suit #	Defendant Suit #
Jewett, J. H.		1774, 1775, 1776, 1777
Jewett, M. M.		1774, 1775, 1776, 1777
Joe, Ah	1305	1238, 1328, 1406
John B. Ellison & Sons	1422	
John, Ah		540
Johns, J. C.		358
Johnson, A.		588
Johnson, Andrew		1424
Johnson, Andrew Bernard		1424
Johnson, Andy		358
Johnson, Ben (Rev.)		358
Johnson, C. T.		358
Johnson, Charles		358
Johnson, D. T.	1802	
Johnson, E.		358
Johnson, E. P. (Mrs.)		358
Johnson, George		2238
Johnson, George A.		358
Johnson, George C.		1209
Johnson, J. R.		358
Johnson, James Charles		2163
Johnson, Jeff		814
Johnson, John		1487
Johnson, M. (Mrs.)		358
Johnson, M. J. (Mrs.)		358
Johnson, Margaret	2163	
Johnson, Mary	2173	
Johnson, Mary Alice		347
Johnson, Orrick		347
Johnson, Richard		1056
Johnson, Robert		1513
Johnson, Robert C.	445, 1740	
Johnson, Sanborn		352, 1468
Johnson, Thomas		304
Johnson, William R.		951
Johnston, Ida	1046	
Jone, C. E.		949
Jones, B. M.	497	
Jones, C. B.		2266

Person/Entity	Plaintiff Suit #	Defendant Suit #
Jones, C. J.	1719	517, 532
Jones, Charles		1751
Jones, Christopher S.	766	
Jones, David	290	
Jones, J. C.		358
Jones, John H.	1688, 1783, 2213	
Jones, Martha		1688
Jones, Peter		338
Jones, Thomas		1351
Jones, Thomas H.		298
Jones, Thomas J.	1719	
Jones, William	629, 840	705
Jones, Winfield S.	90	
Jones, Zue	298	
Joost, John		358
Jordan, J. C.		358
Jordan, J. L.	1392	
Jordan, John		189, 201, 596
Joy, Addison		338
Joy, E. F.		1130, 1186½
Joyce, M.	1582	
Joyce, Martin	387, 951, 1013, 2143	1598
Joyce, Mary F.	1990	
Juan, Louie		1895
Judd, C.		358
Juillard, C. F.		262
Juilliard, C. F.		64, 97, 358, 1052, 1129
Juilliard, L. W.		906
Juilliard, Sarah A.	225	97
Justi, C.		1273
Justi, Charles		1264
Justi, Marie		1264, 1272
Justice, A. L.		358
Justice, Joan		492
Justices Court of Redwood Township		1311
Justin, Felix	2114	2135
Kahn, Louis	214	
Kahn, Moise		856
Kalkman, H. L.	319	

Person/Entity	Plaintiff Suit #	Defendant Suit #
Kamp, N.	1099	
Kane, Chauncey		480
Kane, Michael	115	185
Kane, O'Leary & Co.	115	185
Kasson, James		358
Kastich, Josephine	1046	
Kauffman, Frank	900	
Kauffmann, Phillip L.		1502
Kean, J. B.	1653	
Kean, Serena A.		1653
Kearney, Annie		2261
Kearney, D.		358
Kearney, Dennis H.		2261
Kearney, Elizabeth D.	62	1081
Kearney, John		1081
Kearns, George E.		21, 105
Kearns, James	1030, 1108	
Kearny, D. H.		922
Keay, William	369	343
Kedrolivansky, Alexandra	216, 260	
Kee, Hamilton	343	
Kee, James	588	
Kee, Kon	1436	
Kee, S. J.		369
Kee, William		369
Keegan, Timothy		2052
Keen, A. H.	1159	1657
Keener, J. D.		358
Keim, B. F.		358
Keith, A. D.		2033
Kelleher, P.		358
Kellep, Owen		358
Keller, John		931
Keller, Susie	931	
Kelley, Andrew		358
Kelley, J. W.		1752
Kelley, S. S.		358
Kellogg, C. W.	1883	
Kellogg, Long		358

Person/Entity	Plaintiff Suit #	Defendant Suit #
Kelly, C. A.	1963	
Kelly, C. E.		2234
Kelly, John		18
Kelly, Luke		358
Kelly, Timothy		2001
Kelsey, B.		1254, 1382, 1534
Kendall, Charles Elmer		1818
Kendall, Homer	2134	
Kendall, John	1521	1818, 2291
Kendall, Maria		2291
Kendall, Maria K.		1818
Kennady, D.	1887	
Kenneally, Elizabeth	1652	
Kenneally, James	1652	
Kennedy, C. W.	2137	
Kennedy, Catharine		1961
Kennedy, Charles D.		761
Kennedy, E. H.		2002
Kennedy, Electa		358
Kennedy, Flora		1961
Kennedy, G. H.		2152
Kennedy, George		974
Kennedy, George H.	1931	2014, 2137
Kennedy, James		1779
Kennedy, Nancy A.		1931
Kent, James		358
Kenyon, Edward		34
Kenyon, Edwin	565	
Keran, James N.		1247
Kern, Henry		358
Kerns, Charles		358
Kerr, Hester Ann	976	
Kerr, John		358
Kerr, R. A.		358
Kerr, Robert		976
Keser, L., Jr.	1151	
Keser, Louis, Jr.	1304	2308
Kessing, C.	1716	
Kessing, Clement		810

Person/Entity	Plaintiff Suit #	Defendant Suit #
Kessing, J. F.		1716
Kessler, August	2212	
Ketelsen, Ocke		1750
Key, Harry		1210
Keyes, H. M.		1482, 1741
Keyes, M. M.		1741
Keyes, S. E.		1482
Kidd, E. (Mrs.)		358
Kier, H.	1255, 1593	
Kimball, George H.	1084	1219
Kimball, H. R.		358
Kimble, Jerry W.	1064	
King, Ah		981
King, C. A.		832
King, Flora Ellen		1545
King, G.		1218
King, G. F.		2246
King, George		1327
King, George F.	1929	1026
King, John	459	
King, Joseph		1545
King, Mary E.	1695	
King, N.	1193, 1256, 1393	1590, 1924
King, Samuel	459	
King, William	1695	
King, William M.		358
Kingery, S. S.	372	
Kingsbury, J. T.		302
Kingsland, T. G.		358
Kinkead, C. I.		1503
Kinney, Owen		358
Kinston, J. F.		358
Kirby, Elizabeth		514
Kirby, John	514	
Kirby, John H.		514
Kirch, H.	465	
Kirch, Henry	1034	618
Kirkpatrick, D.	307	
Kirkpatrick, J. M.		358

Person/Entity	Plaintiff Suit #	Defendant Suit #
Kirsh, Joseph		358
Kise, Etta		358
Kiser, Anton	1779	
Kissack, Andrew	1039	
Kissack, Delmar Max		1039
Kissack, Lewin D.		1039
Kizer, A.		433
Kizer, A. N.		1763
Kizer, Abe		851, 852
Kleiser, J. A.		304
Kleiser, James A.	73	
Klute, Anna C.	1170	
Klute, Henry	1170	358
Knapp, A. H.	1056, 1647, 1648	135
Knapp, G. W.		135
Knecht, Frederich		2292
Knight, Dwight		338
Knowles, D. C.	1953	
Knowles, W. A.		2002
Knox, Ellen Walker Johnson		620
Knox, Robert		620
Knust, Charles		2231
Knust, Sarah		2231
Koch, A.		358
Koenig, Ellen		854
Koenig, F.		548
Koenig, Frank	854	
Kohle, August		358
Kohle, Augustina		662
Kohle, Catherine	662	
Kohle, Minnie L.		662
Kohle, William H.		662
Kolb, William		376
Kong, Ah		360
Koop, J. C.		1329
Kopp, William		358
Korbel, A.	164, 546	
Korbel, F.	164, 546	
Korbel, J.	164, 546	

Person/Entity	Plaintiff Suit #	Defendant Suit #
Kortick, James		338
Koster, John L.		1425, 1650
Kraft, E. H.		1751
Kraft, P. E.		358, 674
Kraft, Rosamond	674	
Krager, Isabella G.	1168	
Kreuz, Catherine		1349
Kreuz, Frank P.		1349
Kriecht, F.		358
Kron, Elisabeth	1110, 1187, 1288, 1530	1273
Kroncke, H.	1860	
Krone, Elizabeth		1269
Kronke, H.		358
Krugar, Oscar F.		154
Kruse, E.		2097
Kruse, Edward		275
Kuhfuss, Herman		1699
Kulberg, Andrew	940	941
Kumli, Jacob		358
Kuykendahl, -		358
Kuykendahl, G.		358
Kuykendahl, J.		358
La Société Française d'Epargnes et de Prévoyance Mutuelle	223	
Label, H.	421	149, 318, 358, 452
Lacey, B. T.	1357	
Lachman, H.		1727
Lacock, Driden		783
Lacock, M. A.	783	
Ladd, L. D.		338
Ladd, S. D.		358
Lagomassini, L.		358
Laguna Drainage District	473, 625	
Laik, Ellen V.		1453
Lake, A. B.		222
Lake, Prudence J.	222	
Lamar, W. F.		2237
Lambert George L.		1861
Lambert, C. E.		1861, 1959, 1975
Lambert, C. L.		984

Person/Entity	Plaintiff Suit #	Defendant Suit #
Lambert, Caroline V.		1861
Lambert, Charles L.	462, 471	
Lambert, Frank H.		249
Lambert, Jennie King	1959, 1975	
Lambert, R. F.		1861
Lambert, W. S.	1861	
Lamoreaux, G. W.		821
Lamott, Charles		578
Lampe, William A.		248
Lancel, A.	1276	681, 2285
Lancel, Anselme		2120
Lancel, Anselme H.		1565, 1728, 2254, 2255
Lancel, Anselmo		1294
Lancel, E.	1276	
Lancel, Eugene H.		2254, 2255
Lancel, Eugene Henri		1565
Lancel, Isaiah		1294
Lancel, Leon A.		2254, 2255
Landsborough, Thomas S.	1023	
Landt, P.	1810	
Landt, Paul	865	
Lane, Edward		47
Lang, Ah	1987, 1995	
Langdon, C. W.		584
Langdon, Nora		584
Langdon, Norah		358
Langley, Jacob		2216
Lannan, P.		1036
Lannan, Patrick		857
Larch, J. M.		358
Larson, John		1161
Latapie, E. (Mrs.)		358
Latapie, Edward		593
Latapie, Eleanor L.	788	
Latapie, Eleanora L.		593
Latham, Mary McM.		223
Latham, Milton S.		223
Latimer, L. D.		358
Latson, F. P.		1905

Person/Entity	Plaintiff Suit #	Defendant Suit #
Laughlin, C. W.		1732
Laughlin, J. M.	2031	
Laughlin, John M.		582, 632
Laughlin, L.		1732
Laurence, James A.	1277	
Lauterne, Ferdinand	1363	
Lauterne, M. A.		1363
Lavell, Jane		1861
Lawler, Bridget		2249
Lawler, P.		513
Lawrence, H. E.		1799
Lawrence, J. A.		358
Laws, Robert		322
Lawson, F.		358
Lawson, F. M. (Mrs.)	198	
Lays, Jane	1206	
Lays, Richard	1206	
Layton, G. Richard		1019
Leal, Antoine		1578
Lean, Antoine		1572
Leard, Alfred		1696
Leary, Austin A.		2230
Leary, Minnie	2230	
Leavenworth, Cornelia T.		432
Leavenworth, F. M.		432
Leavenworth, T. M.	784, 1209, 1425, 1650	703, 1273, 1523, 1767
Leavenworth, Thaddeus M.	1272	
LeBarron, Harrison M.	74	
LeClerck, F.		358
Leddy, Patrick		358
Lee, Joe Wah		2023
Lee, Joseph	1668	
Lee, Quong		1224
Lee, Robert		1684
Leek, W. G.		358
Lehman, G.		358
Lehn, Charles		782, 884
Leiby, Fannie K.	903	
Leiby, George		903

Person/Entity	Plaintiff Suit #	Defendant Suit #
Leicher, B.		424
Leicher, N.	424	
Leiding, C. F.	1727	
Leitch, John		1881
Lem, Jacob		358
Lemon, Samuel		358
Lemon, Thomas		358
Leng, Simon		358
Leonard, L.	748	746
Leppo, D.	2015	
Leroy, Oscar		1969
LeRoy, Theodore		223, 1273
Lessel, A.	365	
Letold, J. G.		358
Leveroni, Giovanni	114	
Leveroni, Manuel	508	
Levoroni, Manuella		511
Levroni, Giovanni Battista		114
Levy, M.	1316, 1334	
Lewis H.		1346
Lewis, Eugene	530	522
Lewis, Gilford Howard	1519	
Lewis, H.		1347
Lewis, J.		358
Lewis, James H.		141
Lewis, Mary	1206	
Lewis, Oliver H.		603, 604
Lewis, R. E.		1124, 1751
Lewis, W. A.		1461
Lewis, William		1538, 1547
Lewis, William B.		358
Lewton, Lewis	1380	
Lichon, A. E.		1352
Liebig, F.	491	
Liebman, L.	652, 738	
Light, E. H.		358
Light, William	78	359
Lightner & St. John		955, 1284
Lightner, J. S.		955, 1689

Person/Entity	Plaintiff Suit #	Defendant Suit #
Lightner, John S.		1284
Lilenthal, E. R.		1885
Lilenthal, J. Leo		1885
Lilienthal & Co.		1885
Lillie, C. H.	684	
Lillie, J. H.		358
Lim, Lee	953	
Lin, Yo		694
Lindemood, Israel	900	
Linebaugh, A.	2012	
Linebaugh, Emma		2100
Linebaugh, R. A.	2100	
Ling, Ah	1980	937
Ling, James		358
Lingenfelter, William J.	1287	
Linne, Henry		358
Linville, B.	13	
Linville, J. A.	13	
Lippitt, E. S.	945, 1884, 2243, 2262, 2278	
Litchfield, Durant	900	
Little, H. W.		858
Little, J. D.		690
Little, Joe H.		858
Little, John D.		858
Litton, Agnes D.	2307	
Litton, Walter		358
Liveroni, Augusti	1619	
Liveroni, Catherine	1188	
Liveroni, John	1473	
Liveroni, Manuel		1188
Liverpool & London & Globe Insurance Company		1053
Lloyd, Alice		297
Lock, George	1415	
Lockwood, William	1570, 1571	
Lodge, J. D.	340, 1852	433
Logan, James		358
Logan, John		985
Lohr, G. P.		358

Person/Entity	Plaintiff Suit #	Defendant Suit #
Long, A. S.	842	358
Long, Aaron S.	532	
Long, Catharine		358
Long, Isaac		1811
Long, John		358
Long, L. F.	1699	
Long, Mariam W.	532	
Loomis, Frank		736
Lopez, Bernardo		2127
Lord, Bessie A.	2162	
Lord, Charles A.		1868
Lord, Eva I.	1868	
Lord, F. F.		2162
Lorentino, Antonio		1096
Loucks, A. H.		358
Loucks, Mort	1440	1463
Lougee, Frank W.	1214	
Low, Elizabeth	908	
Low, Ellen N.	908	
Low, Frank E.	908	
Low, Harriet A.		908
Low, Martin L.	908	
Low, N. A. (Mrs.)		358, 1455
Low, William Wallace	908	
Lowe, Ah	1982	
Lowe, George		107, 108, 109, 110
Lowe, George Frederick		1925
Lowe, Jennie Elizabeth	1925	
Lowell, Alphia		1283
Lowell, J. P.		1279, 1283, 1291
Lowery, J. J.	145	
Lowery, M. N.	146	
Lowery, N.	147	
Loy, Wong		1404
Ludolff, Henry		1092
Ludwig, -		52
Ludwig, Mary (Mrs.)		1699
Ludwig, T. J.	406, 1354, 1860	165, 166, 167, 168, 169, 170, 179, 363, 518

Person/Entity	Plaintiff Suit #	Defendant Suit #
Ludwig, Thomas J.	182	163, 164, 503, 1357, 1813
Luedke, J.	566	
Lum, Sam		809
Lunardini, E.		1399
Lunardini, G.		1672
Lung, Ah		767
Lung, Wong Ah		759
Lunibus, John		1519
Lunsford, R. B.	1127	
Luttrell, J. K.		358
Lynch, Charles	244	
Lynch, Ellen	1998	
Lynch, James M.	710	672
Lynch, John	244	
Lynch, Michael	244	
Lynch, Sarah P.	672	1669
Lyndup, P.	1928	
Lyon, A. (Mrs.)		358
Lyon, A. J.	1206	
Lyon, Charles	1206	
Lyon, John H.	1206	
Lyon, Prudence	1206	
Lyon, Robert	1206	
Lyon, Sarah A.	1206	
Lyon, William	1206	
Lyons, Agnes P.		780
Lyons, Thomas M.		780
M. Gradwohl & Co.		66
Maccaby, George		649
Maccaby, Mark		649
Macdonald, D. F.	2242	
Machado, John	740	
Machado, Rosa	740	
Macy, Eliza		267
Macy, J. H.		267
Macy, Martha		267
Maddux, William H.	741	
Madegan, Allie	204	

Person/Entity	Plaintiff Suit #	Defendant Suit #
Madegan, William D.		204
Maderias, A. J.		1521
Magee, Richard	1105	
Magini, Catharine	300	
Magini, Joseph		300
Magnolia and Healdsburg Fruit Company	2192, 2193	
Magoon, H. K.		78
Magoon, W. H.	245	
Maguiness, Thomas		1783
Mahé, Gustave		223
Maher, James	1531	
Mailer, James		358
Maim, William		358
Main & Winchester	1169	
Main, Charles	1169	
Main, Medora		1838
Malloney, Bartholomew	835	
Malloy, John		2234
Malone, Kate		358
Malone, P.		1024
Malone, Peter		257
Maloney, Bartholomew		837
Maltern, F.		358
Manfredini, P.	1795	
Manfredini, Pietro	1827	
Mangini, Catharina	416	
Mangini, Joseph		416
Mann, Edward H.	1168	
Mann, Lulu B.	1541	
Mann, R. F.		933
Mann, Robert J.		1541
Mann, Thomas D.	1168	
Manning, Georgia Ann	446	
Manning, John	824	1454
Manning, Kate		2300
Manning, N. E.		2300
Manning, Robert S.		446
Manzy, S. H.	1660	
Marchisio, Delfino		2142, 2153

Person/Entity	Plaintiff Suit #	Defendant Suit #
Marchisio, Katie	2153	
Marcles, John		121
Marcus C. Hawley & Co.	399	
Marcy, J. G.	2017	
Markell, R. S.		316½, 1881
Markham, Andrew	364	36
Marks, B.		358
Maror, C.		358
Marsh, Henry	200	
Marshall, James		358, 572
Marshall, John		749
Marshall, Lucy A.		2030
Marshall, Robert	749	2182
Marshall, S. A.		430, 505
Marshall, Sarah A.		749
Marshall, W. A.		358
Marsteinstein, Jacob A.	1278	
Marti, M.	801	364, 718
Martin, Adeline	789	
Martin, Angeline B.		123
Martin, C. J.	789	
Martin, Camile	789	
Martin, Eliza Jane	961	
Martin, Ezekiel	1946	
Martin, F. H.	402	
Martin, F. McG.	2236, 2311	
Martin, H. B.	411	358
Martin, Hypolite	789	
Martin, J. M.	754	123
Martin, John	2133	2119
Martin, Joseph P.	1143	
Martin, Mary		1946
Martin, Nathaniel E.		961
Martin, Silas M.	434, 435	
Martinelli, Antonio		598, 599, 600
Martinelli, L.		1474
Mason, Frank L.	2047	
Mason, Jennie F.		2047
Mason, Matthew		1123

Person/Entity	Plaintiff Suit #	Defendant Suit #
Mason, W. C.	881	
Masonic Hall Association		358
Massa, Antonio	2277	
Masterson, John		2286
Matern, F.		683
Mather, J.	169	
Mather, John	467	
Mather, Mary Eloise		467
Mather, S.		358
Mather, Samuel	517	
Mathews, M. (Mrs.)		358
Mathewson, James M.		53
Mathison, George		1481
Matson, J.		358
Mattei, G.	1575	
Mattei, Santina	1575	
Matthews, L. P.		1076
Matthies, Henry	541	
Matthies, Lina	2086	
Matzger, -		358
Mauldin, B. F.		252
Mauzy, S. H.		1655
Maxwell, George H.		2092
May, Edward J.		358
Mayer, August	717, 739, 762, 1148	
Mayer, J. S.		877
Mayer, Jacob F.		766
Mayer, L. W.		877
Mayfield, G. W.		1128
Maynard, F. T.	513	711, 1538, 1547, 1563
Maynard, Frank T.	1277	
Mayne, Joseph		358
McAllester, John		491
McAllister, John	1056	
McAnally, Elsie		731
McAnally, W. W.	731	358
McAnnally, Elsie		736
McAnnally, W. W.	736	
McArthur, D.		1422

Person/Entity	Plaintiff Suit #	Defendant Suit #
McBreen, Mrs.		358
McBride, Georgie	474	
McBrown, John		434, 435
McCabe, A.		2110
McCann, J.		358
McCann, James		358
McCarthy, Charles		726
McCarthy, E. R.	1378, 1615, 1667	
McCaughey, James		1073, 1259
McChristian, James	280, 900	
McChristian, Patrick	1394, 1609	280, 1123
McChristian, Richard	280	
McChristian, Sarah	2308	
McChristian, Sylvester	280	
McClellan, James E.	1589	
McClelland, Buchanan		1289, 1290
McClelland, Elizabeth B.		1289, 1290
McClelland, J. J.	258	358
McClemmy, John	381	1059
McClendon, W. J.		1751
McClish, J. L.		1751
McClish, John N.		1751
McCluskey, W.		1167
McCluskey, William	2245	1211
McClymonds & Fritsch		58
McClymonds, J. W.		58
McCollough, T.		358
McConathy, Frances Ann	316½	
McConathy, James	316½	
McCone, Robert	1634	
McConn, J.		358
McConnell, W. E.		358
McConnell, William E.		1460, 1526, 1770
McCook, John		1785
McCord, James H.	100	
McCormack, William M.	1717	
McCoy, Charles L.	2087	
McCoy, Mary		358
McCracken, Anna P., Jr.		1336

Person/Entity	Plaintiff Suit #	Defendant Suit #
McCracken, Anna P., Sr.		1336
McCracken, Charlotte M.		1336
McCracken, Emma		139, 1034
McCracken, George F.		139, 1034
McCracken, Jasper		139, 1034
McCracken, John		1336
McCracken, John Henry		1336
McCracken, Mary J.		1336
McCracken, Mary Jenkin		1336
McCracken, William D.		1336
McCrea, J.		358
McCrea, William		876
McCullough, C. (Mrs.)		358
McCullough, J. A.		358
McCumisky, James		796
McCune, Ada		793, 1214
McCune, Ada Wakelee		793, 1214
McCune, Alexander		793, 1214
McCune, Alexander Charles		793, 1214
McCune, J. N.		1214
McCune, James N.		793
McCune, James Nelson		793, 1214
McCune, Laura Georgiana		793
McCune, Laura Georgina		1214
McCune, Lena		443
McCune, S.	1261	
McCutchin, William		792
McCutchin, William H.		792
McDaniel, Oliver		1988
McDermott, C. F.		358
McDermott, Charles F.	1216	
McDermott, William		1412
McDevitt Bros.		244
McDevitt, Charles		244
McDevitt, James		244
McDonald, Emma		1772
McDonald, M. L.		167, 358
McDonald, Mark L.	2270	501, 518, 593, 2004, 2021

Person/Entity	Plaintiff Suit #	Defendant Suit #
McDonald, P.		358
McDonell, Alexander		1961
McDonell, Bell		1961
McDonell, Christy		1961
McDonell, Donald		1961
McDonell, Flora		1961
McDonell, G. A.		1961
McDonell, John		1961
McDonell, Maggie		1961
McDonell, Maggie (Mrs.)		1961
McDonell, Margery		1961
McDonell, Mary		1961
McDonell, Mary J.		1961
McDonell, Nancy		1961
McDonell, R. A.		1961
McDonnell, James J.	4	
McDonogh, Thomas	1844	
McDonough, Michael		509
McElarney, Frank	304	1616
McElarney, Jim		1983
McFarland, John		2059
McFarland, Margret	2059	
McGarvey, R.	1885	
McGarvey, Robert		290
McGee, James H.	390, 609, 995	358
McGee, Robert	43	
McGee, Sarah		358
McGeorge, F. B.		358
McGeorge, Robert		358, 1008
McGinty, James		1634
McGovern, D.	606	
McGown & Clarkson	2128	
McGown, J. E.	2128	
McGregor, F. B.		358
McHarvey, Charles	472	
McHeamy, James		1270
McIntosh, J. E.		661
McIntosh, Margaret		661
McIntyre, Emily		20

Person/Entity	Plaintiff Suit #	Defendant Suit #
McKeadney, Hugh		862
McKeadney, Kate	862	
McKean, Hugh		1587
McKeand, Anna		1125
McKenzie, D. W.		684
McKenzie, Eliza	155	172
McKenzie, James	900	
McKenzie, John	155	
McKenzie, John A.	418	172
McKenzie, K.	481	
McKenzie, Kenneth	155	
McKenzie, Kenneth E.		172
McKenzie, Margaret	418	
McKenzie, William A.	155, 418	172
McKnight, J.		358
McLaine, D.		358
McLaren, Daniel		279
McLaren, William D.		279
McLaughlin, William	1446	
McLean, D. J.		148
McLean, Donald		706
McLeane, George M.		1074
McLeane, Ina B.		1074
McMackin, James	760, 1101	1195, 1358, 1763
McMahon, Alexander		358
McManus, J. G.		247
McMeans, A. C.		358
McMillan, H.		1647
McMillan, Sarah Jane	963	
McMillan, Wilson		963
McMillen, Henry		1909
McMinn, J.		338
McMinn, John		81, 82, 88, 89, 258, 358, 1015, 1682
McMinn, Joseph		1015
McNair, -		358
McNair, D.		358
McNamara, B.	2178	1610
McNamara, Bernard		888

Person/Entity	Plaintiff Suit #	Defendant Suit #
McNamara, Ethel May		2115
McNamara, James	2077	
McNamara, James B.		2115
McNamara, James J.		2115
McNamara, Maggie		2115
McNamara, Margaret		2115
McNamara, Thomas B.		2115
McNear, George P.	1350, 1577, 1899, 1941	1804, 1894
McNear, J. A.	1461	
McNear, John A.		1894
McNeil, Elizabeth Ann Kennedy		1779
McNeil, John		281
McNew, Emily	217	
McNew, Z.		278
McPeak, Harmon		850
McPherson, A. W.		933
McPherson, Annie		1988
McPherson, Colborn		1988
McPherson, Early		1985, 1988
McPherson, Ewell		1988
McPherson, Lycurgus	455	462, 471, 1988
McPherson, Mary		1988
McPherson, Miller	1988	
McPhillips, Francis		129
McQuade, John	1259	
McReynolds, Elizabeth	2125	
McReynolds, Jacob	15, 476, 500	
McReynolds, James	255, 1176	358
McReynolds, James (Mrs.)		358
McReynolds, John		255
McReynolds, R. E. L.		2125
McReynolds, William		83
McRossie, James		1717
McRossie, Jane		1717
McVay, James A. J.		1788
McVay, Lucinda	1788	
Meacham, Harrison	434, 435	
Mead, James A.		384
Mead, Sarah J.	1901	

Person/Entity	Plaintiff Suit #	Defendant Suit #
Mead, W. E.		358
Mead, W. H.		206, 358, 406, 516, 525, 654
Mead, W. R.		46, 358
Mead, William E.		1901
Mealy, Jane	922	
Mecartney, A.		2016
Mecartny, A.		1899
Mecham, H.	245, 2131	
Meeker, A. P.	573	1493, 1989
Meeker, C. E.	573	
Meeker, Leslie	573	
Meeker, M. C.		1493, 1989, 2108, 2109, 2177
Meeker, Melvin C.	2258	
Meeker, R. W.	573	
Mego, Toney		1250
Mehan, Daniel		2026
Meinzer, Antoine		1949
Melder, G. M.		1205
Melder, P. A.	1205	
Meldrum, David	501	
Melone, Peter		855
Melson, J. B.		358
Melson, James		358
Melton, Clymena	2210	
Melton, James B.	2210	
Melton, Robert W.	2210	
Melton, William		218
Melton, William W.	2210	
Mendosa, Cerilda		2022
Mendosa, S.		1850
Menefee, S. A.		358
Menihan, Michael	1748	
Merchant, Fred H.	1933	
Merchant, Joel	1890, 1944	388
Merian, Louis		1863
Merriam, Nathan	1826	
Merrill, E. A.		358

Person/Entity	Plaintiff Suit #	Defendant Suit #
Merrill, W. P.		245
Merritt, P. E.		70
Mersereau, H. P.		1084
Metcalf, C. E.	1445, 1512	
Metcalf, J.		358
Metcalf, Phoebe	544	
Methodist Episcopal Church North		358
Methodist Episcopal Church South		358
Methodist Episcopal Church South, Trustees of	1886	
Metzger & Hatimer		358
Metzger Bros.	1138, 1302	1403, 1409
Metzger, A. V.		1409
Metzger, Albert V.	1138	1403
Metzger, E. B.		1409
Metzger, J. E.		1409
Metzger, Joseph E.	1138, 2009	1403
Metzger, W.		358
Metzger, William		358
Meyer, Anton	967, 1580	
Meyer, Caroline Louise		1502
Meyer, Catherine Bertha		1502
Meyer, Charles		358
Meyer, Eleanor W.	900	
Meyer, Elizabeth		1502
Meyer, George S.		730
Meyer, Lorentz	1502	
Meyer, Lorentz, Jr.		1502
Meyer, Margareta Salamona		1502
Meyer, S.	1495	
Meyer, Sam		1402
Meyer, Samuel	1342, 1758	2122
Meyer, William		1081
Meyer, William Jacob		1502
Michael Piezzi & Co.	36	
Micheli, Charles	560, 1396	
Michels, A. W.		95
Michels, Friedlander & Co.		95
Michels, Louis M.		95
Michelssen, Brown & Co.		1121

Person/Entity	Plaintiff Suit #	Defendant Suit #
Michelssen, Edward		1121
Michili, C.		410
Middleton, Eliza F.	220	
Middleton, W. V.		358
Miller, Armelia M.		849
Miller, C. S.		895, 1666
Miller, Charles		232, 1666
Miller, D. E.		7
Miller, Daniel E.		1034
Miller, David		33, 536, 552
Miller, G. T.		2160
Miller, George F.	2078	
Miller, George T.	205, 265, 969, 1492, 1909	
Miller, Ina R.		358
Miller, J. H.		2211
Miller, James R.	849	
Miller, John		1666
Miller, John H.	2078	
Miller, Julia A.	33	
Miller, Mary J.	849	
Miller, Rachel		849
Miller, Rosa A.	846	
Miller, Thomas B.		358
Miller, W. M.		846
Miller, Zerilda		849
Millerick, John		1992, 1993, 2074, 2260, 2279
Millerick, M.		1993
Millerick, M. J.	2279	
Millerick, Michael		6
Millet, A. R.	1798	
Millett, W. H.	464	
Milliken, Daniel		2140
Millikin, Belle	2140	
Mills, E. T.		358
Mills, John	129, 379, 407	358
Mills, Richard		2107
Mills, W. J.		1487

Person/Entity	Plaintiff Suit #	Defendant Suit #
Milon, Alphonse		924
Miltz, Theodore		478
Minear, Henry	384	
Minehan, M.	1588	304
Minges, Peter	927	
Minor, B. M.		1421
Minor, Fidus		1421
Mintzer, A. E.		2234
Mintzer, P. B.		2234
Misner, D. R.		1743
Mitcheli, Charles		1580
Mitchell, Annie C.		90
Mitchell, C. E.	1814	1881, 2025, 2060
Mitchell, D. C.	1375	
Mitchell, John H.		90
Mitchell, Linwood W.		1991
Mitchell, Marcus	705	
Mitchell, Margaret A.	1991	
Mitchell, N. O.		144
Mitchell, R. T.		358
Mitchell, Sadie E.		90
Mitchell, Samuel J.	1642	
Mittchell, G. F.		863
Mize, Aditha		309
Mize, Albert	309	
Mize, Fred		2039
Mize, John		2039, 2040, 2041
Mock, Wesley		1190
Mock, Westly		358
Moeller,-		358
Moffitt, Sarah F.	1206	
Mokes, John		1272
Mokes, Peter		1272
Moler, John S.		358
Molero, Amelia		1042
Moltzen, D. F.	466, 618	465
Monahan, P., Jr.		597, 645
Monahan, P., Sr.	645	597
Monahan, Patrick		1002

Person/Entity	Plaintiff Suit #	Defendant Suit #
Monahan, Patrick, Jr.	1024	
Monahan, Patrick, Sr.	855	
Monfredino, A.		1241
Monroe, E. B.		358
Monroe, Eugene B.		296
Monroe, J. M.		358
Montfort, A. R.	2281	
Montgomery, A.	1443	836
Moody, Richard	2300	
Moody, W. B.		2002
Moor, Justin		358
Moore, A. P.	1512	1595, 1609
Moore, Anastasia	1990	
Moore, C. P.		1751
Moore, Charles	1990	
Moore, Ellen	1990	
Moore, James		290
Moore, James E.	1990	
Moore, Patrick	1627	
Moore, William	1990	
More, Samuel	1207	
Morey, Almeda	1907	
Morey, Mary A.		2051
Morgan, E. P.		358
Morgan, Edward		175
Morgan, G. W.		1937, 1938
Morgan, James		358
Morgan, Mary		358
Morgan, W. C.	522	1937, 1938
Moritz, Michael	124	
Moritz, Miche		856
Moritz, Michel		2220
Morrill, B. D.		59
Morris, Henry Z.		375
Morris, James B.	504	375, 1519
Morris, Joseph		1362
Morris, Mary E.		375
Morris, Miles	1166	
Morris, T. D.		1519

Person/Entity	Plaintiff Suit #	Defendant Suit #
Morris, Thomas D.		351
Morris, W. H.		358
Morrisey, Kate	1439	
Morrison & Curtis	1368	
Morrison, F. G.	440	
Morrison, J.		358
Morrison, J. J.	1368	
Morrison, Oscar		785, 800, 1335
Morrison, S.		358
Morrison, Thomas		2005
Morrow, C. E. (Mrs.)		358
Morrow, E. E.	1858	358, 1905
Morrow, Ellen C.	1990	
Morrow, George P.		1338
Morrow, Hattie B.		1670
Morrow, J. S.		358
Morrow, J., Jr.		358
Morrow, James	1670	
Morrow, James H.		1415
Morrow, Jane Doe		1415
Morrow, Robert F.		1851
Morse, Caroline		358
Morse, E. E.	576	373
Mortier, William		358
Mosely, A. P.	136, 878	
Mott, Charles W.		1219
Moulton, Kate D.		768, 1926
Moulton, W. M.		768
Moulton, William		732
Moulton, William M.		1926
Mount Jackson Quicksilver Mining Company	1053	341, 384, 461
Mowbray, Jane (Mrs.)		1699
Mucio		732½
Muller, Frank		1420
Muller, John		1353, 1924
Müller, John	2296	
Müller, Maria		2296
Muller, Mary		1924
Muller, Mary J.		1353

Person/Entity	Plaintiff Suit #	Defendant Suit #
Mulligan, Margaret		2080
Mulligan, William		2080
Mulvaney, Robert		281
Muma, Aditha	1199	
Muma, Peter		1199
Murdock, L. A.	2034	358
Murphy, Catherine	823	
Murphy, Delia		358
Murphy, H. E.		2011
Murphy, J. E.		2011
Murphy, James		358
Murphy, M. T.	171	
Murphy, Mary T.		358
Murphy, Matt		2150
Murphy, R.		179
Murphy, Rufus	570, 700, 1300, 1629, 1658, 1661	358, 546, 1677
Murphy, Wyman		302, 358, 943, 1005, 2289
Murray, Annie		1158
Murray, Dennis	718	801
Murray, Georgiana	1928	
Murray, Jack		230
Murray, Lena		443
Murray, Patrick		1046
Murray, W. E.	1274, 1286	
Mutch, Isabella	2095	
Muther, Fannie		358
Muther, Fannie M.	274	1710
Muther, Frank	1710	274
Mutual Relief Association of Petaluma	690	1378
Mutz, Henry	810, 973, 1048, 1093	488
Myer, Samuel	1631	
Myers, Dillon P.	601	
Myers, Edgar N.	1371	
Myers, Hannah P.		601
Myers, S.	1425½	
Myers, Sarah Ellen		1371
Nagle, F. G.	539	

Person/Entity	Plaintiff Suit #	Defendant Suit #
Nagle, F. H.		358
Nalley, A. B.	2210	1751
Nally, A. B.		218
Nanyoks, Annie M.	1799	
Napa Wood Company		1038
Nash, W. H.		358
Nason, Abner W.	1826	
Nathanson, Arthur		613
Nathanson, Arthur E.	1083	
Nathanson, Dora L.	1083	
Nathanson, Martin M.	1083	
Nathanson, R. E.	1083	
Naughton, John F.	1595	1525
Nay, L. G.		775, 1050, 1461, 1538, 1547
Nay, S. A.	1759	
Neal, Esther E.		1435
Neal, James M.		1435
Neblett, E.		64, 262, 358, 1129
Neblett, Edward	991	
Neece, A.		753, 772
Neece, Caroline		753
Needham, Festus	770	
Neeley, T. L.	1192	
Neely, L.		497
Neely, Robert	239	
Neely, T. L.	239	
Neff, Susan		850
Nelson, Alfred	1273	
Nelson, Edward		389
Nelson, L.		358
Nelson, W. C.		358
Nelson, William C.		695
Nepper, David		358
Netter, Henry		358
Neustadt, Walter		1606
Neville, John		1706
Nevins, E. M.	1135	
Nevins, William	732	

Person/Entity	Plaintiff Suit #	Defendant Suit #
Newby, Carrie	1496	1852
Newby, H. C.	2035	1225, 1496, 1852
Newmark, M. J.	115	185
Newsome, George F.		1039
Newton, Charles		358
Neyce, J. H.	977	1390, 2320
Niblock, James		1376
Nicholls, Samuel		358
Nichols, Asa C.	2155, 2324	
Nichols, Ellen W.	2324	
Nichols, Thomas	1743	
Nichols, W. K.		1962
Nick, A. D.		2263
Nicoll, D. C.		227
Nissen, E. P.		1090
Nixon, Robert S.		358
Noah, John G.		358
Noethig, William		1820
Noggle, William		358
Noonan & Towey	1309	
Noonan, Alice		1997
Noonan, Frank		1997
Noonan, George P.		408, 1476, 1997
Noonan, P.		358
Noonan, P. H.	1309	358
Noonan, Patrick H.		1997
Norcross, Harriet		358
Nordwell, O. W.		1764, 1773
Norsworthy, John M.		1376
North Coast Stage Company		2097
North Pacific Coast Rail Road Company		1952, 1953
North Pacific Coast Railroad Company		1695, 1889
Northup, E. G.	463	
Norton, Juliette		209
Norton, L. A.	190, 1374, 1434, 1592, 1726, 1978	59
Norton, Lonny		358
Norton, W. H.	1413, 1414, 1937	
Norton, W. M.		531, 1922

Person/Entity	Plaintiff Suit #	Defendant Suit #
Norton, William H.		1525, 1571
Nosler, H. E.		1200
Notti, James		1590
Nottingham, Thomas		358
Nourse, George E.		1443
Nourse, Laura A.		1443
Nowell, Adelia		358
Nowell, C. H.		358
Nowell, Charles	1196	
Nowell, Charles W.		1506
Nowell, Frank C.		1126
Nowell, Hattie	1126	
Nowlan, J. C.		31
Nowlin, S. S.	160	354
Nunan, George P.		358
O'Brien, John		568
O'Brien, John H.		678
O'Brien, Mary		358
O'Brien, Patrick	774	
O'Brien, William		358
O'Connor, Daniel	877	
O'Farrell, Cathal	280	
O'Farrell, Elena	280	
O'Farrell, Florence	280	
O'Farrell, Gerald	280	
O'Farrell, John J.	280	
O'Farrell, Louis	280	
O'Farrell, Minnie	280	
O'Farrell, William	280	
O'Flaherty, Ann		1478
O'Flaherty, Mary		1478
O'Flaherty, Patrick		1478
O'Flaherty, Patrick E.		1478
O'Grady, Thomas	142	131
O'Leary, Bridget		1493
O'Leary, Fergus	115	185
O'Leary, Thomas		1493
O'Neil, Charles		358
O'Neil, Mary		358

Person/Entity	Plaintiff Suit #	Defendant Suit #
O'Rear, W. E.		1943
O'Reilly, Martin	1156, 1842, 1957	1458, 1816
O'Toole, George		358
Oak, Henry L.		358
Oakland Quicksilver Mining Company		100, 1369
Oates, James W.	1719	
Odd Fellows Savings Bank		358
Odlum, Gabrella A.	187	
Odlum, Lorenzo D.		187
Ogden, Eliel		39, 279
Ogilvie, John	1940	
Oliver, Andrew		358
Oliver, Charles P.		358
Oliver, James F.		345
Oliver, Martha		345
Olmstead, J. (Mrs.)		358
Olmstead, O. A.		358, 1465
Olsen, Bernard		1028
Ord, Augustias	856, 2220	
Order of Mutual Companions	1095, 1315, 1333, 1388	1230, 1295, 1296, 1318, 1323, 1338
Ordway, John		358
Orr, John		859½
Orris, William		1836
Ossman, Abner	2248	
Ott, Nicholas		358
Ottis, Frank		358
Overton, A. P.		358, 1730, 1731, 1816
Overton, J. H.		358
Owens, -		358
Owens, George		1835
Owens, R. R.		358
Pabst, Cora	2037	
Pabst, George	2174	2037
Pacific Bank	357	
Pacific Benefit Association	1806	
Pacific Methodist College, President & Board of Trustees of		1830
Pacific Methodist College, President & Trustees of		397
Pacific Mutual Life Insurance Company of California	2116	

Person/Entity	Plaintiff Suit #	Defendant Suit #
Pacific Reclamation Company		370
Paddock, E. S.	1739	
Page, C. A.	1936	
Page, Charles	1352, 1594	
Page, Henry	1352, 1594	
Page, Thomas S.	1352, 1594	
Page, Wilfred	1352, 1594	
Page, Zasela		482
Paine, David	992	
Palmer, J. M.	2187	1194
Palmer, John A.	1416	1412
Panella, G.	949	
Park, George W.	1898	27, 1204, 1905
Parke, L. C.	1357	
Parker, E. C.	1651	
Parker, Emily		2201
Parker, John F.		2201
Parker, Minnie B.		1651
Parks, Abraham H.		1648
Parks, D. H.	1498, 1655	
Parks, D. H., Jr.		1648
Parks, O. B.		1498
Parrazzo, G.		469
Parrazzo, G. B.	447	
Parsons, Isaac	20, 478, 1813	
Parsons, Joseph		996
Partee, B. F.		1010, 1040, 1105
Partee, George		1010
Pasalaqua, Frank	2142	
Patten, Charles W.		714
Patten, Mary C. G.		1141
Patten, R. R.	1141	
Patterson, James		620
Patterson, James H.	1186	717, 739, 762, 1148
Patterson, Margaret		478
Patterson, Mary		1984
Patterson, William	845, 1984	
Pattini, Louis		1239
Paul, H. C.	1186½	1839

Person/Entity	Plaintiff Suit #	Defendant Suit #
Paula, John		740
Pauli, A. F.	1687	
Pauli, Caroline J.	1687	
Pauli, John	2291	
Pauli, Pauline M.	1687	
Payne, William		1469, 2154
Peal, W. J.		1310
Pearce, George	2217	127
Peckinpah, A. R.		41
Peckinpah, David A.		41
Peckinpah, Edward N.		41
Peckinpah, T. E.	997	
Peckinpah, T. Edgar		41
Pedrini, Angelo	2151	
Peffero, Benedetto		1057

Person/Entity	Plaintiff Suit #	Defendant Suit #
People	9, 10, 21, 22, 23, 24, 25, 55, 102, 103, 104, 105, 106, 107, 108, 109, 110, 111, 112, 121, 141, 172, 229, 230, 231, 232, 233, 237, 248, 249, 250, 251, 252, 253, 254, 257, 270, 271, 305, 311, 315, 322, 323, 324, 326, 330, 331, 335, 350, 353, 360, 362, 389, 403, 404, 405, 431, 441, 442, 443, 453, 480, 495, 496, 509, 511, 536, 540, 552, 562, 578, 587, 596, 603, 604, 624, 630, 641, 642, 643, 653, 676, 677, 678, 679, 680, 694, 714, 720, 725, 732½, 733, 734, 747, 757, 758, 759, 763, 771, 781, 804, 805, 808, 809, 814, 822, 832, 833, 837, 838, 847, 848, 851, 852, 853, 867, 880, 885, 886, 890, 910, 914, 920, 936, 937, 944, 948, 950, 959, 966, 974, 975, 980, 981, 985, 987, 990	

Person/Entity	Plaintiff Suit #	Defendant Suit #
People	1028, 1050, 1059, 1060, 1065, 1066, 1067, 1068, 1069, 1080, 1085, 1086, 1096, 1097, 1102, 1103, 1114, 1115, 1116, 1117, 1154, 1161, 1162, 1163, 1165, 1198, 1210, 1217, 1224, 1225, 1226, 1232, 1238, 1239, 1240, 1241, 1242, 1246, 1294, 1308, 1310, 1325, 1328, 1329, 1331, 1332, 1360, 1370, 1372, 1387, 1400, 1401, 1404, 1406, 1407, 1410, 1417, 1423, 1424, 1433, 1442, 1461, 1462, 1463, 1464, 1481, 1485, 1535, 1539, 1547, 1548, 1554, 1555, 1556, 1557, 1563, 1591, 1597, 1598	
People	1600, 1601, 1602, 1603, 1604, 1621, 1622, 1640, 1641, 1649, 1659, 1665, 1673, 1696, 1700, 1701, 1702, 1706, 1707, 1753, 1780, 1784, 1785, 1796, 1797, 1807, 1835, 1836, 1850, 1851, 1865, 1874, 1895, 1920, 1921, 1950, 1951, 1967, 1968, 1969, 1970, 1971, 1983, 2011, 2022, 2023, 2024, 2026, 2039, 2040, 2041, 2049, 2052, 2053, 2054, 2060, 2072, 2073, 2082, 2083, 2102, 2107, 2110, 2111, 2112, 2113, 2119, 2126, 2127, 2135, 2139, 2149, 2150, 2167, 2179, 2196, 2197, 2198, 2199, 2237, 2238, 2239, 2240, 2244, 2263, 2264, 2265, 2266, 2267, 2278, 2286, 2318, 2319, 2320	

Person/Entity	Plaintiff Suit #	Defendant Suit #
Peoples, Nathan		2
Perazzo, G.		1638
Percival Milling Co.	1918	1504
Perinoni, Filippo	1927	
Perinoni, G.		1215
Perkins & Benjamin		745
Perkins, -		745
Perkins, J. J.	933	
Perrin, E. B.	1914	
Perry, A. F.	1823	
Perry, James A.		420, 1823
Perry, John R.	1905	
Perry, William	1572, 1578, 1624, 1841	
Petaluma Savings Bank	370, 711, 1754	119, 128, 1894
Petaluma Turn Verein	5	
Petaluma, Board of Education of the City of		1538, 1547, 1563
Petaluma, Board of Trustees of the City of		1538, 1547, 2243
Petaluma, City of	410, 921, 994, 1235	709, 712, 1547, 2121
Peter, Martin	713	
Peters, John T.	1391	1386, 2303
Peters, Norah		2303
Peters, William		290
Peterson, C.		293
Peterson, Chris		399
Peterson, Christ	470	
Peterson, Edward	1729	
Peterson, Errick		1273
Peterson, Henry C.	460, 483	
Peterson, Jack		771
Peterson, Julius A.	400	
Peterson, Mary	1725	
Petit, A. P.		235
Peugh, Jennie	883	
Peugh, Jennie	1542	
Pfister, Conrad	799, 1869, 2004, 2021	
Pfister, Jacob O.		799
Phariss, P. H.	101, 844	1966
Philips, E.		1921
Philips, Edward	1873	

Person/Entity	Plaintiff Suit #	Defendant Suit #
Philips, H.		1921
Phillips, A. G.	1742	1547, 1563
Phillips, D. D.		2160
Phillips, Fannie E.	1031	
Phillips, Millard F.		1031
Phillips, S. E.		2160
Phillips, Thomas		50
Phillips, Walter	657	1752
Piatt, A.	2096	
Piatt, George A.	2058	
Piatt, J. P.	2062	
Pickett, Catharine B.		2116
Pickett, Mary E.		1273
Pickett, William	1025	2116
Pieper, Leon		2010
Pieratt, A. W.	807	
Pieratt, Gerald	1459	
Pieratt, James		1459
Pieratt, W. B.	807	
Pierce, Henry		1831
Pierine, Valentine	900	
Piezzi, Michael	36	
Piffero, Benedetto		1003, 1712, 1795
Piffero, Virginia	1712	1795
Pimm, Jacob	930	
Pinto, Jose Antonio		1009
Pipher, Andrew		2173, 2184
Pipher, Philip		2095, 2173, 2184
Pitts, William H.		824
Platt, B. C.		611, 647
Platt, Henry B.		836
Platt, John C.		836
Plumley, M. W.	868, 873	
Plumly, Mardon W.	1233	
Plummer, H. W.		872
Plunket, John	1382	
Plunkett, John		1534
Poe, Elihu		210
Poehlman, C.		709, 712, 945

Person/Entity	Plaintiff Suit #	Defendant Suit #
Poehlman, Conrad	1468, 2000	775
Poehlman, Martin	1468	
Polack, Mary	591	686
Polifka, Charles		2191
Polifka, Kreszentia	2191	
Polk, Charles E.		1050
Poly, Isaac	1815	
Pomeroy, George		1361
Pometta, D.		571
Pond, Milo B.	100	
Pool, Abbie	429	
Pool, Kinney D.		429
Poppe, Charles J.	2136	
Porter, J. K.	7	
Porter, J. V.		413
Porter, Thomas		547
Porter, W. W.	280	
Potter, Augusta E.	277	
Potter, Page G.		277
Powell, Moses	382	
Powell, R.	2229	
Powell, Ransom	655, 2294	
Powell, W. V.		349
Powers, David P.		212, 535, 2003
Powers, Frank	1427	
Powers, Jennie		1427
Powers, Jessie	660	
Powers, Lottie		2003
Powers, Mary C.	212, 535	
Praetzel, Albert	2250	
Presby, Elijah		907
Presby, Elizabeth	907	
Pressley, John G.		2048
Preston, J. M.		1194
Prewett, E.		1145
Price, Joseph K.	130	982
Pridham, Charles H.	1509	
Prince, David S.	87	
Prince, Peter	42, 148, 281	

Person/Entity	Plaintiff Suit #	Defendant Suit #
Prindle, Fred		1196
Prindle, Marion Ella		1196
Prindle, Nellie L.		1196
Prindle, William	81	
Pritchett, J. H.		1027
Proctor, Ira		246, 1751
Proctor, T. A.		225
Proletti, Joseph	1179	
Prouse, Daniel		773
Prows, Bettie		1425½
Prows, S. W.	1426	1425½
Prowse, James		2149
Pruett, E.		1278
Pulver, O. H.	2289	
Purrington, Frances		34
Purrington, Joseph		34, 54, 533, 549, 921
Purrington, T. F.	1606	
Purrington, Thomas F.		34
Quackenbush, Albert		330, 331
Quackenbush, Alfred		330, 331
Quackenbush, L. J.	521	
Quackenbush, Mary		964
Quackenbush, R. P.		521
Quackenbush, Russell M.	964	
Quackenbush, Sarah A.		652, 738
Quackenbush, U. P.	564	
Quackenbush, Uriah P.	138	
Quatman, J. H.		1233
Queen, C.		176, 631
Queen, W. D.		1483
Quen, C.		2097
Quigley, Laura		850
Quinlan, John		104, 947
Quinlan, Lydia		947
Quinn, John		595, 1822
Quinn, Margret	1822	
Quinto, J. M.	76	
Quitzow, A.		158
Quitzow, Aug		1022

Person/Entity	Plaintiff Suit #	Defendant Suit #
Quitzow, Augustus		1509
Quong, Sam		1165
R. T. Carroll & Co.	143, 173	
Raabe, M.		2203
Rackliff, Ella C.	1385	1383, 1384
Rackliff, Eugene L.	1383	1384, 1385
Rackliff, W. G.	1384	1383, 1385
Rafael, M. E.	1625	1624
Raffee, Angello		1758
Ragsdale, J. W.	315, 543	901
Railsback, Caleb	434, 435	
Rains, Anna	1576	
Rains, Gallant	911	1576, 2195
Rains, Jasper O'Farrell		1557, 1796
Rains, W. P.		911
Rambo, J. H.		1302
Rambo, Jacob		358
Rambo, Jacob J.		358
Ramsey, Rebecca L.	2032	
Ramsey, William H.		2032
Ranard, J. H.		1536
Randall, James S.	202	
Randolph, Jess	2182	
Raney, A. C.		358
Raney, John	1206	
Raney, O.		358
Raney, Sarah	1206	
Raney, Thomas	1206	
Raschen, John Frederick		1911
Rassmussen, S.	372	
Rawson, G. C.		1492
Rayner, Ann		2118
Rayner, John		2118
Read, Charles		358
Read, J. B.		358
Read, W. B.		822
Redden, Eugene		1665
Redding, B. B.		358
Redman, Dennis	34	

Person/Entity	Plaintiff Suit #	Defendant Suit #
Redman, Pat		358
Redmond, M. D.	452	
Redmond, Martin D.	408	
Redmond, Mary T.		358
Redmond, P.	902	
Reed, Bridget		1736, 2007
Reed, E. S.		1484, 2123
Reed, Ellen	1529	
Reed, J. H.	278	1846
Reed, James		1529
Reed, John	1190	
Reed, John J.		358
Reed, John S.	1699	
Reed, M. F. (Mrs.)		358
Reed, Matthew	2007	
Reed, Michael	1090	1736, 2007
Reed, P. W.	398	
Reed, W. A.		1601
Reed, W. C.		358
Reed, William B.		1380, 1483
Rees, T.	2316	
Reese, Michael		358
Reeves, Ezekiel		358
Regan, James C.		2061
Reghitto, David		919
Rehart, F. M.		2232
Rehart, Fannie M.		2234
Reigenbach, M. F.		303
Reiss, Jacques		967
Rendall, S. A.		358
Renfro, L. C.		397
Renfro, Mary		264
Renfro, Silas W.		264
Renhall, S.		358
Renieri, Mechi		1466
Rennie, William	1821	
Reno, Henry		358
Respini, J.	571	
Respini, Michael		1575

Person/Entity	Plaintiff Suit #	Defendant Suit #
Rex, William		358, 1443
Reynolds, W. B.		901
Rhegetti, Bartolemo		1345
Rhoads, Alphonso A. H.		1213
Rhodehaver, J. P.	1277	
Rhodes, A. J.		583
Rice, -		3
Rich, Abraham		358
Rich, John		358
Rich, John A.		439
Richard, G. W.		2256
Richards, John		338
Richards, Philena		287
Richards, Philena H.	488	
Richards, Phlena (Mrs.)		358
Richards, Victor		358
Richardson, A. J.		358
Richardson, E. H. (Mrs.)		358
Richardson, H. A.	1513	1724
Richardson, H. E.		756
Richardson, Helen E.		670
Richardson, Holena E.		1713
Richardson, J. H.		1713
Richardson, J. W.		358
Richardson, L. B.		756, 1713
Richardson, Maria H.	1510	
Richardson, Marie		2148
Richardson, Nathan W.		1510
Richardson, Thomas H.	1175	
Richardson, W. A.		528
Richey, John		1374, 1434, 1592, 1726
Richey, Virginia E.	1206	
Richliss, P. H.		338
Rickliff, Clinton		1370
Rickliff, P. H.		663
Rickliff, Peter		1417
Rickliffe, P. H.		358
Ridde, James		358
Ridgway, J.		358

Person/Entity	Plaintiff Suit #	Defendant Suit #
Ridgway, J., Jr.		358
Ridgway, J., Sr.		358
Ridgway, Jeremiah	272, 383, 492, 871, 1122, 1142, 1335	
Ridgway, Joseph	492, 871	
Ridgway, Joseph W.	272, 383, 1122, 1335, 1943	
Rien, George E.	1585	
Rien, J. M.	1585	
Rien, Mary A.		176
Rien, Nellie J.	1585	
Rien, S. W.	1585	
Rien, Samuel	39, 40	176
Righitti, Berto Lame	671	
Riley, A. W.		358
Riley, P.		1809
Ring, George E.	153	
Ripley, I. D.	2109	
Risdon, C.		256
Ritchie, John		828
Robbins, Abigail S.	2045	
Robbins, George H.		2045
Robbins, Leander	1408	
Roberts, Benjamin F.	2287	
Roberts, Charles	1736	1090
Roberts, D.	1147	
Roberts, Ella Jane		2287
Roberts, Frank	266	
Roberts, J. W.		929, 1133, 1189
Roberts, Mary		614
Robertson, Albert	1871	
Robertson, Albert B.		1874
Robertson, James Calhoun	1902, 1904, 1976	
Robertson, John T.		1806
Robertson, Mrs.		358
Robertson, Phoebe S.		504
Robertson, Robert		504
Robertson, Sarah Jessie	1902, 1904, 1976	
Robertson, William A.	1902, 1904, 1976	

Person/Entity	Plaintiff Suit #	Defendant Suit #
Robin, Victor G.		817
Robinson, Agnes	1046	
Robinson, J. R.		1727
Robinson, Jacob	174	
Robinson, James		132
Robinson, Laura A.		1727
Robinson, Margaret M. M.		463
Robinson, P. F.		1410
Robinson, William		992
Rockford, Thomas		131
Rodehaver, J. P.	245	420
Rodgers, Edward		2143
Rodgers, W. H.	1608	358
Roeding, F.		1574
Rogers, E.		1615
Rogers, E. A.	2157	
Rogers, Ethan L.	1867	
Rogers, H. G.	1101	
Rogers, J. R.	534	
Rogers, John L.	256	
Rogers, John R.	729	
Rogers, Sarah M.		534, 729
Rohte, Emil	275	
Roix, Charles F.	269	
Romine, Mary	1935	358
Ronald, Margaret	297	
Roney & Prince	42, 148, 281	
Roney, J. M.	42, 148, 281, 696, 1312	358, 1017, 1417, 1505
Rose, James		358
Rose, Joseph	71	393, 433
Ross, D. L. B.		1441
Ross, Elizabeth (Mrs.)		358
Ross, Frank		2046
Ross, Frank C.	1732	
Ross, James Edwin	1997, 2065	
Ross, R. C.		358
Rossi, Peter	1155	
Roth, D.		1121
Rothermel, Mary P.		780

Person/Entity	Plaintiff Suit #	Defendant Suit #
Rothermel, P.		780
Roux, Andrew F.		2106
Roux, M. L.		2106
Rowe, Orena		1614
Rowland, William		755, 1735
Rowshermer, J.		358
Royael, A. (Mrs.)		358
Royal Canadian Insurance Company		72
Royce, Rach		358
Royers, E. A.		358
Rubke, H.	1358	
Rue, James B.		869, 971
Rued, J. C.	1282	
Ruffino & Bianchi	1284	
Ruffino, L. J.	1284	
Ruffner, William		1684
Rugg, Fannie A.		1045
Rugg, William H.	1045	
Rule Mill, Lumber, Wood & Tan-bark Association		1900
Rule, Charles H. S.	1900	
Rule, Charles S.	193	
Rule, Edward J.	193	
Rule, Elizabeth	193, 1900	
Rule, Josephine	193	
Rule, Nannie A.	193	
Rule, Willie J.	193	
Runey, H.		358
Runyon, Alexander N.		209
Runyon, Emma M.		209
Runyon, Frederick M.		209
Runyon, Mary	419	209, 358
Runyon, R. B.		358
Runyon, Soloman		209
Runyon, William N.	209	
Rupe, D. C.	234	145, 146, 147, 314, 355, 622
Rupe, M. (Mrs.)		358
Rupe, Mary J.		622
Rupe, S. H.	289	

Person/Entity	Plaintiff Suit #	Defendant Suit #
Rurbke, H.		1206
Rush, John		1748
Russ, H.		1030, 1108
Russell, Amelia		956, 958
Russell, Henry		2150
Russell, W. F.		1524
Russell, William H.		956, 958
Russian River Land & Lumber Company		223
Rutherford, R. H.		2019
Ryan, Pierce	2005	
Ryan, William		358
Sacramento Bank	1081	
Sacry, D. S.		358
Sacry, Susan		358
Saeger, F.		358
Salsbury, W. H.	1236	
Sam, Ah	1016, 1982, 2132	808, 937
Samuel More & Co.	1207	
Samuels, James	1318	1968
Samuels, Jennie		1968
San Francisco & North Pacific Rail Road Company	63, 120, 179, 339, 516, 525, 567, 579, 582	358, 577, 587, 815, 881, 1611
San Francisco & North Pacific Railway Company	2188, 2189	
San, Yee	767	
Sanborn, E. P.	820	
Sanches, Ramon		1308
Sanders, Inda	1680	
Sanders, John		1680
Sanderson, J. L.		1518
Sanford, J. L.	901	
Sang, Ah		324
Sang, David		735
Sanger, Casker M.	2257	
Santa Rosa & Carquinez Rail Road Company	1762, 1763, 1764, 1765, 1766, 1767, 1768, 1769, 1770, 1771, 1772, 1773, 1774, 1775, 1776, 1777, 1803, 1831, 1877	
Santa Rosa Agricultural Park Association		358
Santa Rosa Alden Fruit Preserving Company		876

Person/Entity	Plaintiff Suit #	Defendant Suit #
Santa Rosa Bank	64, 75, 83, 133, 134, 144, 163, 294, 302, 397, 518, 593, 623, 638, 656, 695, 772, 790, 872, 1043, 1129, 1150, 1421, 1460, 2099, 2171, 2216	171, 358, 419, 960, 1304, 1768
Santa Rosa Fruit Preserving Company		358
Santa Rosa Gas Company		358
Santa Rosa Gas Light Company	2020	
Santa Rosa Manufacturing Company	1908	358
Santa Rosa Packing Company		2228
Santa Rosa Planing Mill & Building Company	1860	1905
Santa Rosa Savings Bank		358, 408
Santa Rosa Street Rail Road Company		358, 1562, 2028
Santa Rosa Water Company		358
Santa Rosa Water Works	580, 620	
Santa Rosa Water Works Company	1919	
Santa Rosa, City of	26, 27, 28, 29, 30, 31, 45, 46, 47, 48, 49, 50, 51, 52, 206, 529, 683, 721, 1448, 1449, 1450, 1451, 1452, 1453, 1454, 1455, 1456, 1465, 1466, 1476, 1562, 2156, 2225, 2226, 2227, 2228	197, 203, 358, 1904, 1976, 2166
Santa Rosa, Common Council of the City of		2128
Sargent, R. C.	1389	
Sartor, Antonio		86
Sartor, Joseph	86	
Sartor, Rosa		86
Sartori, P. G.		1393
Satterlee, George A.		133, 285
Satterlee, William		133
Saul, Anna A.	1055	
Saul, Rodman M.		1055
Savage, G. N.	874	358
Savings & Loan Society		358

Person/Entity	Plaintiff Suit #	Defendant Suit #
Savings Bank of Santa Rosa	334, 859½, 1015, 1021, 1073, 1227, 1245, 1249, 1752, 1846, 2019, 2048, 2055, 2089, 2105, 2295, 2304	73, 1075, 1281, 1508, 1677, 1694, 2156
Sawyer, Lucy H.		1382, 1534
Saxton, W. R.	900	
Schaeffer, Ignatz	506	
Schaeffer, Margaret		506
Scheeline, N.		394
Schell, Georgiana L.		156
Schell, Theodore L.		156
Schetter, Otto	576	373, 1523
Schierhold & Wohlers	1845	
Schierhold, H.	428, 2321	
Schierhold, Herman	1845	
Schillingman, William	1781	
Schintz, J. H.		1421
Schlicker, Frederick	1979	
Schloss, S.	891, 1152, 1367	457, 1303
Schmidlapp Live Oak Distillery Company	1145	
Schmidli, Joseph	1475	
Schmidt, C. H.		358
Schmidt, Mary	1110	
Schmidt, V.	1275	
Schmitt, George	1750	1269, 1979
Schmitt, Mary	1187, 1288, 1530	1269, 1273
Schnicker, -		1978
Schocken, S.	1825	
Schockin, S.		1101
Schoenagel, Babette	829	
Schoenagel, Jacob		829
Schoenwald, August		431
Schrack, George		1490
Schroder, Henry	619	
Schroyer, A.		523, 2097
Schroyer, Aaron		35, 553
Schulte, H. A.	1222	
Schute, Anthony	954	

Person/Entity	Plaintiff Suit #	Defendant Suit #
Schwan, L.		358
Schwan, Leonard	2290	
Schwan, Wilhelmina	2290	
Schwartz, Henry	1263, 1264, 1265, 1266, 1267, 1268, 1269, 1270, 1271	
Scollay, Oceana	1565	
Scott & Staley	1573, 1746	1560, 1564
Scott, Anna		358
Scott, David P. H.		75
Scott, E. W.	415	
Scott, J. D.		1563
Scott, Malinda		1690
Scott, Sylvester	1573, 1746	1560, 1561, 1564, 1566, 1690
Scown, Adoph G.		1635
Sear (an Indian)		1103, 1115
Sear, Gabrial		1115
Sears, Franklin		2222, 2223
Sears, G. C. P.		2222, 2223
Seawell, Alice		2257
Seawell, D. H.		1419
Seawell, D. R.		1419
Seawell, George C.		2257
Seawell, James B.		1419
Seawell, James W.		2257
Seawell, Joseph	2042	
Security Savings Bank		312
Seegelken, A. D.		358
Seegelken, E. A.		358, 2268
Seeley, David	900	
Sellards, Virginia A.	537	
Sellers, Eugene		2111
Sellers, William		1622
Sessions, George W.		1273
Sessions, Ida		1273
Sewell, J. W.		1737
Sewell, James B.		1737
Seymour, L. B.		592

Person/Entity	Plaintiff Suit #	Defendant Suit #
Seymour, L. B.		1589
Shafter, P. J.	1693	1875
Shainwald, Herman	1118	
Shane, Adam		358, 529
Shannon, Mary J.		358
Sharp, John		950
Sharp, M.		358
Sharp, Matt H.	1206	
Sharp, Rebecca C.	1206	
Sharp, Samuel O.	1206	
Sharp, William	965	
Shattuck, Parallee	1206	
Shaw, Bowman & Co.	292	
Shaw, E. H.		1732
Shaw, Elias	1491	
Shaw, Isaac E.	292, 361, 1533	
Shaw, James		484
Shaw, James A.	916	184, 716
Shaw, John		338
Shaw, John George	312	716
Shaw, Melissa		1491
Shea, Con	2029	
Shearer, John	895	
Shedd, Charles		1438
Shedd, Clarence		1438
Shedd, Mary R. J.	1438	
Sheffer, C. M.	486	
Shelton, J. G.		358
Shelton, Parmelia	1206	
Shepherd, A.	197	
Shepherd, Evelyn Manro		1801
Shepherd, J. Avery	1801	
Shepherd, J. S.		775
Shepherd, John B.		271, 496
Sheppard, E. T.		1473
Sheppard, Eli T.	1380	
Sherman, Clay & Co.	869, 971	
Sherman, Hyde & Co.	224	
Sherman, L. S.	224	

Person/Entity	Plaintiff Suit #	Defendant Suit #
Sherman, Leander S.	869	
Sherry, John	1635	
Shetland, Edward	2036	
Sheward, D.		2029
Shields, William S.		555
Shire, Jacob		838
Shirley, Almira C.	1001	
Shirley, J. Q.		1001, 1007
Shiveley, David C.	1139	
Shively, Jennie May	336	
Shively, William B.		336
Shoemake, Susan		665
Shoemake, William	499	55
Shone, Edward		143
Shone, Edwin		173
Shone, Kenrick		143, 173
Shore, G.		696
Shores, Leander		2038
Shorey, F. A.	1128	30, 358
Shorr, A. J.	1277	
Shulte, Henry F.	219	
Shulte, M. E.	313	
Shulte, M. E. (Mrs.)		358
Shulte, Mary E.		294
Sichel, Michael		1413, 1414
Sick, Lee		1242
Sickles, J. E.		1077
Sicott, F.	461	
Sicotte, F.		1532
Siegrist, C.		358
Silva, Francisco	1804	
Silvia, A. J.	752	
Sim, Ah	1982	
Simmons, A. R.		693
Simmons, Alonzo R.	633	
Simmons, Elizabeth		1880
Simmons, J.		358
Simmons, J. C.		397
Simmons, J. R.	363, 819	406

Person/Entity	Plaintiff Suit #	Defendant Suit #
Simmons, James Sylvester		1988
Simmons, Jennette A.		633
Simmons, John		116
Simmons, John R.		1880
Simmons, Thomas		116
Simon, Simon I.		367
Simoni, Giovanni		1464
Simons, J. B.		358
Simple, W. J.		358
Simple, W. S.		358
Simpson, John		1216
Simpson, William		24
Singer Manufacturing Company	1718	
Singleterry, Lillie	1206	
Singley, James		1538, 1547, 1563
Skaggs, A.	1891	
Skaggs, Wilson W.		1631
Skellenger, D. A.		1501
Skellenger, S. R.	1501	
Skillman, Theodore		916, 1193
Skinner, H. R.		358
Slater, M. E. (Miss)		358
Slayton, C. W.	1223	
Slayton, Margaret		1223
Sleadman, S. W. (Mrs.)		358
Slusser, L. S. B.		781
Slusser, Levi S. B.		892
Smallwood, L. B.		358
Smith, A.		338
Smith, A. (Mrs.)		338
Smith, A. H.		358
Smith, C. W.		1347
Smith, Charles A.	1474	
Smith, Dexter	1052	
Smith, Elwood	2182	
Smith, Frank	1133	1389
Smith, Fred		757
Smith, G. H.		358
Smith, H. S.		358

Person/Entity	Plaintiff Suit #	Defendant Suit #
Smith, Harry		1673
Smith, Henry		1086
Smith, Isaac P.	943, 1005	
Smith, J. K.		227, 358
Smith, J. W.		2193
Smith, James		338
Smith, James L.		2295
Smith, James M.		419
Smith, John	1263, 1264, 1265, 1266, 1267, 1268, 1269, 1270, 1271	
Smith, John K.		794, 960, 1245
Smith, Joseph		1114
Smith, Lucinda J.	943, 1005	
Smith, M. J. (Mrs.)		358
Smith, M. V.		358
Smith, Margaret Ann		419
Smith, Mart J.		290
Smith, Mary E.	1251	
Smith, Melvina		419
Smith, Patrick	18	
Smith, R. P.		358
Smith, R. W.		747
Smith, Robert		1351
Smith, T. F.		1251
Smith, T. W.	56	
Smith, Thomas		477
Smith, W. (Mrs.)		358
Smith, W. A.		531
Smith, W. B.		2071
Smith, W. H.		358
Smith, W. H. E.		2312
Smith, W. J.		396
Smith, W. S.		1963
Smith, William P.		372
Smyth, Charles S.		207
Smythe, C. S.		358
Smythe, E. H.		358
Sneed, Peter S.	1206	

Person/Entity	Plaintiff Suit #	Defendant Suit #
Sneed, Richard	1206	
Sneed, Thomas J.	1206	
Snelson, J.	320	
Snelson, John	1811	
Snider, Jane	91	
Snider, John D.		91, 265
Snow, Susana		1675
Snow, Susanna		1493
Snyder, Rachel J.		2222
Society of the Seventh Day Adventist Church of Healdsburg	988, 1379	
Solley, Emely Marcella	1356	
Solley, Stephen J.		1356
Solomon, Arthur	1915	
Somes, Manuel		769
Sonoma & Marin Beneficial Association, Directors of the	635	
Sonoma & Marin Mutual Beneficial Association	715	573
Sonoma & Santa Rosa Rail Road		551½
Sonoma & Santa Rosa Rail Road Company	427	702
Sonoma County Agricultural Park Association		845
Sonoma County Land & Improvement Company		1774, 1775, 1776, 1777
Sonoma County Stock Breeders' Association	2061	
Sonoma County Water Company	2206	813
Sonoma Pacific Coal Company		605, 607
Sonoma Valley Bank	780, 1545, 1833, 2068	965, 1630
Sonoma Valley Improvement Company	1947	
Sonoma Valley Land Company		2017, 2018
Sonoma Valley Rail Road Co.		186, 370, 445, 563, 1157
Sonoma Valley Railroad Co.	119, 128	
Sonoma, Board of Supervisors of the County of		311, 315, 407, 666, 2157, 2311
Sonoma, County of	468, 663, 1017, 1018, 1051, 1395, 1574, 1583, 1893, 1942, 2101, 2166	193, 234, 358, 370, 962, 1330, 1365, 1848, 1849, 2236
Soules, Albert		1524
Soules, L. O.		1524
Southerland, C. (Mrs.)		358
Southwick, E. B.		358
Southwick, Helen	544	
Souza, Manuel	1613	

Person/Entity	Plaintiff Suit #	Defendant Suit #
Sozer, Manuel		1608
Sparks, G. W.		1101
Sparks, George W.		784
Sparrow, E. D.	1213	
Sparrow, Edward D.		1596
Spaulding, George S.		290
Spaulding, Kimball D.		1755
Spaulding, Laura B.	1755	
Spaulding, Mary		1045
Spear, Charles		1659
Speck, L. P.		42
Spencer, B. M.		358
Spencer, Byron M.	1826	
Spencer, David		290
Spencer, Jane		358
Spencer, Mary C.		358, 478
Spencer, Thomas		478
Sperry & Co.	1504	
Spinetti, A.		469
Sponogle, F. M.		1972
Sponogle, J. C.		1559
Spotswood, A.	1461	
Spotswood, Andrew	1277	
Spotswood, George W.		67
Sprengel, Christian		1274, 1286
Spridgeons, J.		358
Springer, C.		358
Springer, Jason	1236	
Sproul, Lena		1045
Spudgrave, -		338
Squires, John S.		371
Squires, Mary E.	371	
Sroufe, John		284
St John, A.		955
St. Clair, Frank C.	1985	
St. Clair, George	929	
St. Clair, Nancy E.	1985	
St. John, A. C.		1284
St. Pierre, Alfred	166	

Person/Entity	Plaintiff Suit #	Defendant Suit #
Stahl, C.		358
Staley, Isaac	1573, 1746	1069, 1560, 1564, 1566, 1690
Stamner, Julius Caesar		1978
Stanford, Leland		905
Stanley, Neblett & Company		262, 358
Stanley, W. B.	291	64, 262, 358, 1129
Stanley, William B.		876
Stapleton, Patrick		2005
Stapp, I. N.	16	1751
Stapp, James T.		811
Stapp, Margaret	811	
Stapp, Martha A.		16
Stapp, Mary A.	687	
Starger, Andrew		1951, 1970
Stargroom, Emily		1273
Stargroom, Marc L.		1273
Starke & Edwards		1884
Starkie, F.	303	
Starr, Theodore C.		2310
Starratt, Handley	900	
Starrett & Gliddon		1300, 1537
Starrett, John		1300, 1537
Steadman, Amos D.	89	
Steadman, Mary G. W.	89	
Stearns, F. R.		909
Stedman, George W.	938	
Steele, T. H. B.		358
Stegman, William		954
Steiger, Edward		1168
Steiger, W. H.		933
Stein, Henry		2024
Steitz, John		358
Stephens, A. L.		272
Stephens, William	1042, 1489	
Sterger, Andrew	1956	
Stevens, Charles Louis		1343
Stevens, François	1343	
Stevens, Russell		250

Person/Entity	Plaintiff Suit #	Defendant Suit #
Stewart & Hall		15
Stewart, C.	14	
Stewart, Charles		15
Stewart, J. H.		2254
Stewart, John	634	628
Stewart, K. M.	1819	
Stewart, K. M. (Mrs.)		1810
Stewart, Sarah	634	
Stiles, John		1272
Stiles, Peter		1272
Stiles, Rueben T.	900	
Stites, A. H.		1751
Stoddard, J.		358
Stoetz, Charles		229
Stofen, John J.		1833
Stofen, Peter N.	1527	1833
Stoffel, Philip		140
Stone & Weaver	1330	
Stone, J. S.	1330	
Stone, James		1387
Stone, N. J.		358
Stone, Nathan J.	1149	1304
Stoner, John H.		807
Stoner, Sarah E.	923	
Stoner, Zachariah R.		923
Stormes, Mattie	1903	
Stormes, S. H.		1903
Storni, Giacomina	952	
Storni, Peter	636	952
Stratton, Hannah M.		44
Stratton, William A. T.		44
Strode, C. E.	1100	
Strode, John	1173	
Strom, William		358
Strong, J.		358
Strong, Jennie	1628	
Strong, John		502
Strother, R. S. (Mrs.)		358
Stuart, Absalom B.	1880	

Person/Entity	Plaintiff Suit #	Defendant Suit #
Stuart, Anabel McGaughey	1880	
Stuart, Antoinette R.		1273
Stuart, Charles D.		554, 1272, 1273
Stuart, Charles D. (Mrs.)		1263
Stuart, Edwin		1675
Stuart, Ellen M.		1272, 1273
Stuart, Isabel		1273
Stuart, James F.		100
Stuart, Jane Doe		1263
Stuart, Jane Roe		1263
Stuart, John Doe		1263
Studdert, Michael		2121
Stump, James		12
Sturdevant, Edward		1513
Suang, Ang Ah		1442
Suart, F. S.		358
Sue, Ah		1232
Suie, Ah		990
Sullivan, James	889	1577, 1627
Sullivan, James G.	1581	
Sullivan, Mary		1627
Sullivan, P. J.		358, 1258, 1375
Sullivan, T. J.		932, 1766
Summit Mills		2002
Sutherland, Frank B.	1506	
Sutherland, J. J.	401	
Sutliff, Henry	1219	
Sutton, Cornelia		850
Sutton, Hannah	712	
Sutton, Hiram D.		34
Sutton, Owen P.		34
Swain, R. M.	1956	2234
Swank, J. W.	1254	358
Swanson, V.		358
Swanwell, F.		679
Sweeney, Patrick		659
Sweet, James		776
Sweetzer, J. N.	228	
Swett & Crane		977

Person/Entity	Plaintiff Suit #	Defendant Suit #
Swett, F. H.	1292	977
Swift, N. E.		358
Swygert, Sarah	2103	
Sylvester, D. W.		1100
Symonds & Lamoreaux		821
Symonds, C. W.		821
T. G. Cockrill & Company	12	
Taboas, F. C.		1040
Taboas, M. M.	1144	
Tachella, Pietro		918, 919
Taft, H. D.		358
Taft, S. A.		358
Taggart, Henry		959
Taggart, John	1478	
Taggart, John, Jr.	928	
Taggart, John, Sr.	457	
Tai, Ah		1442
Talbot, Mary W.		358
Tan, W. A.		1072
Tann, James		288
Tarbett, B. F.		358
Tarrant, H. F.		1271, 1273, 1768
Tarrant, John Doe		1272
Tarrant, Sophie Adele		1768
Tarwater, M. W.		211
Tarwater, Martin		1281
Tarwater, Martin W.		1569
Tate, Frank		1762
Tatum, Henry L.	1092	
Taylor, C. D.		358
Taylor, Clay		2239, 2240
Taylor, Cordelia		1045
Taylor, Despard		650, 843
Taylor, Ernest M.		1045
Taylor, George M.	836	
Taylor, J.		358
Taylor, J. S.		358
Taylor, John	1262	
Taylor, John Franklin		1045

Person/Entity	Plaintiff Suit #	Defendant Suit #
Taylor, John S.	354	160
Taylor, Medora A.		1045
Taylor, O. A.	2276	
Taylor, Orson A.	730	
Taylor, Paul Chester		1045
Taylor, W. F.	1322	
Taylor, W. H.		1718
Taylor, William	1487	
Teague, C. P.		2226
Teague, O. D.		358
Tembley, M. J. (Mrs.)		358
Tempel, C.		1799
Temple, C.		1338
Temple, Conrad	1966	1014
Temple, J. W.	616	
Templeton, M. L.		358
Templeton, Milo F.	79	
Templeton, Milo L.	79	
Terry, J. W.	548	
Tharp, J. B.		999
Tharp, J. W.		1053½, 1781
Thayer, F. L.	1311	1159
Thayer, Franklin L.		1657
Thelan, Jane Doe		1267
Thelan, John J.		1267, 1273, 1425
Thelen, J. J.	1662	
Thelen, John J.	1691	1650
Thierkoff, Anna	702	
Thierkoff, F. G.	702	
Thierkoff, Frank G.		1766
Thierkoff, M. A.		1766
Thing, Arthur	498	218, 489, 538
Thomas, J.		358
Thomas, John		641
Thomas, Thompson		358
Thomas, William	226	
Thompson, A. C.	1689	
Thompson, A. W.		1552
Thompson, Amelia		544

Person/Entity	Plaintiff Suit #	Defendant Suit #
Thompson, Amelia S.		756
Thompson, Amelie L.		1735
Thompson, C. H.		358
Thompson, Charles P.		1336
Thompson, Charles T.	1516	
Thompson, Elizabeth		19
Thompson, F. P.		282
Thompson, Frank P.		268
Thompson, G. W.	165	19, 358, 876
Thompson, George W.	88	
Thompson, Hannah J.	900	
Thompson, J.		358
Thompson, John		1432
Thompson, L.		1677
Thompson, L. L.		358
Thompson, Marion S.		134, 1021, 2105
Thompson, Mary		268
Thompson, May C.	355	
Thompson, R. A.		358, 390
Thompson, S. G.		756
Thompson, T. P.		358
Thompson, Thomas L.		133, 134, 213, 220, 285, 1021, 2048, 2105
Thompson, W. A.		1748
Thomson, F. M.		1754
Thomson, J. P.		1754
Thorn, Frank		1967
Thorne, Mary A.		2044, 2051
Thornley, George D.	188, 737	
Thornley, John W.	188, 737	
Thornley, William H.	188, 737	
Thornton, G. A.		358
Thornton, George F.	1914	
Thorpe, Louise E.	8	
Thrift, Mary O.	778	
Thrift, Sabin D.	675, 697, 719, 778	644
Throop, James H.		1447
Throop, Rachel C.	1447	
Tibbetts, David	520	

Person/Entity	Plaintiff Suit #	Defendant Suit #
Tighe, Kelly	488, 839	287, 576, 752, 2194
Tighe, Thomas W.	1849	
Tilgner, Ferdinand Joseph Hugo		1349
Tilgner, Franz Ferdinand	1349	
Tilley, G. W.		358
Tilley, William J.		1882, 1897
Tilton, B. F.	280	
Tilton, Benjamin F.	554	
Timms, Ann	2071	
Timperly, Nickolas		1068
Tinson, G. E.	98	
Titus, I. S., Jr.	1786	
Tivnen, John	576, 1002, 2005	373
Tobin, Edward		2086
Todd, Judith A.	1335	
Todd, William S.		2082, 2083
Tolles, D. H.		358
Tomasini, G.	325	
Tomasini, Julian	982	
Tomassini, G.	35	
Tomblin, David		2315
Tomblinson, John	1910	
Tomblinson, Samuel	1704	
Tomlinson, John		1202
Toney, C.		358
Tong, Ah		1154
Toon, Ah	1996	
Torliatt, Peter	1863	
Torrance, S. H.	1532	
Torrence, Joseph L.	423	
Torrence, Rosa		423
Torrence, S. H.		878
Torrence, Shubal H.		1247
Torres, Joaquin	449	
Torri, Lorenzo	469	
Torri, Pasqual	469	
Totten, Samuel	1413, 1414, 1938	1570
Totton, Samuel		2089
Towey, P.	1309	

Person/Entity	Plaintiff Suit #	Defendant Suit #
Towne, Charles		948
Townsend, Horace R.	1202	
Toy, Ah	1982	
Traback, B. A.		77
Travis, John		22
Travis, Wirt		22
Tremblay, Alfred		691
Trescony, Alberto	1467	
Trewholtz, E. M.		1275
Tripp, Clinton C.	338, 358	411
Trosper, Thomas		1896
Trosper, Thomas G. W.	1553	1507
Truell, George	1499	
Truett, M. F.		236
Truitt, E. R.		2294
Truitt, John R.		1398
Truitt, R. K.		968, 1208, 1307, 2210, 2294
Truitt, Roland K.	669	
Truitt, Sarah E.	1398	
Trush, W.		358
Tuck, Charles E.		1262
Tucker, M. W.		2131
Tucker, Mary E.		1878
Tucker, Morgan G.	1878, 1881	
Tucker, W. B.	273	256
Tuggles, Eliza Ann	1206	
Tuite, Christopher	594	362, 507
Tuite, Julia	507	
Tully, Frances	590	
Tumblin, David		2248
Tunly, B.		2227
Tunzi, Domenico	1146	
Tunzi, Dominico		1399
Tunzi, Ellen	1618	
Tunzi, Geiessippi		1146
Tunzi, Giuseppi	1856	1399
Tuomey, B.		1888
Tuomey, Catharine	1888	

Person/Entity	Plaintiff Suit #	Defendant Suit #
Tupper, G. A.	2144	358, 1869
Tupper, George A.		810, 1801
Tupper, Harriet E.		1869
Tupper, James H.		338
Turner, G. J.		687
Turner, N.		358
Turner, Peter		385
Turner, W. J.		109, 110, 490
Turri, G.		1790
Ty, Ah	1579	
Uhlhorn, H. B.		653
Underhill, Gilbert E.		188
Underhill, J.		358
Underhill, John		307
Ursuline Community	332, 1011, 2088	
Urton, Sarah		1377
Urton, W. L.		317, 699, 727, 1377
Vaell, R. S.		358
Valaningham, Rachel E.		2067
Valentine, Mary G.		358
Vallejo, Benicia F.	482	1480
Vallejo, Ignacio		482
Vallejo, Lus		482
Vallejo, Mariano G.		1480
Vallejo, Platon		482
Valley, Rachel		358
Van Alen, William		1756
Van Allen, William	1711	
Van Doran, John S.		1602, 1603, 1604, 1649
Van Doren, J. S.	215, 1644, 1656	921
Van Doren, John S.	279	1554, 1555, 1556
Van Doren, W. L.	1295	
Van Dyke, Samuel P.	275	
Van Voast, W. H.		993
Van Vorst, John		1127
Van Winkle, I. S.		127
Vance, James M.		1718
Vance, John B.		1194
Vandergrift, E. W.	2115	

Person/Entity	Plaintiff Suit #	Defendant Suit #
Vanderhoof, M. V.	864	754
Vanderlieth, Elizie	828	
Vanderlieth, John	828	
Vandervoort, G. J.	821	
Vaughn, E. K.	2160	1492
Veale, William R.		775
Velasco, Maria Loretto	1044	
Velasco, Ysidro		1044
Velleggia, Giulio	1393	
Venaia, Michele F.		1596
Verano Land Company		2092
Vestal, Lewis	139	
Vestal, Louis		1960
Vincienzo, Muzzi		732½
Von Geldern, Joseph		2164
Von Geldern, Minnie Francisca Elizabeth	2164	
Von Rotz, Joseph		1148
Von Schroder, Mary Ellen	1480	
Von Schroeder, Mary Ellen	2303	
Vorhees, James	493	
W. Zartman & Co.	1277	
Waddel, A. J.	547	
Wagele, Conrad		1978
Waldier, Charles		1792
Waldier, Katie R.	1792	
Walk, H. L.		1408
Walk, J. J.		1408
Walker, D. W.	669	1588
Walker, J.		320
Walker, J. D.	666	
Walker, John	436, 861	144
Walker, John L.	1558	
Walker, Joseph		1488
Walker, L. W.		764
Walker, Louisa	1488	
Walker, Louise C.		1558
Walkup, W. B.		689
Walls, David	1082	
Walsh, David		1850, 2022

Person/Entity	Plaintiff Suit #	Defendant Suit #
Walsh, M.		709, 712, 945, 1041, 1050, 1461
Walsh, Michael	2161	1538, 1547
Walters, Soloman	1617	
Walters, Solomon	205, 1713	
Ward, Catherine		259
Ward, Charles		259
Ward, Charles H.	1930	
Ward, Francis M.		1131
Ward, H. J.	1120	
Ward, J. A.	1637	
Ward, James		198
Ward, John W.	1037, 1317	
Ward, N.	617	
Ward, T. B.		358
Ward, Thomas	80	
Ware, A. B.		358
Ware, M. M.		358
Ware, P.		358
Warfield, John Doe		1265
Warfield, K. F.		1265
Warfield, Kate		1272, 1273
Warfield, Kate F.		1662
Warfield, R. H.		418
Warner, Alexander	2254, 2255	
Warner, Caroline W.	1516½	
Warner, Edward H.		1029
Warner, G.		528
Warner, Gustavus	434, 435	
Warner, J. J.	77	
Warner, James	57, 1176	358, 1516½, 2029, 2055
Warner, Rebecca J.	1029	
Warren, Frank		914
Washer, H.		49
Washer, J. A. (Mrs.)		358
Watriss, Emma	1483	
Watriss, Franklin	1483	
Watriss, George	1483	
Watriss, Martha C.	1483, 1484, 2123	

Person/Entity	Plaintiff Suit #	Defendant Suit #
Watson, Charles N.	2247	2177
Watson, G.		1237
Watson, Green		283, 284
Watson, J. A.		872, 1160, 1646
Watson, James		823
Watson, John		823
Watson, Mary		823
Watson, Mary C.	276	
Watson, Milton		276
Watson, Samuel		823
Watts, Elizabeth	159	
Watts, George		159
Watts, J. B.		358
Watts, Richard	750	
Wayman, John V.	1038, 1131	
Weatherington, H.		358
Weatherington, R.		358
Weaver, C. W.	1330	
Webster, Adrian		1125
Webster, Anna		1125
Webster, Jane Roe		1125
Webster, Joseph		1125
Webster, Joseph L.		1125
Webster, Perry		1125
Wedemeyer, Elizabeth	1738	
Wedemeyer, Frederick William		1738
Weeks, Rosetta L.	863	
Weeks, T. E.		358
Wegener, Ed	978	
Wegner, Ed	347, 693, 817	
Wehrspon, A.		2101
Wehrspon, August	1124	1704
Weill, D. H.	2079	
Weimer, P. W. (Mrs.)		51
Weise, Christian		1212
Weise, George Frederick		1212
Weise, Lisette	1212	
Welch, Annie E.	310	
Welch, Charles		310

Person/Entity	Plaintiff Suit #	Defendant Suit #
Welch, M. E.	2194	
Welch, Matilda		1942
Welch, Patrick	2194	
Weller, Silas		358
Wellman, Bela	1882, 1897	
Wellman, Ruth A.	1882, 1897	
Wellman, William B.	1882, 1897	
Wells Fargo & Company		370, 905
Wells, Clark	333	
Wells, E.	904	
Wells, J. W.		358
Wells, John		1116
Wells, S. O.		358
Welsh, Mary		358
Werden, John		495
Wescott, Oliver	785, 800	
West, Charles	1669	
West, Fred	1669	
West, John	1669	1203
West, Mary	1590	
West, R.		772
West, Robert		256
Westcoat, Oliver		1127
Weston, H. L.		1338
Wetmore, F. R.		1244
Wetmore, Frederick R.		1130, 1186½
Wetmore, Georgiana A.		1130, 1186½, 1244
Wetmore, Henry D.	1244	
Wetmore, J. L.	314, 417	2002
Wetmore, W. P.		2002
Weyl, Henry	551½, 563, 1072, 1157	576, 2068
Wharton, C. V.		358
Wheaton, J. B.		1119
Wheeler, Abram		338
Wheeler, D. R.	1390	
Wheeler, Edward	941	940
Wheeler, H. William		338
Wheeler, Jacob	267, 296, 756, 1340, 1744, 1913	358, 2156

Person/Entity	Plaintiff Suit #	Defendant Suit #
Wheeler, James P.		192
Wheeler, Jamima J.	123, 267, 296	
Wheeler, Jemima J.	756	358
Wheeler, K. (Mrs.)		358
Wheeler, M. (Mrs.)		28
Wheeler, Matilda M.	192	
Wheeler, William H.		338
Wheelock, Daniel	1566	
Wheelock, David		1690
Whight, J. M.		358
White, Carlos		723
White, D. L.		358
White, E.		358
White, George E.	235	313
White, J. H.	1113	
White, J. M.		1943
White, N.		1113
White, Samuel		1351
White, W. H.		1088
White, William H.		379, 403, 476, 500
Whitehead, G. C.	773	
Whitehead, S. A.	773	
Whitehouse, W. B.		861
Whiting, J. W.	224	
Whitlock, M. J.	158	
Whitman, H. H.	1038	
Whitman, J. H.		680, 1882
Whitman, Joseph H.		1897
Whitman, S.		358
Whitney, A. L.		1609
Whitney, A. P.	54, 183, 533, 549, 775	582
Whitney, C. E.		1609
Whitney, C. L.	1939	
Whitney, Calvin E.		1338
Whitney, Susan D.		1338
Whitson, Frank		1806
Whittaker, G. N.		358
Whittier, J. T.		358
Whitton, Charles W.		261

Person/Entity	Plaintiff Suit #	Defendant Suit #
Whitton, Sarah E.	261	
Whychoff, G. H.		934
Wickersham, Fred A.		1891
Wickersham, I. G.	131, 137, 528, 794, 945, 1441, 1525, 1614, 1759½, 2222, 2223	358
Wickersheimer, August		1580
Wiedersheim, H.		1751
Wieland, John	724	
Wiester, W. H.	2201	
Wieszeniewski, Alexandre		216, 260
Wightman, Silas	344	
Wilbur, Rebecca (Mrs.)		358
Wilde, L.		358
Wiles, J. M.	1830	
Wiley, H.		1382
Wiley, Harriet	1534	
Wilgues, Lola	2325	
Wilgues, Lorenzo D.	2325	
Wilkerson, Jeremiah	627	
Wilkins, P.		358
Wilkinson, J.		650
Wilkinson, R.		358
Williams, Albert		1187, 1268, 1273
Williams, Alfred		1269
Williams, Benjamin F.	2046	
Williams, Bridget		1187, 1268, 1269, 1288
Williams, Bridget K.		1273, 1530
Williams, C. B.	999, 1730, 1731, 1960	
Williams, Charles H.		1429
Williams, Elizabeth	1986	
Williams, Frank		1986
Williams, G. H.		358
Williams, George H.		606, 1872
Williams, George R.	2003, 2122	
Williams, Harriet	2176	
Williams, J. A.		358
Williams, J. M.		358
Williams, James		1110

Person/Entity	Plaintiff Suit #	Defendant Suit #
Williams, Joe		183
Williams, John A.	900	651
Williams, Joseph		1273
Williams, Joseph A.		1288
Williams, Mary A.	1429	
Williams, Robert B.	892	
Williams, Sophia		1187, 1268, 1269
Williams, Sophia A.		1273
Williamson, S. A.		492
Williamson, Sarah		358
Willis, Thomas N.		17
Willis, Viana J.	17	
Willits, W. H.	942, 993	819, 1351
Willitts, William H.		700
Wilmerding, J. C.	673	
Wilsey, Frankie Jane		1045
Wilsey, H.	1934	
Wilsey, Hayes		1045
Wilsey, Henry		1045
Wilsey, Henry Martin		1045
Wilsey, Mary Elizabeth		1045
Wilsey, Sarah M.		1045
Wilson Bros.		1905
Wilson, Caroline		716
Wilson, Emma Jane		1854
Wilson, George		1539
Wilson, Goldfish & Co.	1279	
Wilson, H. M.	59	1735
Wilson, H. S.		358
Wilson, Henry		2053, 2054
Wilson, J. B.		2179
Wilson, J. H.		1826
Wilson, J. K.		2179
Wilson, J. L.		290
Wilson, John	1854	
Wilson, John R.	1130	1186½
Wilson, Louisa	32	
Wilson, Mary		358
Wilson, Nellie		1826

Person/Entity	Plaintiff Suit #	Defendant Suit #
Wilson, Robert		32
Wilson, S. H.		358
Wilson, Susan		1826
Wilson, Thomas		2197
Wilson, W. P.	2018	
Wilson, W. Y.		358
Wilson, William	1107, 1160, 1279, 1283, 1289, 1290, 1306, 1646, 1682, 1749	
Wilson, William Y.	368	
Winans, J. L.		1461, 1538, 1547, 1759
Winchcomb, Harry M.	689	
Winchester, E. H.	1169	
Wing, Ah		360
Wing, Amanda F.	698	
Wing, Fong	797	
Wing, Tong	803	804
Wing, W. H.		933
Wing, William		698
Winkle, Henry	561	
Winslow, A. J.		860
Winslow, E. C. (Mrs.)		860
Winslow, Emma I.		957
Winslow, George	692	957
Winslow, Jane Doe		860
Winslow, John Doe		860
Winter, Anne		1471, 1551
Winter, Thomas P.	1471, 1551	
Winters, Charles	1125	
Winters, Dennis	1324	
Winters, Ellen	1324	
Wise & Goldfish	178, 306, 753	
Wise, -	753	
Wise, H.	178	
Wise, Henry	306	
Wise, Mary		358
Wisecarver, J. R.		198, 1751
Wiswell, J. A.		775
Witham, Charles H.		1637

Person/Entity	Plaintiff Suit #	Defendant Suit #
Witham, George T.		776
Witham, Josephine		1838
Withers, Mary E.	1206	
Withington, Hannah B.		1
Withington, James R.		2
Wohler, Ana M. G.		1042
Wohlers, Theodor	1845	
Wohlers, Theodore	2321	
Woman's Relief Association	1664	
Wood, B. S.		402
Wood, Ben S.	2010, 2256	468, 853
Wood, Ellen		2205
Wood, Frank	1623, 1626	1640
Wood, Guy Mead	438	
Wood, J. L.		894
Wood, John		438
Wood, Joseph D.		2205
Wood, Robin W.		761
Wood, Rosa L.	894	
Wood, Rosanna		761
Wood, Wesley		558
Woods, Isaac		1960
Woods, James A.	1666	
Woods, John		358
Woods, John Doe		1960
Woods, Wesley		632
Woodward, M. J. (Mrs.)		358
Woodward, M. W.		992
Wordward, C. W.		358
Wordward, O. T.		358
Worth, Charles		867
Worth, Eusebia R.		1119
Worth, Frances H.		387
Worth, Reuben G.		387
Wright, A. S.		358
Wright, B. F.		1751
Wright, Emma A.	795	958
Wright, Fannie L.	1722, 1879	1227, 2006
Wright, H. C. (Mrs.)		358

Person/Entity	Plaintiff Suit #	Defendant Suit #
Wright, Isaac	1430	1521
Wright, J. E.		358
Wright, James A.		795
Wright, Joseph	614	233, 235, 338, 358
Wright, L. R.		499
Wright, S.		358
Wright, S. B.		570
Wright, Sampson B.		1227, 1722, 1879
Wright, Samson B.	2006	
Wright, W. S. M.	592	338, 358, 1245, 1249
Wright, Winfield S. M.	345	
Wrightson, Francis	2231	
Wristen, W. D.		358
Yancey, Henrietta	84	
Yancey, L. M.		84
Yandle & Glynn	2280	
Yandle, T. J.	2280	
Yarbrough, Crockett D.		1593
Yates, C. H.	1005	
Yates, Charles H.		1802
Yeat, Ah	1579	
Yon, Ah	798, 806	805
Yonker, S. N.	2268	
Yorka, Nancy Ann	451	
Yorka, Philip		451
Young, B. S.		358
Young, Charles	929	
Young, Charles H.		2069
Young, F. N.		358
Young, George		1751
Young, Henry		139, 189, 1034
Young, J. B.	425	358
Young, J. S.	2203	1433
Young, James B.		2200, 2204
Young, John		1095
Young, John D.	2067	
Young, John E.		2204
Young, Maria E.		915
Young, Mary L.	2200, 2204	

Person/Entity	Plaintiff Suit #	Defendant Suit #
Young, Rebecca		1095
Yow, Ah	906	
Yung, Ah		981
Zane, A. J.	1972	
Zartman, W. H.	1277	
Zartman, William	775, 825, 945, 1277, 1461	582
Zeile, John		370
Zimmerman, G. H.		1063
Zimmerman, George	1215	
Zimmerman, J. M.		1142
Zimmerman, John M.		995
Zuver, J. H.	669	

Suit #	Plaintiffs	Defendants	Cause of Suit	Register of Actions Volume: page(s)	Action Date
1	Cluff, William B.	Withington, Hannah B.	Foreclosure	1: 32-33	5 Jan 1880
2	Cluff, William B. & DeWitt, Mortimer (dba Cluff & DeWitt)	Withington, James R. & Peoples, Nathan	Assumpsit	1: 34-35	5 Jan 1880
3	Barnes, Aaron	Hinckley, George E.; Haight, George W.; Rice, -	Foreclosure	1: 36-37	5 Jan 1880
4	McDonnell, James J.	Dinwiddie, James L.	Replevin	1: 38-39	5 Jan 1880
5	Petaluma Turn Verein		Application to mortgage real estate	1: 40-41	5 Jan 1880
6	Henley, Patrick	Millerick, Michael	Appeal	1: 40-41	5 Jan 1880
7	Porter, J. K.	Miller, Daniel E.	Appeal	1: 42-43	5 Jan 1880
8	Thorpe, Louise E.	Grove, William H.	Appeal	1: 42-43	5 Jan 1880
9	People	Drice, Manuel	Burglary	1: 44-45	26 Jan 1880
10	People	Frahm, Frank	Assault with a deadly weapon	1: 44-45	26 Jan 1880
11	Jackson, Evaline	Jackson, E. N. B.	Divorce	1: 46-47	9 Jan 1880
12	Cockrill, T. G. & Homer, James L. (dba T. G. Cockrill & Co.)	Stump, James	At law	1: 194-195	10 Jan 1880
13	Linville, B. & Linville, J. A. (dba B. Linville & Son)	Corbaley, Richard	Appeal	1: 196-197	12 Jan 1880
14	Stewart, C.	Hoag, J. W	Attachment	1: 198-199	12 Jan 1880
15	McReynolds, Jacob	Stewart, Charles & Hall, C. T. (dba Stewart & Hall)	Attachment	1: 200-201	15 Jan 1880
16	Stapp, I. N.	Stapp, Martha A.	Divorce	1: 202-203	16 Jan 1880
17	Willis, Viana J.	Willis, Thomas N.	Divorce	1: 204-205	19 Jan 1880
18	Smith, Patrick	Kelly, John	Equity	1: 206-207	19 Jan 1880
19	Barnes, Aaron	Thompson, G. W.; Thompson, Elizabeth, his wife; Bell, Robert W.	Foreclosure	1: 208-209	21 Jan 1880
20	Parsons, Isaac	Bond, Mary Elizabeth; Bond, William Hammet; McIntyre, Emily; Bond, Thomas I.; Bond, Lewis Butler	Foreclosure	1: 210-211	22 Jan 1880

Suit #	Plaintiffs	Defendants	Cause of Suit	Register of Actions Volume: page(s)	Action Date
21	People	Kearns, George E.	Felony-voting more than once at one election	1: 212-213	26 Jan 1880
22	People	Travis, Wirt & Travis, John	Murder	1: 214-215	26 Jan 1880
23	People	Cnopias, John & Cnopias, Lewis	Misdemeanor-resisting an officer	1: 216-217	29 Jan 1880
24	People	Simpson, William	Petit larceny	1: 218-219	29 Jan 1880
25	People	Butterly, F. S.	Petit larceny	1: 220-221	30 Jan 1880
26	Santa Rosa, City of	Darden, John	Tax	1: 222-223	27 Jan 1880
27	Santa Rosa, City of	Park, George W.	Tax	1: 224-225	27 Jan 1880
28	Santa Rosa, City of	Wheeler, Mrs. M.	Tax	1: 226-227	27 Jan 1880
29	Santa Rosa, City of	Conrad, Charles	Tax	1: 228-229	27 Jan 1880
30	Santa Rosa, City of	Shorey, F. A.	Tax	1: 230-231	27 Jan 1880
31	Santa Rosa, City of	Nowlan, J. C.	Tax	1: 232-233	27 Jan 1880
32	Wilson, Louisa	Wilson, Robert	Divorce	1: 234-235	28 Jan 1880
33	Miller, Julia A.	Miller, David	Divorce	1: 236-237	2 Feb 1880
34	Redman, Dennis	Purrington, Thomas F.; Sutton, Owen P.; Sutton, Hiram D.; Purrington, Frances; Purrington, Joseph; Baxter, Ellen Louise; Kenyon, Edward	Equity	1: 238-239; 2: 244-245	2 Feb 1880
35	Tomassini, G.	Schroyer, Aaron	Appeal	1: 240-241	2 Feb 1880
36	Michael Piezzi & Co.	Markham, Andrew	Appeal	1: 242-243	4 Feb 1880
37	Hinds, Julia	Hinds, H. B.	Divorce	1: 244-245	5 Feb 1880
38	Carr, Frances A. Watts Hensworth	Carr, James	Divorce	1: 250-251	7 Feb 1880
39	Rien, Samuel	Ogden, Eliel & Brimigian, S.	Attachment	1: 252-253	7 Feb 1880
40	Rien, Samuel	Brimigian, S.	Attachment	1: 254-255	7 Feb 1880
41	Grover, J. & Grover, B. P. (dba Grover Bros.)	Peckinpah, A. R.; Peckinpah, David A.; Peckinpah, Edward N.; Peckinpah, T. Edgar	At law	1: 256-257	9 Feb 1880
42	Roney, J. M. & Prince, Peter (dba Roney & Prince)	Speck, L. P.	At law	1: 258-259	11 Feb 1880

Suit #	Plaintiffs	Defendants	Cause of Suit	Register of Actions Volume: page(s)	Action Date
43	McGee, Robert	Gaver, Andrew P.	At law	1: 260-261	17 Feb 1880
44	Baxter, Ellen Louise	Stratton, William A. T. & Stratton, Hannah M.	Foreclosure	1: 262-263	17 Feb 1880
45	Santa Rosa, City of	Hayden, James	Tax	1: 264-265	10 Feb 1880
46	Santa Rosa, City of	Mead, W. R.	Tax	1: 266-267	10 Feb 1880
47	Santa Rosa, City of	Lane, Edward	Tax	1: 268-269	10 Feb 1880
48	Santa Rosa, City of	Jacques, J. F.	Tax	1: 270-271	10 Feb 1880
49	Santa Rosa, City of	Washer, H.	Tax	1: 272-273	10 Feb 1880
50	Santa Rosa, City of	Phillips, Thomas	Tax	1: 274-275	10 Feb 1880
51	Santa Rosa, City of	Weimer, P. W. (Mrs.)	Tax	1: 276-277	10 Feb 1880
52	Santa Rosa, City of	Duncan & Ludwig	Tax	1: 278-279	19 Feb 1880
53	Giovannini, Daniel	Mathewson, James M. & Jesson, Samuel	Unlawful detainer	1: 280-281	20 Feb 1880
54	Whitney, A. P.	Purrington, Joseph	At law	1: 282-283	21 Feb 1880
55	People	Shoemake, William	Appeal	1: 284-285	24 Feb 1880
56	Smith, T. W.	His Creditors	Insolvency	1: 286-287	24 Feb 1880
57	Warner, James	Cannon, James	Foreclosure	1: 288-289	24 Feb 1880
58	Fritsch, John	McClymonds, J. W. & Fritsch, J. R. (dba McClymonds & Fritsch)	At law	1: 290-291	24 Feb 1880
59	Wilson, H. M.	Norton, L. A.; Hutton, Charles E.; Brainard, H. P.; Morrill, B. D.; Chapman, I. N.; Emmerson, J. P.	Injunction	1: 296-297	1 Mar 1880
60	Case, A. B.	Colburn, W. R.	At law	1: 298-299	1 Mar 1880
61	Bank of Healdsburg	Howell, John G.	Lien	1: 300-301	25 Feb 1880
62	Kearney, Elizabeth D.		Sole trader	1: 302-303	1 Mar 1880
63	San Francisco & North Pacific Railroad Co.	Dinwiddie, James L. (Sheriff)	Injunction	1: 304-305	28 Feb 1880
64	Santa Rosa Bank	Stanley, W. B.; Neblett, E.; Juilliard, C. F.	Assumpsit	1: 306-307	4 Mar 1880
65	Gibbs, Sarah A.	Gibbs, Frank W.	Divorce	1: 308-309; 2: 518-519	5 Mar 1880
66	Fine, Joff	M. Gradwohl & Co.	Appeal	1: 310-311	9 Mar 1880
67	Fuller, V. R.	Calder, A. E. & Spotswood, George W.	Appeal	1: 312-313	15 Mar 1880
68	Cogill, C. W.	Coffey, William & Baker, Albert	Equity	1: 314-315	15 Mar 1880

Suit #	Plaintiffs	Defendants	Cause of Suit	Register of Actions Volume: page(s)	Action Date
69	Fraser, Thomas A.	Fish, F. B.	Ejectment	1: 316-317	15 Mar 1880
70	Duncans Mills Land and Lumber Company	Merritt, P. E.	Attachment	1: 318-319	16 Mar 1880
71	Rose, Joseph	Corliss, Albert & Collins, Frank	Equity	1: 320-321	19 Mar 1880
72	Emerson, Henry	Royal Canadian Insurance Company	At law	1: 322-323	20 Mar 1880
73	Kleiser, James A.	Cook, Charles; Cook, Johanna; Savings Bank of Santa Rosa	Foreclosure	1: 324-325	22 Mar 1880
74	Brown, James H. & LeBarron, Harrison M. (dba Brown & LeBarron)	Dinwiddie, James L.	Replevin	1: 326-327	22 Mar 1880
75	Santa Rosa Bank	Scott, David P. H.	Foreclosure	1: 328-329	23 Mar 1880
76	Quinto, J. M.	Dinwiddie, James L.	Appeal	1: 330-331	29 Mar 1880
77	Warner, J.J.	Biaggi, D. & Traback, B. A.	Appeal	1: 332-333	31 Mar 1880
78	Light, William	Magoon, H. K.	Foreclosure	1: 336-337	30 Mar 1880
79	Templeton, Milo F. (name also given as Templeton, Milo L.)	Jensen, Ole Chris	Foreclosure	1: 338-339	1 Apr 1880
80	Ward, Thomas	Fitzgerald, A.	Appeal	1: 340-341	3 Apr 1880
81	Prindle, William	McMinn, John	Attachment	1: 342-343	3 Apr 1880
82	Gray, J. W.	McMinn, John	Attachment	1: 344-345	3 Apr 1880
83	Santa Rosa Bank	Duncan, James P. & McReynolds, William	At law	1: 346-347	6 Apr 1880
84	Yancey, Henrietta	Yancey, L. M.	Divorce	1: 350-351	7 Apr 1880
85	Fitch, Joseph	Fitch, Joseph	Equity	1: 352-353	9 Apr 1880
86	Sartor, Joseph	Sartor, Rosa (Executrix Last Will Antonio Sartor); Sartor, Rosa; Barsocchini, Antonio	Quiet title	1: 354-355	10 Apr 1880
87	Prince, David S.	His Creditors	Insolvency	1: 356-357	12 Apr 1880
88	Thompson, George W.	McMinn, John	Attachment	1: 358-359	13 Apr 1880
89	Steadman, Mary G. W. (Adm. Est. Amos D. Steadman)	McMinn, John	Attachment	1: 360-361	14 Apr 1880
90	Jones, Winfield S.	Chisholm, Duncan R.; Mitchell, John H.; Ebner, Charles; Mitchell, Annie C. (wife of John H. Mitchell and wrongly complained of as Sadie E. Mitchell)	Foreclosure	1: 362-363	22 Apr 1880
91	Snider, Jane	Snider, John D.	Divorce	1: 364-365	23 Apr 1880
92	Henderson, James W.	Henderson, Sarah E.	Divorce	1: 366-367	17 Apr 1880

Suit #	Plaintiffs	Defendants	Cause of Suit	Register of Actions Volume: page(s)	Action Date
93	Barry, Julia	Harris, Richard	Replevin	1: 368-369	26 Apr 1880
94	Ames, Mary Ann	Barnes, Aaron; Doe, John; Roe, Richard	Ejectment	1: 370-371	26 Apr 1880
95	Berger, M.	Dinwiddie, James L. & Michels, A. W.; Friedlander, M.; Michels, Louis M. (dba Michels, Friedlander & Co.)	Trespass	1: 372-373	26 Apr 1880
96	Healdsburg Institute		Petition to sell or mortgage property	1: 374-375	27 Apr 1880
97	Ham, E. D.	Juilliard, C. F. & Juilliard, Sarah A., his wife	Foreclosure	1: 376-377; 3: 299	29 Apr 1880
98	Tinson, G. E.	Grobb, Henry	Ejectment	1: 378-379	3 May 1880
99	Burchfield, Sarah	Burchfield, James R.	Divorce	1: 380-381	3 May 1880
100	McCord, James H.; Gibbs, William H.; Griffith, C. C.; Pond, Milo B.	Oakland Quicksilver Mining Co.; Stuart, James F.; Doe, John; Roe, Richard; Black, James		1: 382-383	6 May 1880
101	Pharris, P. H.	Harris, T. M.	Replevin	1: 384-385	7 May 1880
102	People	Hill, A. B.	Grand larceny	1: 386-387	5 May 1880
103	People	Hill, A. B.	Grand larceny	1: 386-387	7 May 1880
104	People	Quinlan, John	Assault with intent to commit murder	1: 388-389	6 May 1880
105	People	Kearns, George E.	Felony-voting more than once at one election	1: 390-391	6 May 1880
106	People	Hayes, George H. & Hayes, Emma	Murder	1: 392-393	7 May 1880
107	People	Bolden, S. & Lowe, George	Arson	1: 394-395	7 May 1880
108	People	Bolden, S. & Lowe, George	Arson	1: 396-397	7 May 1880

Suit #	Plaintiffs	Defendants	Cause of Suit	Register of Actions Volume: page(s)	Action Date
109	People	Turner, W. J.; Bolden, S.; Lowe, George	Felony-burning insured property with intent to defraud the insurer	1: 398-399	7 May 1880
110	People	Turner, W. J.; Bolden, S.; Lowe, George	Felony-burning insured property with intent to defraud the insurer	1: 400-401	7 May 1880
111	People	Hill, A. B.	Grand larceny	1: 402-403	11 May 1880
112	People	Hill, A. B.	Grand larceny	1: 404-405	14 May 1880
113	Demetz, Henry	His Creditors	Insolvency	1: 406-407	7 May 1880
114	Leveroni, Giovanni	Leveroni, Giovanni Battista	At law	1: 408-409	14 May 1880
115	Kane, Michael; O'Leary, Fergus; Gruenberg, Max; Newmark, M. J. (dba Kane, O'Leary & Co.)	Duffey, Thomas	At law	1: 410-411	14 May 1880
116	Hayes, Thomas & Hayes, Mary T.	Simmons, John & Simmons, Thomas	Ejectment	1: 412-413	14 May 1880
117	Bollman, F. H.	Engelhart, F. & Engelhart, Mary	At law	1: 414-415	15 May 1880
118	Duffy, Thomas	His Creditors	Insolvency	1: 416-417	18 May 1880
119	Sonoma Valley Railroad Co.	Bihler, William & Petaluma Savings Bank	Right of way	1: 418-419	18 May 1880
120	San Francisco & North Pacific Railroad Co.	Dinwiddie, J. L. (Sheriff & *ex officio* Tax Collector of Sonoma County)	Injunction	1: 420-421	21 May 1880
121	People	Alvarado, Joaquin (aka Marcles, John)	Assault with intent to commit murder	1: 422-423	14 Apr 1880

145

Suit #	Plaintiffs	Defendants	Cause of Suit	Register of Actions Volume: page(s)	Action Date
122	Hitchcock, Hollis	Gobbi, Paul	At law	1: 424-425	19 May 1880
123	Wheeler, Jamima J.	Martin, J. M. & Martin, Angeline B.	Foreclosure	1: 426-427	19 May 1880
124	Moritz, Michael	His Creditors	Insolvency	1: 428-429; 2: 316-317	24 May 1880
125	Farmer, J. A.	Boggs, G. M.	At law	1: 430-431	26 May 1880
126	Edwards, James	His Creditors	Insolvency	1: 432-433	28 May 1880
127	Cavanagh, John	Dinwiddie, J. L.; Van Winkle, I. S.; Pearce, George; Duncan, R. H.	Equity	1: 436-437	1 Jun 1880
128	Sonoma Valley Railroad Co.	Bihler, William & Petaluma Savings Bank	Right of way	1: 438-439	20 May 1880
129	Mills, John	McPhillips, Francis	Foreclosure	1: 440-441	2 Jun 1880
130	Price, Joseph K.	His Creditors	Insolvency	1: 442-443	4 Jun 1880
131	Wickersham, I. G.	O'Grady, Thomas & Rockford, Thomas	At law	1: 444-445	4 Jun 1880
132	Collean, Dan	Robinson, James	Appeal	1: 446-447	5 Jun 1880
133	Santa Rosa Bank	Thompson, Thomas L.; Satterlee, George A.; Satterlee, William	At law	1: 448-449; 2: 536-537	5 Jun 1880
134	Santa Rosa Bank	Thompson, Thomas L. & Thompson, Marion S.	At law	1: 450-451	5 Jun 1880
135	Bloomfield Masonic Hall Association	Knapp, G. W. & Knapp, A. H.	Appeal	1: 452-453	7 Jun 1880
136	Mosely, A. P.	Bennett, N.	Foreclosure	1: 454-455	7 Jun 1880
137	Wickersham, I. G.	Grant, John D. & Goodwin, Mary E.	At law	1: 456-457	8 Jun 1880
138	Quackenbush, Uriah P.	Duncan, Florence B. & Duncan, Samuel M.	Foreclosure	1: 458-459	10 Jun 1880
139	Vestal, Lewis	Young, Henry; Groshong, Celia; Hershberger, Emily; Hershberger, Charles; Hershberger, Frank; Hershberger, Jeremiah; McCracken, Jasper; McCracken, George F.; McCracken, Emma	Quiet title	1: 460-461	10 Jun 1880
140	Hasbrouck, A. A.	Ferguson, James & Stoffel, Philip	Appeal	1: 462-463	10 Jun 1880
141	People	Lewis, James H.	Grand larceny	1: 466-467	3 Jun 1880
142	O'Grady, Thomas	His Creditors	Insolvency	1: 468-469	11 Jun 1880
143	Carroll, R. T. (dba R. T. Carroll & Co.)	Shone, Edward & Shone, Kenrick (dba E. & K. Shone)	Attachment	1: 470-471	14 Jun 1880
144	Santa Rosa Bank	Mitchell, N. O. & Walker, John	Appeal	1: 472-473	14 Jun 1880
145	Lowery, J. J.	Rupe, D. C.	Appeal	1: 474-475	19 Jun 1880

Suit #	Plaintiffs	Defendants	Cause of Suit	Register of Actions Volume: page(s)	Action Date
146	Lowery, M. N.	Rupe, D. C.	Appeal	1: 476-477	19 Jun 1880
147	Lowery, N.	Rupe, D. C.	Appeal	1: 478-479	19 Jun 1880
148	Roney, J. M. & Prince, Peter (dba Roney & Prince)	Duval, O. & McLean, D. J.	At law	1: 480-481	17 Jun 1880
149	Conrad, Charles	Label, H.	Appeal	1: 482-483	17 Jun 1880
150	Alley, Bowen & Co.	Edelman, G. W.	Appeal	1: 484-485	21 Jun 1880
151	Clark, James P.	Carr, Jesse D.	Accounting	1: 486-487	21 Jun 1880
152	Allen, Robert	Howe, C. W. & Field, W. A.	Foreclosure	1: 488-489	22 Jun 1880
153	Ring, George E.	Bradbury, John Q.	Attachment	1: 490-491	23 Jun 1880
154	Farmers and Mechanics Bank	Gamble, A. W.; Krugar, Oscar F.; Jenkins, W. J.	Ejectment	1: 492-493	23 Jun 1880
155	McKenzie, William A.; McKenzie, Kenneth; McKenzie, John; McKenzie, Eliza	Hunter, R. E.	Mandamus	1: 494-495	24 Jun 1880
156	Akers, Stephen	Hale, Henry M. & Schell, Georgiana L. (Executors of Will of Theodore L. Schell)	Ejectment	1: 496-499, 640-641	28 Jun 1880
157	Grangers Business Association	Beeson, William S.	At law	1: 498-499	29 Jun 1880
158	Whitlock, M. J.	Quitzow, A.	Appeal	1: 500-501	2 Jul 1880
159	Watts, Elizabeth	Watts, George	Divorce	1: 504-505	3 Jun 1880
160	Nowlin, S. S.	Taylor, John S.	Damages	1: 506-507	1 Jul 1880
161	Beggs, Thomas J.	Fraser, A.	Attachment	1: 508-509	1 Jul 1880
162	Bank of Healdsburg	Bailhache, John N. & Bailhache, Josephine	Quiet title	1: 510-511	2 Jul 1880
163	Santa Rosa Bank	Ludwig, Thomas J. & Guerne, George E. (dba Guerne & Ludwig)	Attachment	1: 512-513	6 Jul 1880
164	Korbel, F.; Korbel, A.; Korbel, J. (dba F. Korbel & Bros.)	Ludwig, Thomas J. & Guerne, George E. (dba Guerne & Ludwig)	Attachment	1: 514-515	6 Jul 1880
165	Thompson, G. W.	Guerne, George E. & Ludwig, T. J. (dba Guerne & Ludwig)	Attachment	1: 516-517	6 Jul 1880
166	St. Pierre, Alfred	Guerne, George E. & Ludwig, T. J. (dba Guerne & Ludwig)	Attachment	1: 518-519	6 Jul 1880
167	Armstrong, S.	Guerne, George E.; Ludwig, T. J.; McDonald, M. L.	Attachment	1: 520-521	6 Jul 1880
168	Bloom, Jonas & Cohen, Samuel (dba Bloom & Cohen)	Guerne, George E. & Ludwig, T. J. (dba Guerne & Ludwig)	Attachment	1: 522-523	6 Jul 1880

Suit #	Plaintiffs	Defendants	Cause of Suit	Register of Actions Volume: page(s)	Action Date
169	Mather, J. & Heiser, Robert (dba J. Mather & Co.)	Guerne, George E. & Ludwig, T. J. (dba Guerne & Ludwig)	Attachment	1: 524-525	7 Jul 1880
170	Davis, George A.	Guerne, George E. & Ludwig, T. J. (dba Guerne & Ludwig)	Attachment	1: 526-527	7 Jul 1880
171	Murphy, M. T.	Boyce, J. F.; Boyce, M. A.; Santa Rosa Bank	Foreclosure	1: 528-529	6 Jul 1880
172	People	McKenzie, John A.; McKenzie, William A.; McKenzie, Kenneth E.; McKenzie, Eliza	Appeal	1: 530-531	7 Jul 1880
173	Carroll, R. T. (dba R. T. Carroll & Co.)	Shone, Edwin & Shone, Kenrick (dba E. & K. Shone)	At law	1: 532-533	8 Jul 1880
174	Robinson, Jacob	Byxbee, John F.; Duncans Mills Land & Lumber Co.; Duncan, Alexander; Doe, John; Roe, Richard; Doe, Peter; Doe, William	Foreclosure	1: 534-535	8 Jul 1880
175	Hawkins, Joseph	Morgan, Edward; Hassett, John D.; Gilbride, R.	Foreclosure	1: 536-537	8 Jul 1880
176	Dutton, Warren	Rien, Samuel; Rien, Mary A.; Queen, C.	At law	1: 538-539	8 Jul 1880
177	Hood, Eliza Ann (wife of William Hood)		Sole trader	1: 540-541	7 Jul 1880
178	Wise, H. & Goldfish, B. (dba Wise & Goldfish)	Boggs, George W.	At law	1: 542-543	8 Jul 1880
179	San Francisco & North Pacific Railroad Co.	Guerne, George E.; Murphy, R.; Ludwig, T. J. (dba Guerne, Murphy & Ludwig)	At law	1: 544-545	9 Jul 1880
180	Bloom, Jonas & Cohen, Samuel (dba Bloom & Cohen)	Goddard, Daniel	At law	1: 546-547	12 Jul 1880
181	California Savings & Loan Society	Aitken, Jane (formerly Collins, Jane)	Foreclosure	1: 548-549	12 Jul 1880
182	Guerne, George E. & Ludwig, Thomas J. (dba Guerne & Ludwig)		Involuntary insolvency	1: 550-551, 612-613	13 Jul 1880
183	Whitney, A. P.	Williams, Joe	Appeal	1: 552-553	10 Jul 1880
184	Hettich, Christian	Shaw, James A.	At law	1: 554-555	15 Jul 1880
185	Hopkins, Mary	Dinwiddie, J. L.; Duffy, Mary; Duffy, Thomas; Greenberg, Max; Newmark, M. J.; O'Leary, Fergus & Kane, Michael (dba Kane, O'Leary & Co.)	Foreclosure	1: 556-557	3 Aug 1880
186	Bihler, William	Sonoma Valley Rail Road Company	Injunction	1: 558-559	23 Jul 1880
187	Odlum, Gabrella A.	Odlum, Lorenzo D.	Divorce	1: 560-561	28 Jul 1880
188	Thornley, William H.; Thornley, John W.; Thornley, George D.	Underhill, Gilbert E.	Partition	1: 562-563	28 Jul 1880

Suit #	Plaintiffs	Defendants	Cause of Suit	Register of Actions Volume: page(s)	Action Date
189	Downs, Vernon	Frost, C. W.; Jordan, John; Young, Henry	At law	1: 564-565	28 Jul 1880
190	Norton, L. A.	Dana, Mary E. & Herman, Rudolph (Adms. Est. George S. Dana); Divine, Michael	Foreclosure	1: 566-567	29 Jul 1880
191	Ames, Lucy	Hoyt, Austin & Anderson, W. L.	Foreclosure	1: 568-569	30 Jul 1880
192	Wheeler, Matilda M.	Wheeler, James P.	Divorce	1: 570-571	4 Aug 1880
193	Rule, Elizabeth (Widow); Rule, Edward J.; Rule, Nannie A.; Rule, Josephine; Rule, Charles S. & Rule, Willie J. (Minors by guardian *ad litem* Charles G. Ames)	Sonoma, County of	Damages	1: 572-573	4 Aug 1880
194	Frehe, Louis		Insolvency	1: 574-575	4 Aug 1880
195	Hill, Louise J.	Hill, A. B.	Divorce	1: 576-577	5 Aug 1880
196	Ginella, L.	Frasier, A. H.	Appeal	1: 578-579	5 Aug 1880
197	Shepherd, A.	Santa Rosa, City of	At law	1: 580-581	9 Aug 1880
198	Lawson, F. M. (Mrs.)	Ward, James & Wisecarver, J. R.	Unlawful detainer	1: 582-583	12 Aug 1880
199	Haering, Frederick	Haering, Helen	Divorce	1: 584-585	13 Aug 1880
200	Marsh, Henry	Ellison, L. M.	Replevin	1: 586-587	14 Aug 1880
201	Crilly, Nicholas	Jordan, John	Appeal	1: 588-589	16 Aug 1880
202	Randall, James S.	Briggs, George S.	At law	1: 590-591	15 Jul 1880
203	Hatton, Charles B.	Santa Rosa, City of	At law	1: 592-593	18 Aug 1880
204	Madegan, Allie	Madegan, William D.	Divorce	1: 594-595	24 Aug 1880
205	Miller, George T. & Walters, Solomon	Flack, John	Foreclosure	1: 596-597	25 Aug 1880
206	City of Santa Rosa	Mead, W. H.	Tax	1: 598-599	25 Aug 1880
207	Atterbury, William B.	Smyth, Charles S. (Superintendent of Public Instruction of Sonoma County)	Injunction	1: 600-601	25 Aug 1880
208	Buzzell, Lucinda	Buzzell, Albert A.	Divorce	1: 602-603	25 Aug 1880
209	Runyon, William N.	Runyon, Mary; Boyer, Elizabeth; Norton, Juliette; Runyon, Alexander N.; Runyon, Soloman; Hall, Amelia A.; Brown, Victoria A.; Runyon, Frederick M.; Runyon, Emma M.	Partition	1: 604-605	26 Aug 1880
210	Bank of Healdsburg	Jacobs, G. H.; Hassett, Aaron; Poe, Elihu	At law	1: 606-607	27 Aug 1880

149

Suit #	Plaintiffs	Defendants	Cause of Suit	Register of Actions Volume: page(s)	Action Date
211	Durham, Thomas S.	Tarwater, M. W.	Appeal	1: 608-609	28 Aug 1880
212	Powers, Mary C.	Powers, David P.	Divorce	1: 610-611	28 Aug 1880
213	Briscoe, John	Thompson, Thomas L. & Boyce, John F.	At law	1: 614-615	1 Sep 1880
214	Kahn, Louis	Ballman, F. H. & Dinwiddie, J. L. (Sonoma County Sheriff)	Quiet title	1: 616-617	2 Sep 1880
215	Van Doren, J. S.	Dardis, Andrew	At law	1: 618-619	4 Sep 1880
216	Kedrolivansky, Alexandra	Wieszeniewski, Alexandre	Detainer	1: 620-621	6 Sep 1880
217	McNew, Emily	Bancroft, A. L. & Ink, W. P.	Equity	1: 622-623	31 Aug 1880
218	Farmers and Mechanics Bank of Healdsburg	Bostwick, N. W.; Thing, Arthur; Nally, A. B.; Barnes, E. H. (Executors Est. William Melton); Brown, H. K.	Foreclosure	1: 624-625	2 Sep 1880
219	Shulte, Henry F.		Insolvency	1: 626-627	3 Sep 1880
220	Middleton, Eliza F.	Thompson, Thomas L. & Holmes, Henderson P.	At law	1: 628-629	4 Sep 1880
221	Dardis, Andrew		Insolvency	1: 630-631	7 Sep 1880
222	Lake, Prudence J.	Lake, A. B.	Divorce	1: 632-633	8 Sep 1880
223	La Société Française d'Epargnes et de Prévoyance Mutuelle	Russian River Land & Lumber Co.; Latham, Milton S.; Latham, Mary McM., his wife; Doherty, John W.; LeRoy, Theodore (Successor trustee Gustave Mahé, dec'd); Eastland, Joseph G.; Coleman, John W.; Freeborn, James	Foreclosure	1: 634-635	14 Sep 1880
224	Clay, C. C.; Whiting, J. W.; Sherman, L. S. (dba Sherman, Hyde & Co.)	Glynn, E. (Mrs.)	Replevin	1: 636-637	14 Sep 1880
225	Juilliard, Sarah A.	Proctor, T. A. & Harris, Thomas M.	Appeal	1: 638-639	2 Sep 1880
226	Thomas, William	Adkisson, Joseph	Foreclosure	1: 640-641	17 Sep 1880
227	Barnes, Aaron	Nicoll, D. C. & Smith, J. K.	Foreclosure	1: 642-643	18 Sep 1880
228	Sweetzer, J. N.	Hammel, H. H.	Attachment	1: 644-645	20 Sep 1880
229	People	Stoetz, Charles	Obstructing highway	2: 2-3	21 Jun 1880
230	People	Murray, Jack	Manslaughter	2: 2-3	13 Jul 1880
231	People	Hansen, Joaquin	Grand larceny	2: 4-5	3 Sep 1880
232	People	Miller, Charles	Burglary	2: 6-7	20 Sep 1880

Suit #	Plaintiffs	Defendants	Cause of Suit	Register of Actions Volume: page(s)	Action Date
233	People	Wright, Joseph	Appeal	2: 8-9	22 Sep 1880
234	Rupe, D. C.	Sonoma, County of	Appeal	2: 10-11	7 Sep 1880
235	White, George E.	Petit, A. P.; Wright, Joseph; Ferguson, E. C.; Boyce, J. F.; Clark, James P.; Brown, John	At law	2: 12-13	24 Sep 1880
236	Bank of California	Truett, M. F.	Ejectment	2: 14-15	27 Sep 1880
237	People	Fook, Ah	Felony-offering a bribe to an executive officer	2: 16-17	28 Sep 1880
238	Curtis, Lousia C.	Curtis, James	Divorce	2: 18-19	2 Oct 1880
239	Neely, T. L. (Adm. Est. Robert Neely)	Hooten, M. V.	Attachment	2: 20-21	4 Oct 1880
240	Cox, Fathy	Cox, Jordan	Divorce	2: 22-23	4 Oct 1880
241	Fell, Erastus	Fairbanks, H. T.	Damages	2: 24-25	4 Oct 1880
242	Bailhache, John N.		Insolvency	2: 26-27	5 Oct 1880
243	Bank of Healdsburg	Bailhache, John N.	At law	2: 28-29	28 Sep 1880
244	Lynch, Charles; Lynch, John; Cleary, Thomas J. (Executors Est. Michael Lynch)	McDevitt, James & McDevitt, Charles (dba McDevitt Bros.)	At law	2: 30-31	8 Oct 1880
245	Mecham, H.; Hammell, H.; Rodehaver, J. P.; Hasbrouck, A.; Finch, H. P.; Holly, S. B. & Magoon, W. H. (dba Holly & Magoon)	Dickinson, C.; Drummond, Donald; Merrill, W. P.	At law	2: 32-33	8 Oct 1880
246	Bailhache, Josephine	Proctor, Ira	Replevin	2: 34-35	30 Sep 1880
247	Haigh, Mary & Haigh, Edwin (Adms. Est. John B. Haigh)	McManus, J. G.	Foreclosure	2: 36-37	11 Oct 1880
248	People	Lampe, William A.	To cancel certificate	2: 38-39	11 Oct 1880
249	People	Lambert, Frank H.	To cancel certificate	2: 40-41	11 Oct 1880
250	People	Stevens, Russell	To cancel certificate	2: 42-43	11 Oct 1880

Suit #	Plaintiffs	Defendants	Cause of Suit	Register of Actions Volume: page(s)	Action Date
251	People	Boardman, H. J.	To cancel certificate	2: 44-45	11 Oct 1880
252	People	Mauldin, B. F.	To cancel certificate	2: 46-47	11 Oct 1880
253	People	Carr, Sam; Billings, John; Brown, H. E.; Gaunce, George (indicted under the name of Gauntz, George)	Murder	2: 48-49	9 Oct 1880
254	People	Carr, Sam; Billings, John; Brown, H. E.; Gaunce, George (indicted under the name of Gauntz, George)	Murder	2: 50-51	9 Oct 1880
255	McReynolds, James	McReynolds, John	Foreclosure	2: 52-53	13 Oct 1880
256	Rodgers, John L.	Caruthers, T. C.; Risdon, C.; Tucker, W. B.; West, Robert	At law	2: 54-55	18 Oct 1880
257	People	Malone, Peter	Appeal	2: 56-57	19 Oct 1880
258	McClelland, J. J.	McMinn, John	At law	2: 58-59	20 Oct 1880
259	Barnes, Aaron	Hinckley, George E.; Hinckley, Mary R.; Ward, Charles; Ward, Catherine, his wife	Foreclosure	2: 60-61	25 Oct 1880
260	Kedrolivansky, Alexandra	Wieszeniewski, Alexandre	Unlawful detainer	2: 62-63	26 Oct 1880
261	Whitton, Sarah E.	Whitton, Charles W.	Divorce	2: 64-65	27 Oct 1880
262	Feusier, Louis	Stanley, W. B.; Neblett, E.; Juilliard, C. F. (dba Stanley, Neblett & Co.)	Foreclosure	2: 66-67	27 Oct 1880
263	Hooten, M. V.		Insolvency	2: 68-69	28 Oct 1880
264	Brown, Samuel	Renfro, Silas W. & Renfro, Mary	Foreclosure	2: 70-71	1 Nov 1880
265	Miller, George T.	Snider, John D.	Foreclosure	2: 72-73	1 Nov 1880
266	Roberts, Frank	Caseres, Cyrus	Appeal	2: 74-75	3 Nov 1880
267	Wheeler, Jacob (Executor Est. Jamima J. Wheeler)	Ink, W. P.; Macy, Eliza; Macy, J. H.; Macy, Martha; Jackson, E. N. B.; Jackson, Evaline	Foreclosure	2: 76-77	4 Nov 1880
268	California Savings & Loan Society	Thompson, Frank P. & Thompson, Mary, his wife	Foreclosure	2: 78-79	5 Nov 1880
269	Roix, Charles F.		Insolvency	2: 80-81	26 Oct 1880
270	People	Hansen, Joaquin	Grand larceny	2: 82-83	18 Oct 1880
271	People	Shepherd, John B.	Grand larceny	2: 84-85	22 Oct 1880

Suit #	Plaintiffs	Defendants	Cause of Suit	Register of Actions Volume: page(s)	Action Date
272	Ridgway, Jeremiah & Ridgway, Joseph W.	Duncan, J. P.; Childers, Arnold & Duncan, J. P. (Adm. Est. A. L. Stephens)	Foreclosure	2: 86-87	26 Oct 1880
273	Tucker, W. B.	Muther, Frank	Insolvency	2: 88-89	8 Nov 1880
274	Muther, Fannie M.		Divorce	2: 90-91	10 Nov 1880
275	Rohte, Emil & Van Dyke, Samuel P.	Helmke, Frederick; Helmke, Arabella; Kruse, Edward; Hanson, Charles; Collins, George H.	Foreclosure	2: 92-93	11 Nov 1880
276	Watson, Mary C.	Watson, Milton	Divorce	2: 94-95	11 Nov 1880
277	Potter, Augusta E.	Potter, Page G.	Divorce	2: 96-97	11 Nov 1880
278	Reed, J. H.	McNew, Z.	Appeal	2: 98-99	13 Nov 1880
279	Van Doren, John S.	McLaren, William D.; McLaren, Daniel; Ogden, Eliel; Crist, George F.	Foreclosure	2: 100-101	15 Nov 1880
280	McChristian, James; McChristian, Richard; McChristian, Sylvester; Tilton, B. F.; O'Farrell, William; O'Farrell, Elena; O'Farrell, John J.; O'Farrell, Minnie & O'Farrell, Louis; O'Farrell, Cathal; O'Farrell, Florence; O'Farrell, Gerald (infants by their guardian W. W. Porter)	McChristian, Patrick	Detainer	2: 102-103	26 Nov 1880
281	Roney, J. M. & Prince, Peter (dba Roney & Prince)	McNeil, John & Mulvaney, Robert	Foreclosure	2: 104-105	26 Nov 1880
282	Fulkerson, Richard	Thompson, F. P.	Foreclosure	2: 106-107	27 Nov 1880
283	Bank of Sonoma County	Watson, Green	At law	2: 108-109	29 Nov 1880
284	Bank of Sonoma County	Watson, Green & Sroufe, John	At law	2: 110-111	29 Nov 1880
285	First National Gold Bank of Petaluma	Thompson, Thomas L.; Satterlee, George A.; Henley, Barclay	At law	2: 112-113	30 Nov 1880
286	Bard, Samuel	Dardis, Andrew; Dardis, Lawrence; Dinwiddie, J. L. (Assignee)	Foreclosure	2: 114-115	10 Nov 1880
287	Brown, John	Tighe, Kelly	Appeal	2: 116-117	30 Nov 1880
288	Burgtorff, C. W.	Tann, James	Appeal	2: 118-119	3 Dec 1880
289	Rupe, S. H. (Adm. Est. of W. T. Cocke)	Cocke, W. E.	Equity	2: 120-121	3 Dec 1880

Suit #	Plaintiffs	Defendants	Cause of Suit	Register of Actions Volume: page(s)	Action Date
290	Jones, David	Carothers, Thomas L.; Corder, C.; Wilson, J. L.; Moore, James; Hale, Joseph; Spencer, David; Hall, A. W.; McGarvey, Robert; Iverson, Niles; Peters, William; Spaulding, George S.; Smith, Mart J.	Damages	2: 122-123	4 Dec 1880
291	Stanley, W. B.		Insolvency	2: 124-125	6 Dec 1880
292	Shaw, Isaac E.; Bowman, John H.; Harmon, John B. (dba Shaw, Bowman & Co.)	Isbell, William	At law	2: 126-127	7 Dec 1880
293	Fine, Emsley	Henry, John & Peterson, C. (dba Henry & Peterson)	Appeal	2: 128-129	9 Dec 1880
294	Santa Rosa Bank	Shulte, Mary E. & Dobbins, Thomas	At law	2: 130-131	11 Dec 1880
295	Benham, A. M.	Conrad, Charles	Replevin	2: 132-133	13 Dec 1880
296	Wheeler, Jacob (Executor Est. Jamima J. Wheeler)	Monroe, Eugene B.	Foreclosure	2: 134-135	14 Dec 1880
297	Ronald, Margaret	Lloyd, Alice	Foreclosure	2: 136-137	6 Dec 1880
298	Jones, Zue	Jones, Thomas H.	Divorce	2: 138-139	18 Dec 1880
299	Burchfield, Sarah	Burchfield, James R.	Divorce	2: 140-141	18 Dec 1880
300	Magini, Catharine	Magini, Joseph	Divorce	2: 142-143	18 Dec 1880
301	Huntington, Rosanna	Huntington, C. A.	Divorce	2: 144-145	18 Dec 1880
302	Santa Rosa Bank	Kingsbury, J. T.; Murphy, Wyman; Hoag, O. H.	Appeal	2: 146-147	20 Dec 1880
303	Starkie, F. (Adm. Est. W. Dahlman)	Reigenbach, M. F.	Appeal	2: 148-149	20 Dec 1880
304	McElarney, Frank	Cloverdale, Town of; Johnson, Thomas; Minehan, M.; Brush, W. T.; Kleiser, J. A.; Bowman, J. H.	Damages	2: 150-151	27 Dec 1880
305	People	Bond, Edward W.	Forgery	2: 152-153	28 Dec 1880
306	Wise, Henry & Goldfish, B. (dba Wise & Goldfish)	Feehan, William	At law	2: 154-155	31 Dec 1880
307	Kirkpatrick, D.	Underhill, John	At law	2: 156-157	3 Jan 1881
308	Coolbroth, Samuel W.		Insolvency	2: 158-159	3 Jan 1881
309	Mize, Albert	Mize, Aditha	Divorce	2: 160-161	4 Jan 1881
310	Welch, Annie E.	Welch, Charles	Divorce	2: 162-163	5 Jan 1881
311	People (ex rel. J. B. Christie)	Sonoma, Board of Supervisors of the County of	Mandate	2: 164-165	7 Jan 1881
312	Shaw, John George	Security Savings Bank	At law	2: 166-167	10 Jan 1881
313	Shulte, M. E.	White, George E.	Appeal	2: 168-169	10 Jan 1881
314	Wetmore, J. L.	Rupe, D. C.	Replevin	2: 170-171	18 Dec 1880

154

Suit #	Plaintiffs	Defendants	Cause of Suit	Register of Actions Volume: page(s)	Action Date
315	People (ex rel. J. W. Ragsdale)	Sonoma, Board of Supervisors of the County of	Certiorari	2: 172-173	11 Jan 1881
316	Flack, John		Insolvency	2: 174-175	11 Jan 1881
316½	McConathy, Frances Ann & McConathy, James	Markell, R. S.	Damages	2: 178-179	13 Jan 1881
317	Hefner, Philip	Urton, W. L.	Foreclosure	2: 176-177	11 Jan 1881
317½	Hildburgh, L. & Hildburgh, D. (dba Hildburgh Bros.)	Davis, Levi	At law	2: 180-181	14 Jan 1881
318	Caldwell, F. M.	Label, H.	Appeal	2: 182-183	15 Jan 1881
319	Kalkman, H. L.	Bliss, W. D.	At law	2: 184-185	15 Jan 1881
320	Snelson, J.	Walker, J.	Appeal	2: 186-187	17 Jan 1881
321	Bank of Healdsburg	Emerson, J. P. & Emerson, N. S.	Foreclosure	2: 188-189	17 Jan 1881
322	People	Laws, Robert	Grand larceny	2: 190-191	20 Dec 1880
323	People	Casey, Matt	Grand larceny	2: 192-193	21 Dec 1880
324	People	Sang, Ah & Chung, Ah	Burglary	2: 194-195	21 Dec 1880
325	Tomasini, G.		Application to be released from bond	2: 196-197	17 Dec 1880
326	People	Fitzpatrick, A.	Appeal	2: 198-199	20 Dec 1880
327	Fay, Sarah L.	Fay, Julius A.	Divorce	2: 200-201	20 Jan 1881
328	Cheney, D.		Insolvency	2: 202-203	24 Jan 1881
329	Cheney, R. J.		Insolvency	2: 204-205	24 Jan 1881
330	People	Quackenbush, Albert & Quackenbush, Alfred	Murder	2: 206-207	24 Jan 1881
331	People	Quackenbush, Albert & Quackenbush, Alfred	Murder	2: 208-209	24 Jan 1881
332	Ursuline Community		To sell land	2: 210-211	27 Jan 1881
333	Wells, Clark	Bassett, James A.	Ejectment	2: 212-213	21 Jan 1881
334	Savings Bank of Santa Rosa	Dixon, James & Fairfax, Ada (dba Dixon & Fairfax)	At law	2: 214-215	1 Feb 1881
335	People	Davis, Giles	Appeal	2: 216-217	3 Feb 1881
336	Shively, Jennie May	Shively, William B.	Divorce	2: 218-219	4 Feb 1881
337	Cutter, James H.	Coleman, James	At law	2: 220-221	8 Feb 1881
338	Tripp, Clinton C.	Davidson, J. E. et al.	Ejectment	2:222-223	9 Feb 1881
339	San Francisco & North Pacific Rail Road Co.	Dinwiddie, James L. (Sheriff and *ex officio* tax collector of Sonoma County)	At law	2: 224-225; 3: 60	9 Feb 1881

Suit #	Plaintiffs	Defendants	Cause of Suit	Register of Actions Volume: page(s)	Action Date
340	Lodge, J. D.	Jacobi, John	At law	2: 226-227	12 Feb 1881
341	Hutton, Charles E.	Mount Jackson Quicksilver Mining Company	Foreclosure	2: 228-229	15 Feb 1881
342	Foreman, John	Gelman, R. H.	Lien	2: 230-231	15 Feb 1881
343	Kee, Hamilton	Keay, William	Appeal	2: 232-233	17 Feb 1881
344	Wightman, Silas	Abbott, J. M.; Grosse, Guy E.; Edouard, Carl L.; Cassels, Everard L.	Foreclosure	2: 234-235	17 Feb 1881
345	Wright, Winfield S. M.	Oliver, James F.; Oliver, Martha, his wife; Finley, John	Foreclosure	2: 236-237	18 Feb 1881
346	Austin, Percy	Harris, Thomas L.	Equity	2: 238-239	17 Feb 1881
347	Wegner, Ed	Johnson, Mary Alice & Johnson, Orrick	Foreclosure	2: 240-241	19 Feb 1881
348	Hegler, Gerhard	Castens, Henry	Accounting	2: 246-247	23 Feb 1881
349	Dooly, E. & Duncan, E. H.	Powell, W. V.	At law	2: 248-249	25 Feb 1881
350	People	Cassidy, Martin	Assault to commit rape	2: 250-251	25 Feb 1881
351	Butler, Joanna L.	Morris, Thomas D.	Unlawful detainer	2: 252-253	25 Feb 1881
352	Denman, Ezekiel	Johnson, Sanborn & Hill, William	Foreclosure	2: 254-255	1 Mar 1881
353	People	Bosqui, William A.	Assault with a deadly weapon	2: 256-257	3 Mar 1881
354	Taylor, John S.	Nowlin, S. S.	At law	2: 258-259	4 Mar 1881
355	Thompson, May C.	Rupe, D. C.	Replevin	2: 260-261	4 Mar 1881
356	Foster, John F.	Hamlet, John	At law	2: 262-263	8 Mar 1881
357	Pacific Bank	Cook, Algernon M. (Surviving partner of I. & A. M. Cook); Cook, Katie W. (Executrix Est. Isaac Cook); Cook, Irving B.; Roe, John; Roe, Richard	Foreclosure	2: 264-265	8 Mar 1881
358	Tripp, Clinton C.	Santa Rosa Street Rail Road et als.	Ejectment	2: 266-267, 614-643	9 Mar 1881
359	Coleman, James	Light, William	Damages	2: 268-269	10 Mar 1881
360	People	Wing, Ah & Kong, Ah	Felony	2: 270-271	11 Mar 1881
361	Shaw, Isaac E.	Ballard, - & Hall, - (dba Ballard & Hall)	At law	2: 272-273	11 Mar 1881

Suit #	Plaintiffs	Defendants	Cause of Suit	Register of Actions Volume: page(s)	Action Date
362	People	Tuite, Christopher	Assault with a deadly weapon	2: 274-275	11 Mar 1881
363	Simmons, J. R.	Guerne, George E. & Ludwig, T. J.	Appeal	2: 276-277	12 Mar 1881
364	Markham, Andrew	Marti, M.	At law	2: 278-279	16 Mar 1881
365	Lessel, A.		Insolvency	2: 280-281	18 Mar 1881
366	Englehart, Fred		Insolvency	2: 282-283	19 Mar 1881
367	Burckhalter, A.	Simon, Simon I.	Setting aside patent	2: 284-285	19 Mar 1881
368	Wilson, William Y.		Application to be released from bond	2: 286-287	3 Mar 1881
369	Keay, William	Kee, William & Kee, S. J.	Appeal	2: 288-289	24 Mar 1881
370	Petaluma Savings Bank	Bihler, William; Zeile, John; Pacific Reclamation Co.; Somoma, County of; Sonoma Valley Rail Road Co.; Wells Fargo & Co.	Foreclosure	2: 290-291	26 Mar 1881
371	Squires, Mary E.	Squires, John S.	Divorce	2: 292-293	25 Mar 1881
372	Kingery, S. S. & Rassmussen, S.	Smith, William P.	Foreclosure	2: 294-295	28 Mar 1881
373	Glover, Charles	Tivnen, John; Morse, E. E.; Schetter, Otto (Board of Commissioners of the City of Sonoma) & Harned, J. A. M.	Equity	2: 296-297	31 Mar 1881
374	Colvin, Mary A.	Colvin, W. J.	Divorce	2: 298-299	2 Apr 1881
375	Hill, William	Morris, James B.; Morris, Mary E. (Adm. Est. Henry Z. Morris)	Foreclosure	2: 300-301	6 Apr 1881
376	Claussen, George	Kolb, William	Dissolution of partnership	2: 304-305	11 Apr 1881
377	Ackerman, O. B.	Bryan, Thomas J. & Bryan, Elizabeth	Foreclosure	2: 306-307	18 Apr 1881
378	Bloomington, L. J.	Cook, I. F.	Appeal	2: 308-309	19 Apr 1881
379	Mills, John	White, William H.	At law	2: 310-311	21 Apr 1881
380	Byrne, Bridget	Byrne, M.	Divorce	2: 312-313	21 Apr 1881

Suit #	Plaintiffs	Defendants	Cause of Suit	Register of Actions Volume: page(s)	Action Date
381	McClemmy, John	Hinkston, Green	Attachment	2: 314-315	23 Apr 1881
382	Powell, Moses		Insolvency	2: 318-319	27 Apr 1881
383	Ridgway, Jeremiah & Ridgway, Joseph W.	Childers, Spencer & Dinwiddie, J. L.	Foreclosure	2: 320-321	28 Apr 1881
384	Minear, Henry	Mount Jackson Quicksilver Mining Co. & Mead, James A.	Damages	2: 322-323	30 Apr 1881
385	Campbell, John T.	Turner, Peter	Foreclosure	2: 324-325	30 Apr 1881
386	Gifford, J.	Espey, J. H.	Appeal	2: 328-329	30 Apr 1881
387	Joyce, Martin	Worth, Rueben G. & Worth, Frances H.	Foreclosure	2: 330-331	4 May 1881
388	Case, A. B.	Merchant, Joel	At law	2: 332-333	4 May 1881
389	People	Nelson, Edward	Assault to commit rape	2: 334-335	5 May 1881
390	McGee, James H.	Thompson, R. A.	Appeal	2: 336-337	5 May 1881
391	Hill, James M.	Hill, Sarah	Divorce	2: 338-339	6 May 1881
392	Boyes, Polly H.	Boyes, John B.	Divorce	2: 340-341	7 May 1881
393	Collins, F. M.	Rose, Joseph	Appeal	2: 342-343	9 May 1881
394	Fine, Joff	Scheeline, N.	Appeal	2: 344-345	9 May 1881
395	Carriger, Sophronia J.	Carriger, A. B.	Divorce	2: 346-347	10 May 1881
396	Hutchinson, Samuel	Smith, W. J.	Foreclosure	2: 348-349	11 May 1881
397	Santa Rosa Bank	Pacific Methodist College, President & Trustees of; Renfro, L. C.; Simmons, J. C. et al.	Foreclosure	2: 350-351	17 May 1881
398	Reed, P. W.	Colusa, Lake & Mendocino Telegraph Co.	Appeal	2: 352-353	19 May 1881
399	Marcus C. Hawley & Co.	Peterson, Chris & Henry, John	Attachment	2: 354-355	23 May 1881
400	Peterson, Julius A. & Davidson, James	Dinwiddie, J. L. (Sheriff)	Replevin	2: 356-357	26 May 1881
401	Sutherland, J. J.		Insolvency	2: 358-359	27 May 1881
402	Martin, F. H.	Wood, B. S. (Co-Auditor)	Mandamus	2: 360-361	26 May 1881
403	People	White, William H.	Appeal	2: 362-363	31 May 1881
404	People	Holcomb, L. D.	Grand larceny	2: 364-365	1 Jun 1881
405	People	Holcomb, L. D.	Grand larceny	2: 366-367	1 Jun 1881
406	Ludwig, T. J.	Simmons, J. R. & Mead, W. H.	Injunction	2: 368-369	3 Jun 1881
407	Mills, John	Sonoma, Board of Supervisors of the County of	Certiorari	2: 370-371	4 Jun 1881

158

Suit #	Plaintiffs	Defendants	Cause of Suit	Register of Actions Volume: page(s)	Action Date
408	Redmond, Martin D.	Noonan, George P. & Savings Bank of Santa Rosa	Damages	2: 372-373; 3: 19	7 Jun 1881
409	Cockrill, Damie	Hall, Henry	Assumpsit	2: 374-375; 4: 289	7 Jun 1881
410	Petaluma, City of	Michili, C. &Greiss, George (dba C. Michili & Co.)	At law	2: 376-377	8 Jun 1881
411	Hill, William & Martin, H. B.	Castro, Victor; Carrillo, Julio; Tripp, Clinton C. et als.		2: 378-379	8 Jun 1881
412	Caldwell, Amanda J.	Caldwell, F. M.	Divorce	2: 380-381	11 Jun 1881
413	Cook, Sarah Ann (By her guardian Elinor Bassett)	Porter, J. V.	Foreclosure	2: 382-383	14 Jun 1881
414	Ingham, A. H.	Holmes, Calvin H.	Lien	2: 384-385	14 Jun 1881
415	Scott, E. W.	Heffelfinger, W. J.; Heffelfinger, Laura; Frame, David; Hassett, Aaron	Foreclosure	2: 386-387	16 Jun 1881
416	Mangini, Catharina	Mangini, Joseph	Divorce	2: 388-389	18 Jun 1881
417	Wetmore, J. L.	Deller, C. W.	Forfeiture of lease	2: 390-391	21 Jun 1881
418	McKenzie, John A.; McKenzie, William A.; McKenzie, Margaret	Warfield, R. H. & Jacobs, George H.	Equity	2: 392-393	21 Jun 1881
419	Runyon, Mary	Smith, James M.; Smith, Margaret Ann; Smith, Melvina; Santa Rosa Bank	Foreclosure	2: 394-395	22 Jun 1881
420	Bank of Sonoma County	Hicok, J. J.; Rodehaver, J. P.; Hicok, C. C.; Perry, James A.	Attachment	2: 396-397	22 Jun 1881
421	Label, H.		Insolvency	2: 326-327, 398-399; 3: 15	22 Jun 1881
422	Ashley, William T.		Insolvency	2: 400-401	23 Jun 1881
423	Torrence, Joseph L.	Torrence, Rosa	Divorce	2: 402-403	24 Jun 1881
424	Leicher, N.	Leicher, B.	Divorce	2: 404-405	27 Jun 1881
425	Young, J. B.	Beckner, W. S.	Assumpsit	2: 406-407	27 Jun 1881
426	Atkins, William G.	Atkins, Nancy T.	Equity	2: 408-409	5 Jul 1881
427	Sonoma & Santa Rosa Rail Road Co.	Enos, Susie & Enos, J. S.	Condemnation	2: 410-411	6 Jul 1881
428	Schierhold, H.		Insolvency	2: 412-413	7 Jul 1881
429	Pool, Abbie	Pool, Kinney D.	Divorce	2: 414-415	14 Jul 1881
430	Burrus, G. W.	Marshall, S. A.	Nuisance	2: 416-417	20 Jul 1881

Suit #	Plaintiffs	Defendants	Cause of Suit	Register of Actions Volume: page(s)	Action Date
431	People	Schoenwald, August	Grand larceny	2: 418-419	21 Jul 1881
432	Appleton, H. & Appleton, Eliza	Leavenworth, F. M. & Leavenworth, Cornelia T.	Equity	2: 420-421	23 Jul 1881
433	Corliss, A.	Rose, Joseph; Lodge, J. D.; Kizer, A.	Appeal	2: 422-423	25 Jul 1881
434	Martin, Silas M.; Denman, Ezekiel; Railsback, Caleb; Warner, Gustavus; Meacham, Harrison	McBrown, John	Damages	2: 424-425	25 Jul 1881
435	Martin, Silas M.; Denman, Ezekiel; Railsback, Caleb; Warner, Gustavus; Meacham, Harrison	McBrown, John	Damages	2: 426-427	25 Jul 1881
436	Walker, John	Boyce, J. F. & Boyce, Martha A.	Foreclosure	2: 428-429	26 Jul 1881
437	Cooper, Hattie H.	Cooper, George W.	Divorce	2: 430-431	26 Jul 1881
438	Wood, Guy Mead	Wood, John	At law	2: 432-433	28 Jul 1881
439	Campbell, John T.	Rich, John A.	Foreclosure	2: 434-435	29 Jul 1881
440	Morrison, F. G.	Beatty, John C.	Appeal	2: 436-437	29 Jul 1881
441	People	Alexander, Peter	Murder	2: 438-439	1 Aug 1881
442	People	Cope, James	Burglary	2: 440-441	1 Aug 1881
443	People	McCune, Lena (aka Murray, Lena)	Appeal	2: 442-443	3 Aug 1881
444	Amerman, H. J.		Insolvency	2: 444-445	3 Aug 1881
445	Johnson, Robert C.	Sonoma Valley Rail Road Company	Ejectment	2: 446-447	3 Aug 1881
446	Manning, Georgia Ann	Manning, Robert S.	Divorce	2: 448-449	5 Aug 1881
447	Parrazzo, G. B.		Petition to be discharged on writ of habeas corpus	2: 450	6 Aug 1881
448	Dingley, C. L. & Bihler, William	Houser, S. R.	Injunction	2: 452-453	11 Aug 1881
449	Torres, Joaquin		Petition to be discharged on writ of habeas corpus	2: 454-455	12 Aug 1881
450	Harlow, James	Hoag, David & Hoag, Charles	Assumpsit	2: 456-457	15 Aug 1881
451	Yorka, Nancy Ann	Yorka, Philip	Divorce	2: 458-459	16 Aug 1881
452	Redmond, M. D.	Dinwiddie, J. L.; Hermann, M.; Label, H.	Appeal	2: 460-461	17 Aug 1881

Suit #	Plaintiffs	Defendants	Cause of Suit	Register of Actions Volume: page(s)	Action Date
453	People	Fung, Lui	Assault with intent to commit murder	2: 462-463	20 Aug 1881
454	Brooks, E. L.		Insolvency	2: 464-465	22 Aug 1881
455	McPherson, Lycurgus		Insolvency	2: 466-467; 3: 161	26 Aug 1881
456	Fiori, Joseph & Fiori, Juditha, his wife	Corrippo, Peter	Damages	2: 468-469	27 Aug 1881
457	Taggart, John, Sr.	Schloss, S.	Appeal	2: 470-471	29 Aug 1881
458	Foy, Ah		Application for writ of habeas corpus	2: 472-473	29 Aug 1881
459	King, John & King, Samuel		Insolvency	2: 474-475	29 Aug 1881
460	Peterson, Henry C.		Insolvency	2: 476-477	1 Sep 1881
461	Sicott, F. et al.	Mount Jackson Quicksilver Mining Co.	Arbitration	2: 478-479	1 Sep 1881
462	Lambert, Charles L.	McPherson, Lycurgus	Foreclosure	2: 480-481	1 Sep 1881
463	Northup, E. G.	Curtis, Ellen M. & Robinson, Margaret M. M.	Equity	2: 484-483	2 Sep 1881
464	Millett, W. H.		Application for writ of habeas corpus	2: 484-485	5 Sep 1881
465	Kirch, H.	Moltzen, D. F.	Attachment	2: 486-487	6 Sep 1881
466	Moltzen, D. F.		Involuntary insolvency	2: 488-489; 3: 47	8 Sep 1881
467	Mather, John	Mather, Mary Eloise	Divorce	2: 490-491	10 Sep 1881
468	Sonoma, County of	Wood, Ben S. (Recorder)	Submission	2: 494-493	10 Sep 1881
469	Torri, Lorenzo & Torri, Pasqual	Spinetti, A. & Parrazzo, G.	Appeal	2: 494-495	12 Sep 1881
470	Peterson, Christ	Henry, John	Accounting	2: 496-497	14 Sep 1881
471	Lambert, Charles L.	McPherson, Lycurgus & Dinwiddie, J. L.	Foreclosure	2: 498-499	14 Sep 1881
472	McHarvey, Charles & Hope, Valentine	Gaffnie, John & Gaffnie, Annie	Foreclosure	2: 500-501	21 Sep 1881
473	Laguna Drainage District	Giovannini, D.	Foreclosure	2: 502-503	21 Sep 1881
474	McBride, Georgie	Chapman, William S.	Foreclosure	2: 504-505	24 Sep 1881

161

Suit #	Plaintiffs	Defendants	Cause of Suit	Register of Actions Volume: page(s)	Action Date
475	Haas, C. H.; Haas, K.; Haas, William (dba Haas Bros.)	Hildburgh, L. & Hildburgh, D. H. (dba Hildburgh Bros.)	Attachment	2: 506-507	27 Sep 1881
476	McReynolds, Jacob	White, William H.	Attachment	2: 508-509	27 Sep 1881
477	Fowler, John H.	Smith, Thomas	Assumpsit	2: 510-511	29 Sep 1881
478	Parsons, Isaac	Spencer, Mary C.; Spencer, Thomas; Miltz, Theodore; Patterson, Margaret	Foreclosure	2: 512-513	30 Sep 1881
479	Bank of Sonoma County	Eaton, I. F. & Eaton, A. J.	Assumpsit	2: 514-515	30 Sep 1881
480	People	Kane, Chauncey	Robbery	2: 516-517	29 Sep 1881
481	McKenzie, K.		Application for writ of habeas corpus	2: 522	4 Oct 1881
482	Vallejo, Benicia F.	Vallejo, Lus; Vallejo, Ignacio; Frisbie, Felicita; Page, Zasela; Vallejo, Platon; Frisbie, Anatilde; Doe, John; Roe, Richard	To quiet title	2: 524-525	4 Oct 1881
483	Peterson, Henry C.		Insolvency	2: 526-527	6 Oct 1881
484	Hettich, Christ	Shaw, James	At law	2: 528-529	7 Oct 1881
485	Crose, J. M.		Insolvency	2: 530-531	7 Oct 1881
486	Sheffer, C. M.	Austin, M. A. & Austin, Catherine	Attachment	2: 532-533	6 Oct 1881
487	Gibney, Martha C.	Gibney, George	Divorce	2: 534-535	8 Oct 1881
488	Tighe, Kelly (Adm. Est. Philena H. Richards)	Mutz, Henry	Ejectment	2: 538-539	12 Oct 1881
489	Hassett, J. D.	Thing, Arthur	Attachment	2: 540-541	12 Oct 1881
490	Bolden, Samuel	Turner, W. J.	At law	2: 542-543	12 Oct 1881
491	Liebig, F.	McAllester, John	Accounting	2: 544-545	13 Oct 1881
492	Ridgway, Jeremiah & Ridgway, Joseph	Williamson, S. A. & Justice, Joan	Attachment	2: 546-547	17 Oct 1881
493	Vorhees, James	Hall, Albert A.	Attachment	2: 548-549	17 Oct 1881
494	Beaver, J. L.	Beaver, Belle	Divorce	2: 550-551	22 Oct 1881
495	People	Werden, John	Burglary	2: 552-553	24 Oct 1881
496	People	Shepherd, John B.	Grand larceny	2: 554-555	25 Oct 1881
497	Jones, B. M.	Neely, L.	Equity	2: 556-557	25 Oct 1881
498	Thing, Arthur		Insolvency	2: 558-559; 3: 16	29 Oct 1881
499	Shoemake, William	Wright, L. R.	Foreclosure	2: 560-561	31 Oct 1881

162

Suit #	Plaintiffs	Defendants	Cause of Suit	Register of Actions Volume: page(s)	Action Date
500	McReynolds, Jacob	White, William H.	Injunction	2: 562-563	31 Oct 1881
501	Meldrum, David	McDonald, Mark L.	Assumpsit	2: 564-565	1 Nov 1881
502	Hugues, Ernest	Strong, John	At law	2: 566-567	2 Nov 1881
503	Heald, T. T.	Ludwig, Thomas J.	Assumpsit	2: 568-569	2 Nov 1881
504	Morris, James B.	Robertson, Phoebe S. & Robertson, Robert	At law	2: 570-571	2 Nov 1881
505	Barnes, E. H.	Marshall, S. A.	Nuisance	2: 572-573	3 Nov 1881
506	Schaeffer, Ignatz	Schaeffer, Margaret	Divorce	2: 574-575	4 Nov 1881
507	Barry, Julia (alias Tuite, Julia)	Tuite, Christopher	Divorce	2: 576-577	7 Nov 1881
508	Leveroni, Manuel		Application for writ of habeas corpus	2: 578	10 Nov 1881
509	People	Archambeau, Charles & McDonough, Michael	Grand larceny	2: 580-581	11 Nov 1881
510	Burris, L. W.	Head, R.	Injunction	2: 582-583; 3: 48, 115	12 Nov 1881
511	People	Levoroni, Manuella	Appeal	2: 584-585	14 Nov 1881
512	Holly, S. B.		Insolvency	2: 586-587; 3: 59	21 Nov 1881
513	Maynard, F. T.	Lawler, P.	Appeal	2: 588-589	21 Nov 1881
514	Kirby, John	Kirby, John H. & Kirby, Elizabeth, his wife	Equity	2: 590-591	22 Nov 1881
515	Hunter, Sarah A.	Hunter, Robert E.	Divorce	2: 592-593	22 Nov 1881
516	San Francisco & North Pacific Rail Road Co.	Mead, W. H. (Constable)	Injunction	2: 594-595	25 Nov 1881
517	Mather, Samuel	Jones, C. J.	Ejectment	2: 596-597	26 Nov 1881
518	Santa Rosa Bank	McDonald, Mark L. & Ludwig, T. J.	Attachment	2: 598-599	28 Nov 1881
519	Caldwell, Amanda J.	Caldwell, F. M.	Attachment	2: 600-601	5 Dec 1881
520	Tibbetts, David	Hall, Henry	Attachment	2: 602-603	5 Dec 1881
521	Quackenbush, L. J.	Quackenbush, R. P.	Divorce	2: 604-605	5 Dec 1881
522	Morgan, W. C.	Lewis, Eugene	Attachment	2: 606-607	5 Dec 1881
523	Bassi, Vincenza	Schroyer, A.	Accounting	2: 608-609	12 Dec 1881
524	Clark, James P.	Davisson, D. D.	Assumpsit	2: 610-611	12 Dec 1881
525	San Francisco & North Pacific Rail Road Co.	Mead, W. H.		2: 612-613	5 Dec 1881
526	Glynn, F. B.	Dearborn, M. S. & Berka, John	Equity	3: 1	13 Dec 1881

Suit #	Plaintiffs	Defendants	Cause of Suit	Register of Actions Volume: page(s)	Action Date
527	Beaver, J. L.	Beaver, Belle	Divorce	3: 2	22 Dec 1881
528	Wickersham, I. G.	Richardson, W. A. & Warner, G.	At law	3: 3	19 Dec 1881
529	Santa Rosa, City of	Shane, Adam	Tax	3: 4	20 Dec 1881
530	Lewis, Eugene		Insolvency	3: 5	28 Dec 1881
531	Clover, Amanda	Norton, W. M. & Smith, W. A.	At law	3: 6	28 Dec 1881
532	Long, Mariam W. & Long, Aaron S.	Jones, C. J. & Glenn, Robert	At law	3: 7	31 Dec 1881
533	Whitney, A. P.	Purrington, Joseph	Accounting	3: 8	31 Dec 1881
534	Rogers, J. R.	Rogers, Sarah M.	Divorce	3: 9	4 Jan 1882
535	Powers, Mary C.	Powers, David P.	Divorce	3: 10	4 Jan 1882
536	People	Miller, David	Murder	3: 11	4 Jan 1882
537	Sellards, Virginia A.		Sole trader	3: 12	6 Jan 1882
538	Hitchcock, Hollis	Hassett, John D. (Assignee of Arthur Thing)	At law	3: 13	7 Jan 1882
539	Nagle, F. G.	Henderson, J. J.	Appeal	3: 14	7 Jan 1882
540	People	Chung, Ah (informed against as Ah John)	Burglary	3: 17	10 Jan 1882
541	Matthies, Henry	Cadden, John	Appeal	3: 18	16 Jan 1882
542	Coon, R. W.		Insolvency	3: 20	16 Jan 1882
543	Ragsdale, J. W.	Hutchinson, Henry	At law	3: 21	16 Jan 1882
544	Metcalf, Phoebe & Southwick, Helen	Thompson, Amelia	Complaint at law	3: 22	16 Jan 1882
545	Gardella, Lorenzo	Grove, C.	Appeal	3: 23	19 Jan 1882
546	Korbel, F.; Korbel, A.; Korbel, J. (dba F. Korbel & Bros.)	Guerne, George E. & Murphy, Rufus (dba Guerne & Murphy)	Injunction	3: 24	21 Jan 1882
547	Waddel, A. J.	Porter, Thomas	Accounting	3: 25	21 Jan 1882
548	Terry, J. W.	Koenig, F.	Foreclosure of mechanic's lien	3: 26	23 Jan 1882
549	Whitney, A. P.	Purrington, Joseph		3: 28, 290	25 Jan 1882
550	Current, Martha E.	Current, Thomas D.	Divorce	3: 29	25 Jan 1882
551	Beardein, Martha E.	Beardein, James M.	Divorce	3: 30	25 Jan 1882
551½	Weyl, Henry	Sonoma & Santa Rosa Rail Road	Injunction	3: 11	28 Jan 1882

164

Suit #	Plaintiffs	Defendants	Cause of Suit	Register of Actions Volume: page(s)	Action Date
552	People	Miller, David	Murder	3: 31	30 Jan 1882
553	Bassi, Allesia	Schroyer, Aaron	Appeal	3: 32	30 Jan 1882
554	Tilton, Benjamin F.	Clark, John & Stuart, Charles D. (Adm. Est. Ann J. Clark)	Foreclosure	3: 33	30 Jan 1882
555	Jewell, A.	Shields, William S. et als.	Abstract of judgment & supplemental proceedings	3: 34	18 Oct 1881
556	Case, A. L.	Glass, Phillip	Attachment	3: 35	7 Feb 1882
557	Darrow, William H.	Darrow, Addie	Divorce	3: 36	9 Feb 1882
558	Espey, John H.	Wood, Wesley	Transfer from Justice Court	3: 37	11 Feb 1882
559	Daniels, Elmon	Coleman, A. & Charles, G. W.	Assumpsit	3: 38	13 Feb 1882
560	Micheli, Charles	Dinwiddie, J. L. & Brush, G. M.	Claim & delivery	3: 39	13 Feb 1882
561	Winkle, Henry	Griffith, A. (Mrs.) & Griffith, Albert	Appeal	3: 40	13 Feb 1882
562	People	Blackinton, Emmet	Information for felony	3: 41	14 Feb 1882
563	Weyl, Henry	Sonoma Valley Rail Road Co. & Donahue, Peter	Restitution & damages	3: 42, 291	15 Feb 1882
564	Quackenbush, U. P.		Involuntary insolvency	3: 43, 80, 265	15 Feb 1882
565	Kenyon, Edwin	Cooper, H. H. & Cooper, Betsey M.	Foreclosure	3: 44	20 Feb 1882
566	Luedke, J.		Involuntary insolvency	3: 45, 143	20 Feb 1882
567	San Francisco & North Pacific Rail Road Co.	Dinwiddie, J. L. (Tax Collector)	Injunction	3: 46	25 Feb 1882
568	Cheney, Thomas & Cheney, Thomas H.	O'Brien, John	Nuisance	3: 49	27 Feb 1882
569	Glass, Phillip		Insolvency	3: 50, 116	27 Feb 1882
570	Guerne, George E. & Murphy, Rufus	Wright, S. B.	Appeal	3: 51	27 Feb 1882
571	Respini, J.	Pometta, D.	Attachment	3: 52	2 Mar 1882

Suit #	Plaintiffs	Defendants	Cause of Suit	Register of Actions Volume: page(s)	Action Date
572	Gianella, L.	Frazier, A. H. & Marshall, James	Injunction	3: 53, 117	2 Mar 1882
573	Meeker, C. E.; Meeker, R. W.; Meeker, Leslie (By their guardian A. P. Meeker)	Sonoma & Marin Mutual Beneficial Association	Assumpsit	3: 54	3 Mar 1882
574	Bailhache, Josephine	Dinwiddie, J. L.		3: 55	6 Mar 1882
575	Barnett, Alexander		Change of name	3: 56	7 Mar 1882
576	Tivnen, John; Morse, E. E.; Schetter, Otto	Weyl, Henry & Tighe, Kelly	Appeal	3: 57	8 Mar 1882
577	Guerra, Giuseppe	San Francisco and North Pacific Rail Road Company	Appeal	3: 58	20 Mar 1882
578	People	Charles, Lamott	Burglary	3: 61	27 Mar 1882
579	San Francisco & North Pacific Rail Road Co.	Dinwiddie, J. L. (Tax Collector of Sonoma County)	Injunction	3: 62	27 Mar 1882
580	Santa Rosa Water Works	Dinwiddie, J. L. (Tax Collector of Sonoma County)	At law	3: 63	30 Mar 1882
581	Howe, Elijah	Howe, Edwin A. & Howe, Ann Frances	Foreclosure	3: 64	4 Apr 1882
582	San Francisco & North Pacific Rail Road Co.	Dinwiddie, J. L.; Denman, E.; Hill, William; Fritsch, John; Zartman, William; Whitney, A. P.; Laughlin, John M.; De Turk, I.; Fulkerson, Richard	At law	3: 65	7 Apr 1882
583	Gamble, John	Rhodes, A. J.		3: 66	8 Apr 1882
584	Barnes, Aaron	Langdon, Nora; Langdon, C. W.; Brown, John	Appeal	3: 67	12 Apr 1882
585	Allen, Ault	Allen, Achilles	Divorce	3: 68	13 Apr 1882
586	Griffin, Rose	Bloom, Jonas	Damages	3: 69, 109, 214	20 Apr 1882
587	People	San Francisco & North Pacific Rail Road Co.	Attachment	3: 70	21 Apr 1882
588	Kee, James	Johnson, A.	Appeal	3: 71	21 Apr 1882
589	Banguess, Eliza M.	Banguess, Lafayette	Divorce	3: 72	26 Apr 1882
590	Tully, Frances		Insolvency	3: 73	27 Apr 1882
591	Polack, Mary	Forsythe, W.	Ejectment	3: 74	28 Apr 1882
592	Wright, W. S. M.	Seymour, L. B.	Ejectment	3: 75	28 Apr 1882
593	Santa Rosa Bank	Boggs, George W.; Boggs, Alabama; McDonald, Mark L.; Latapie, Eleanora L.; Latapie, Eleanora L. (Executrix Est. Edward Latapie)	Foreclosure	3: 76	24 Apr 1882
594	Tuite, Christopher	Barry, Julia	Appeal	3: 77	29 Apr 1882
595	Fine, Joff	Quinn, John	Appeal	3: 78	29 Apr 1882

Suit #	Plaintiffs	Defendants	Cause of Suit	Register of Actions Volume: page(s)	Action Date
596	People	Jordan, John	Misdemeanor- living in a state of open & notorious cohabitation & adultery	3: 79	1 May 1882
597	Cornelius, George H. H.	Monahan, P., Sr. & Monahan, P., Jr.	Attachment	3: 81	1 May 1882
598	Bonnetti, Caterina	Martinelli, Antonio	Attachment	3: 82	3 May 1882
599	Bonnetti, Claudina	Martinelli, Antonio	Attachment	3: 83	3 May 1882
600	Bonnetti, Filomena	Martinelli, Antonio	Attachment	3: 84	3 May 1882
601	Myers, Dillon P.	Myers, Hannah P.	Divorce	3: 85	3 May 1882
602	Alderson, Annie	Alderson, H. E.	Divorce	3: 86	3 May 1882
603	People	Lewis, Oliver H.	Grand larceny	3: 87	3 May 1882
604	People	Lewis, Oliver H.	Grand larceny	3: 88	3 May 1882
605	Bryant, William J.	Sonoma Pacific Coal Company	Attachment	3: 89	4 May 1882
606	McGovern, D.	Williams, George H.	Appeal	3: 90	5 May 1882
607	Bryant, William J.	Sonoma Pacific Coal Company	Attachment	3: 91	6 May 1882
608	Healdsburg Lodge, No. 64, I. O. O. F., Trustees of		Application to sell real estate	3: 92	9 May 1882
609	McGee, James H. (Assignee of Philip Glass, an insolvent debtor)	Griess, George; Griess, Catherine; Glass, Philip; Glass, Margaret	Equity	3: 93; 4: 64	11 May 1882
610	Beckner, William S.		Insolvency	3: 94	15 May 1882
611	Glenn, Robert	Platt, B. C.	Accounting	3: 95	15 May 1882
612	Hitchcock, Hollis	Bloom, Jonas	Complaint on delivery	3: 96, 292	18 May 1882
613	Edwards, James	Nathanson, Arthur	Appeal	3: 97	19 May 1882
614	Wright, Joseph	Roberts, Mary	Appeal	3: 98	20 May 1882
615	Atkins, Nancy J.	Atkins, W. G.	Ejectment	3: 99	22 May 1882
616	Temple, J. W.	Durand, Victor		3: 100	22 May 1882

Suit #	Plaintiffs	Defendants	Cause of Suit	Register of Actions Volume: page(s)	Action Date
617	Ward, N.	Bailey, M. C. et als.	Foreclosure of mechanic's lien	3: 101	22 May 1882
618	Campbell, J. T. (Assignee of D. F. Moltzen, insolvent)	Dinwiddie, J. L. (Sheriff of Sonoma County) & Kirch, Henry		3: 102	23 May 1882
619	Brickwedel, Henry; Hencken, Martin; Schroder, Henry (dba Henry Brickwedel & Co.)	Brown, William	Attachment	3: 103	25 May 1882
620	Santa Rosa Water Works	Gibb, Thomas Murray; Patterson, James (Executor Last Will Daniel Gibb); Patterson, James (Adm. Est. William Gibb); Forbes, Alexander; Knox, Robert; Knox, Ellen Walker Johnson	Equity	3: 104	25 May 1882
621	Frounson, Peter		Application for writ of habeas corpus	3: 105	29 May 1882
622	Barnes, Aaron	Rupe, Mary J. & Rupe, D. C.	Foreclosure	3: 106	29 May 1882
623	Santa Rosa Bank	Carpenter, George	Attachment	3: 107	31 May 1882
624	People	Carpenter, George	Forgery	3: 108	2 Jun 1882
625	Laguna Drainage District	Giovannini, D.	At law	3: 110	3 Jun 1882
626	Body, Mark	Head, William	Accounting	3: 111	6 Jun 1882
627	Wilkerson, Jeremiah		Insolvency	3: 112	6 Jun 1882
628	Bradford, A. C.	Stewart, John	Accounting	3: 113, 308	9 Jun 1882
629	Jones, William (Executor Est. James Harlow)	Hall, Henry	Attachment	3: 114	10 Jun 1882
630	People	Hansen, Joaquin	Assault to commit rape	3: 118	19 Jun 1882
631	Allman, John	Allman, George & Queen, C. (dba Allman & Queen)	Assumpsit	3: 119	26 Jun 1882
632	Espey, John	Woods, Wesley & Laughlin, John M.	To quiet title	3: 120	27 Jun 1882
633	Simmons, Alonzo R.	Simmons, Jennette A.	Divorce	3: 121	27 Jun 1882
634	Stewart, John & Stewart, Sarah	Bradford, L. W. (Mrs.)	Foreclosure	3: 122	1 Jul 1882

168

Suit #	Plaintiffs	Defendants	Cause of Suit	Register of Actions Volume: page(s)	Action Date
635	Sonoma & Marin Beneficial Association, Directors of the		Application to dissolve the corporation	3: 123	5 Jul 1882
636	Storni, Peter	Calanchini, Giacomina	Divorce	3: 124	10 Jul 1882
637	Crosby, James		Insolvency	3: 125	10 Jul 1882
638	Santa Rosa Bank	Frost, C. W.	Ejectment	3: 126	12 Jul 1882
639	Gilbert, T. A.	Carey, Joseph & Carey, Margaret	Foreclosure	3: 127	15 Jul 1882
640	Heath, Adaline J.	Heath, George A.	Divorce	3: 128	17 Jul 1882
641	People	Thomas, John	Misdemeanor- obtaining money by false pretenses	3: 129	17 Jul 1882
642	People	Deeds, Adam E.	Grand larceny	3: 130	17 Jul 1882
643	People	Charlie (A Chinaman)	Grand larceny	3: 131	17 Jul 1882
644	Hughes, R.	Thrift, Sabin D.	Forcible entry & detainer	3: 132	18 Jul 1882
645	Monahan, P., Sr.	Monahan, P., Jr.	Appeal	3: 133	20 Jul 1882
646	Geurkink, B. W.	Charles, J. M.	Injunction	3: 134	20 Jul 1882
647	Glenn, Robert	Platt, B. C.	Attachment	3: 135	25 Jul 1882
648	Comstock, B. F.	Comstock, L. N.	Divorce	3: 136	26 Jul 1882
649	Fletcher, Andrew & Fletcher, Duncan	Maccaby, George & Maccaby, Mark	Injunction	3: 137	26 Jul 1882
650	Bank of Tomales	Wilkinson, J. & Taylor, Despard	Appeal	3: 138	28 Jul 1882
651	Foster, D. A.	Williams, John A.	Equity	3: 139	3 Aug 1882
652	Liebman, L. (Assignee)	Quackenbush, Sarah A.	Equity	3: 140	3 Aug 1882
653	People	Uhlhorn, H. B.	Appeal	3: 141	3 Aug 1882
654	Giovannini, J.	Mead, W. H.		3: 142	3 Aug 1882
655	Powell, Ransom	Bailhache, John N.; Bailhache, Josephine; Frisbie, Levi C.	Equity	3: 144	5 Aug 1882
656	Santa Rosa Bank	Bryant, William J.	Assumpsit	3: 145	24 Jul 1882

Suit #	Plaintiffs	Defendants	Cause of Suit	Register of Actions Volume: page(s)	Action Date
657	Phillips, Walter		Resignation as trustee	3: 146	24 Jul 1882
658	Cornett, Agnes	Cornett, George	Divorce	3: 147	5 Aug 1882
659	Burdell, Mary A.	Sweeney, Patrick	Injunction	3: 148	7 Aug 1882
660	Powers, Jessie	Howard, Mary C.	Appeal	3: 149	7 Aug 1882
661	Hicks, M. C.	McIntosh, J. E. & McIntosh, Margaret	Ejectment	3: 150, 301	8 Aug 1882
662	Kohle, Catherine	Kohle, William H.; Kohle, Minnie L.; Kohle, Augustina (a minor)	Equity	3: 151	9 Aug 1882
663	Sonoma, County of	Rickliff, P. H.	Condemnation	3: 152	9 Aug 1882
664	Bank of Ukiah	Caughey, Robert	Assumpsit	3: 153	12 Aug 1882
665	Bank of Ukiah	Shoemake, Susan (Executrix)	Assumpsit	3: 154	12 Aug 1882
666	Walker, J. D.	Sonoma, Board of Supervisors of the County of		3: 155	14 Aug 1882
667	Hitchcock, Hollis	Genazzi, John	Appeal	3: 156, 241	15 Aug 1882
668	Black, Richard	Dooley, John C.	Appeal	3: 157	18 Aug 1882
669	Truitt, Roland K.; Zuver, J. H.; Walker, D. W.	Frazier, James & Frazier, E. H.	Appeal	3: 158	18 Aug 1882
670	Bayler, Karolina	Richardson, Helena E.	Foreclosure	3: 159	18 Aug 1882
671	Righitti, Berto Lame	Bertolo, Paolo	Appeal	3: 160	19 Aug 1882
672	Lynch, Sarah P.	Lynch, James M.	Divorce	3: 162	26 Aug 1882
673	Wilmerding, J. C.	Bihler, William	Attachment	3: 163	30 Aug 1882
674	Kraft, Rosamond	Kraft, P. E.	Divorce	3: 164	2 Sep 1882
675	Thrift, Sabin D.	Hughes, Roland & Case, W. P.	Damages	3: 165	2 Sep 1882
676	People	Bush, David	To cancel certificate	3: 166	5 Sep 1882
677	People	Gallagher, John P.	To cancel certificate	3: 167	5 Sep 1882
678	People	O'Brien, John H.	To cancel certificate	3: 168	5 Sep 1882
679	People	Swanwell, F.	To cancel certificate	3: 169	5 Sep 1882

Suit #	Plaintiffs	Defendants	Cause of Suit	Register of Actions Volume: page(s)	Action Date
680	People	Whitman, J. H.	To cancel certificate	3: 170	5 Sep 1882
681	Gobbi, Peter	Lancel, A.	Appeal	3: 171	7 Sep 1882
682	Happy, John	Caseres, Cero	Appeal	3: 172	9 Sep 1882
683	Santa Rosa, City of	Matern, F.	Tax	3: 173	9 Sep 1882
684	Lillie, C. H.	McKenzie, D. W.	Assumpsit	3: 174	11 Sep 1882
685	Denk, Frank	Gundlach, Jacob	Appeal	3: 175	11 Sep 1882
686	Chapman, William S.	Polack, Mary & Forsythe, William	Ejectment	3: 176	12 Sep 1882
687	Stapp, Mary A.	Turner, G. J.	Foreclosure	3: 177	12 Sep 1882
688	Carrillo, Mary	Carrillo, Joaquin	Divorce	3: 178	13 Sep 1882
689	Winchcomb, Harry M.	Walkup, W. B. & Hamilton, John Doe	Ejectment	3: 179	13 Sep 1882
690	Mutual Relief Association of Petaluma	Little, J. D. & Hopkins, S. J.	Foreclosure	3: 180	14 Sep 1882
691	Charron, Francis	Tremblay, Alfred	Attachment	3: 181	15 Sep 1882
692	Winslow, George		Insolvency	3: 182	16 Sep 1882
693	Wegner, Ed	Simmons, A. R.	Appeal	3: 183	16 Sep 1882
694	People	Lin, Yo	Burglary	3: 184	18 Sep 1882
695	Santa Rosa Bank	Nelson, William C.	Promissory note	3: 185	18 Sep 1882
696	Roney, J. M.	Shore, G.	Promissory note	3: 186	18 Sep 1882
697	Thrift, Sabin D.	Hughes, Roland	Ejectment	3: 187	20 Sep 1882
698	Wing, Amanda F.	Wing, William	Divorce	3: 188	20 Sep 1882
699	Hefner, Philip	Urton, W. L.	Ejectment	3: 189	23 Sep 1882
700	Guerne, George E. & Murphy, Rufus (dba Guerne & Murphy)	Willits, William H.	Injunction	3: 190, 364; 4: 52	26 Sep 1882
701	Bush, James		Application for writ of habeas corpus	3: 191	28 Sep 1882
702	Thierkoff, F. G. & Thierkoff, Anna	Sonoma & Santa Rosa Rail Road Co.	At law	3: 192	28 Sep 1882
703	Appleton, H.	Leavenworth, T. M.	Appeal	3: 193	26 Sep 1882

171

Suit #	Plaintiffs	Defendants	Cause of Suit	Register of Actions Volume: page(s)	Action Date
704	Cumberland Presbyterian Church of Santa Rosa		Application to sell property	3: 194	3 Oct 1882
705	Mitchell, Marcus	Jones, William	At law	3: 195	6 Oct 1882
706	Ducker, William	McLean, Donald	Foreclosure	3: 196	6 Oct 1882
707	Hatfield, Amanda		Application for writ of habeas corpus	3: 197	6 Oct 1882
708	Grangers Business Association	Capell, B. B.	Assumpsit	3: 198	14 Oct 1882
709	Geurkink, B. W.	Hickey, Morris; Walsh, M.; Doyle, M.; Fairbanks, H. T.; Poehlman, C.; Ayres, William (Trustees of the City of Petaluma) & Petaluma, City of	Injunction	3: 199	16 Oct 1882
710	Lynch, James M.	Forsyth, William H.	Damages	3: 200	17 Oct 1882
711	Petaluma Savings Bank	Fritsch, John; Maynard, F. T.; Cox, W. E.; Bowman, J. C.	Assumpsit	3: 201	19 Oct 1882
712	Sutton, Hannah	Hickey, Morris; Walsh, M.; Doyle, M.; Fairbanks, H. T.; Poehlman, C.; Ayres, William (Trustees of the City of Petaluma) & Petaluma, City of	Injunction	3: 202	21 Oct 1882
713	Peter, Martin	Hooper, George F.	Damages	3: 203	23 Oct 1882
714	People	Patten, Charles W.	Assault with intent to commit murder	3: 204	23 Oct 1882
715	Sonoma & Marin Mutual Beneficial Association		Application to disincorporate	3: 205	26 Oct 1882
716	Hudson, Elizabeth	Shaw, John George; Shaw, James A.; Hood, Eliza A.; Wilson, Caroline	Equity	3: 206	31 Oct 1882
717	Mayer, August	Patterson, James H.	Injunction	3: 207, 293	31 Oct 1882
718	Murray, Dennis	Marti, M.	Appeal	3: 208	13 Nov 1882
719	Thrift, Sabin D.	Delaney, James	Ejectment	3: 209	6 Nov 1882
720	People	Berman, Jacob	Petit larceny	3: 210	6 Nov 1882

172

Suit #	Plaintiffs	Defendants	Cause of Suit	Register of Actions Volume: page(s)	Action Date
721	Santa Rosa, City of	Gillespie, H.	Tax suit	3: 211	14 Nov 1882
722	Howe, Abbie E.	Howe, C. W.	Divorce	3: 212	17 Nov 1882
723	Armstrong, J. B.	White, Carlos	Appeal	3: 213	18 Nov 1882
724	Wieland, John	Agster, John	Attachment	3: 215	20 Nov 1882
725	People	Heisel, Paul	Assault with intent to commit murder	3: 216	20 Nov 1882
726	Berger, M.	McCarthy, Charles	Appeal	3: 217	20 Nov 1882
727	Dougherty, John	Urton, W. L.	Appeal	3: 218	22 Nov 1882
728	Guerne, A. L.		Insolvency	3: 219	24 Nov 1882
729	Rogers, John R.	Rogers, Sarah M.	Divorce	3: 220	24 Nov 1882
730	Taylor, Orson A.	Meyer, George S.		3: 221	27 Nov 1882
731	McAnally, W. W.	McAnally, Elsie	Divorce	3: 222	28 Nov 1882
732	Nevins, William	Moulton, William		3: 223	27 Nov 1882
732½	People	Mucio (alias Vincienzo, Muzzi)	Burglary	3: 224	4 Dec 1882
733	People	Antonio, José	Burglary	3: 225	4 Dec 1882
734	People	Haas, Herman	Attempt to commit arson	3: 226	4 Dec 1882
735	Chamberlain, David	Sang, David	Foreclosure	3: 227	4 Dec 1882
736	McAnally, W. W.	Loomis, Frank C. & McAnnally, Elsie	To quiet title	3: 228, 320	4 Dec 1882
737	Thornley, William H.; Thornley, John W.; Thornley, George D.	Boyce, John F. & Boyce, Martha A.	Ejectment	3: 229, 365	5 Dec 1882
738	Liebman, L. (Assignee)	Quackenbush, Sarah A.		3: 230	5 Dec 1882
739	Mayer, August	Patterson, James H.	At law	3: 231	5 Dec 1882
740	Machado, John & Machado, Rosa, his wife	Paula, John	Slander	3: 232	6 Dec 1882
741	Maddux, William H.		Insolvency	3: 233	6 Dec 1882
742	Hayes, Mary T.	Hayes, Thomas	Divorce	3: 234	9 Dec 1882
743	Elwell, Charles S.	Hudoff, C. D. & Hudoff, Theresa	At law	3: 235	9 Dec 1882
744	Henley, Barclay	Edgerton, Henry	Assumpsit	3: 236	15 Dec 1882

Suit #	Plaintiffs	Defendants	Cause of Suit	Register of Actions Volume: page(s)	Action Date
745	Cassidy, J. W.	Perkins, - & Benjamin, A. M. (dba Perkins & Benjamin)	Assumpsit	3: 237	15 Dec 1882
746	Fine, Joff	Leonard, L.	Equity	3: 238	15 Dec 1882
747	People	Smith, R. W.	Grand larceny	3: 239	16 Dec 1882
748	Leonard, L.	Fine, Joff	Equity	3: 240	18 Dec 1882
749	Marshall, Robert	Marshall, Sarah A. (Executrix Est & Will John Marshall)	Equity	3: 242	21 Dec 1882
750	Watts, Richard	Driscoll John; Driscoll, Hannah; Hallinan, James S.	Foreclosure	3: 243	23 Dec 1882
751	Brotherton, Woodley (By his guardian *ad litem* T. W. Brotherton)	Gunn, J. H.	Slander	3: 244	30 Dec 1882
752	Silvia, A. J.	Tighe, Kelly (Adm. Est. Mannassah Hunt)	Appeal	3: 245	2 Jan 1883
753	Wise & Goldfish	Neece, A. & Neece, Caroline	Assumpsit	3: 246	2 Jan 1883
754	Martin, J. M.	Vanderhoof, M. V.	Claim & delivery	3: 247, 331	3 Jan 1883
755	Bailhache, Josephine	Rowland, William	To quiet title	3: 248	8 Jan 1883
756	Wheeler, Jacob (Executor Est. Jemima J. Wheeler)	Richardson, H. E.; Richardson, L. B.; Thompson, S. G.; Thompson, Amelia S.	Foreclosure	3: 249	8 Jan 1883
757	People	Smith, Fred	Assault to murder	3: 250	10 Jan 1883
758	People	Ging, Wong Loo (alias Gain, Ah)	Assault to murder	3: 251	10 Jan 1883
759	People	Lung, Wong Ah	Murder	3: 252	10 Jan 1883
760	McMackin, James	Gaffnie, John	Ejectment	3: 253	12 Jan 1883
761	Goodman, George R.	Wood, Robin W.; Wood, Rosanna; Kennedy, Charles D.	Foreclosure	3: 254	12 Jan 1883
762	Mayer, August	Patterson, James H.	Unlawful detainer	3: 255	13 Jan 1883
763	People	Hembree, Albert	Assault with intent to commit murder	3: 256	15 Jan 1883
764	Edwards, Benjamin	Walker, L. W.	Arbitration	3: 257	15 Jan 1883

174

Suit #	Plaintiffs	Defendants	Cause of Suit	Register of Actions Volume: page(s)	Action Date
765	Crook, Hiram	Crook, Ida	Divorce	3: 258	15 Jan 1883
766	Jones, Christopher D.	Mayer, Jacob F.	Foreclosure	3: 259	17 Jan 1883
767	San, Yee	Lung, Ah & Burris, L. W.	Appeal	3: 260	17 Jan 1883
768	Campbell, Joseph H.	Moulton, Kate D. & Moulton, W. M.	Ejectment	3: 261, 347	19 Jan 1883
769	Fagas, Joseph F. & wife	Somes, Manuel	Appeal	3: 262	22 Jan 1883
770	Needham, Festus	Boylan, Mary (Adm. Est. Terrence Boylan)	Appeal	3: 263	22 Jan 1883
771	People	Peterson, Jack (An Indian)	Grand larceny	3: 264	24 Jan 1883
772	Santa Rosa Bank	Neece, A. & West, R.	Renewal of Judgment	3: 266	24 Jan 1883
773	Whitehead, G. C. & Whitehead, S. A., his wife	Prouse, Daniel	To quiet title	3: 267	25 Jan 1883
774	O'Brien, Patrick	Cadden, John	Appeal	3: 268	29 Jan 1883
775	Fairbanks, H. T.; Atwater, H. H.; Zartman, William; Whitney, A. P.	Wiswell, J. A.; Crane, J. H.; Hutton, C. E.; Poehlman, Conrad; Nay, L. G.; Blackburn, C.; Hatch, C. P.; Ellsworth, L.; Veale, William R.; Hedges, N. M.; Brooks, S.; Shepherd, J. S. (Trustees)	Equity	3: 269	5 Feb 1883
776	Farrell, Martin	Foster, Joseph; Sweet, James; Witham, George T.	At law	3: 270	6 Feb 1883
777	Crewdson, A. L.	Crewdson, George F.	Divorce	3: 271	6 Feb 1883
778	Thrift, Sabin D. & Thrift, Mary O., his wife	Hughes, Roland & Case, W. P.	Damages	3: 272	7 Feb 1883
779	Brotherton, Woodley (By his guardian ad litem)	Gunn, J. H.	Slander	3: 273	30 Jan 1883
780	Sonoma Valley Bank	Rothermel, P.; Rothermel, Mary P.; Lyons, Thomas M.; Lyons, Agnes P.	At law	3: 274	9 Feb 1883
781	People	Slusser, L. S. B.	Assault to murder	3: 275	12 Feb 1883
782	Franchi, C.	Lehn, Charles	Damages	3: 276	16 Feb 1883
783	Lacock, M. A.	Lacock, Driden	Divorce	3: 277	16 Feb 1883
784	Leavenworth, T. M.	Sparks, George W. (Constable)	Restraining order	3: 278	17 Feb 1883
785	Wescott, Oliver	Morrison, Oscar	Order to show cause	3: 279	19 Feb 1883
786	Fine, Joff		Insolvency	3: 280	19 Feb 1883

Suit #	Plaintiffs	Defendants	Cause of Suit	Register of Actions Volume: page(s)	Action Date
787	Cereghino, A.	Cuneo, A.	Assumpsit	3 : 281	19 Feb 1883
788	Latapie, Eleanor L.	Duncan, James P.	At law	3 : 282	21 Feb 1883
789	Delzell, David H.; Delzell, William R.; Delzell, Milton A.; Martin, Hypolite; Martin, Camille; Martin, Adeline (By their guardian C. J. Martin)	Gamble, John		3 : 283	20 Feb 1883
790	Santa Rosa Bank	Insurance Company of North America	Damages	3 : 284	20 Feb 1883
791	Guerne, A. L.		Insolvency	3 : 285	20 Feb 1883
792	Campbell, Joseph H.	McCutchin, William H. & McCutchin, William	Appeal	3 : 286	23 Feb 1883
793	Fritsch, John & Fritsch, Walter	McCune, Alexander & McCune, Ada (Executors Est. James N. McCune); McCune, Ada; McCune, Laura Georgiana (a minor); McCune, Alexander Charles (a minor); McCune, James Nelson (a minor); McCune, Ada Wakelee (a minor); Doe, John; Roe, Richard; Snow, Susanna	To quiet title	3 : 287	23 Feb 1883
794	Wickersham, I. G.	Smith, John K.	Foreclosure	3 : 288	23 Feb 1883
795	Wright, Emma A.	Wright, James A.	Divorce	3 : 289	24 Feb 1883
796	Bloomington, L. J.	McCumisky, James	Breach of contract	3 : 294	28 Feb 1883
797	Wing, Fong		Application for writ of habeas corpus	3 : 295	28 Feb 1883
798	Yon, Ah		Application for writ of habeas corpus	3 : 296	28 Feb 1883
799	Pfister, Conrad	Pfister, Jacob O.	On judgment	3 : 297	3 Mar 1883
800	Wescott, Oliver	Morrison, Oscar	Appeal	3 : 298	5 Mar 1883
801	Marti, M.	Murray, Dennis	Ejectment	3 : 300	5 Mar 1883
802	Fitch, John B.	Fitch, Libbie	Divorce	3 : 302	9 Mar 1883

176

Suit #	Plaintiffs	Defendants	Cause of Suit	Register of Actions Volume: page(s)	Action Date
803	Wing, Tong		Application for writ of habeas corpus	3: 303	12 Mar 1883
804	People	Wing, Tong	Appeal	3: 304	12 Mar 1883
805	People	Yon, Ah	Appeal	3: 305	12 Mar 1883
806	Yon, Ah		Application for writ of habeas corpus	3: 306	14 Mar 1883
807	Pieratt, A. W. & Pieratt, W. B.	Stoner, John H.	At law	3: 307	14 Mar 1883
808	People	Sam, Ah	Appeal	3: 308	15 Mar 1883
809	People	Lum, Sam	Appeal	3: 309	15 Mar 1883
810	Mutz, Henry	Tupper, George A. & Kessing, Clement	Renewal of Judgment	3: 310	21 Mar 1883
811	Stapp, Margaret	Stapp, James T.	Divorce	3: 311	22 Mar 1883
812	Brotherton, T. Woodly (Minor, by guardian *ad litem* T. W. Brotherton)	Gunn, J. H.	Slander	3: 312	22 Mar 1883
813	Fairbanks, H. T.	Sonoma County Water Company	Petition	3: 313	23 Mar 1883
814	People	Johnson, Jeff	Grand larceny	3: 314	24 Mar 1883
815	Bernhard, Isaac	San Francisco & North Pacific Railroad Company	Damages	3: 315	24 Mar 1883
816	Davis, Ira		Insolvency	3: 316	26 Mar 1883
817	Wegner, Ed	Robin, Victor G.	Attachment	3: 317	27 Mar 1883
818	Brookfield, Mary R.	Brookfield, Arthur C.	Divorce	3: 318	30 Mar 1883
819	Simmons, J. R.	Willitts, W. H.	Ejectment	3: 319	31 Mar 1883
820	Sanborn, E. P.	Glenn, Robert	Damages	3: 321	2 Apr 1883
821	Vandervoort, G. J.	Symonds, C. W. & Lamoreaux, G. W. (dba Symonds & Lamoreaux)	Claim & delivery	3: 322	3 Apr 1883
822	People	Read, William B.	Appeal	3: 323	5 Apr 1883
823	Murphy, Catherine	Watson, James; Watson, John; Brown, Mary (formerly Mary Watson); Watson, Samuel; Jenkins, Wesley & Jenkins, Mary (children of Rebecca Jenkins)	To quiet title	3: 324	7 Apr 1883

Suit #	Plaintiffs	Defendants	Cause of Suit	Register of Actions Volume: page(s)	Action Date
824	Manning, John	Pitts, William H.	Attachment	3: 325	9 Apr 1883
825	Zartman, William	Elkins, I. B.	Appeal	3: 326	9 Apr 1883
826	Day, A. L.	Hall, Henry	Appeal	3: 327	10 Apr 1883
827	Cerini, John	Boyd, William		3: 328	10 Apr 1883
828	Vanderlieth, John & Vanderlieth, Elizie	Ritchie, John		3: 329	12 Apr 1883
829	Schoenagel, Babette	Schoenagel, Jacob	Divorce	3: 330	12 Apr 1883
830	Allen, B. B.	Allen, Ann W.	To quiet title	3: 332	16 Apr 1883
831	Hill, Amanda E.	Hill, John W.	Divorce	3: 333	19 Apr 1883
832	People	King, C. A.	Forgery	3: 334	23 Apr 1883
833	People	Candido, José	Assault with intent to commit murder	3: 335	23 Apr 1883
834	Crawford, S. G.	Cox, J. C.	Appeal	3: 336	20 Apr 1883
835	Malloney, Bartholomew		Petition for habeas corpus	3: 337	24 Apr 1883
836	Taylor, George M.	Platt, Henry B.; Platt, John C.; Montgomery, A.	Injunction	3: 338; 4: 134	25 Apr 1883
837	People	Maloney, Bartholomew	Assault with intent to murder	3: 339	26 Apr 1883
838	People	Shire, Jacob	Assault to murder	3: 340	26 Apr 1883
839	Tighe, Kelly (Pub. Adm. Est. Manasah Hunt)	Berger, M.; Berger, Jennette; Berger, Lewis; Berger, Agusta; Berger, Caroline; Berger, Mary A.; Berger, Rachel; Berger, Edith; Berger, Isaac	Foreclosure	3: 341	27 Apr 1883
840	Jones, William		Insolvency	3: 342, 363, 366	1 May 1883
841	Heffelfinger, W. J.		Insolvency	3: 343	1 May 1883
842	Long, A. S.	Glenn, Robert	Damages	3: 344	2 May 1883
843	Guglielmetti, P. C.	Taylor, Despard		3: 345	4 May 1883

Suit #	Plaintiffs	Defendants	Cause of Suit	Register of Actions Volume: page(s)	Action Date
844	Pharris, P. H.	Baker, Livingston L. & Hamilton, Robert M. (dba Baker & Hamilton)	At law	3: 346	5 May 1883
845	Patterson, William	Sonoma County Agricultural Park Association	Submission to arbitration	3: 348	10 May 1883
846	Miller, Rosa A.	Miller, W. M.	Divorce	3: 349	11 May 1883
847	People	Bohen, Miles	Appeal	3: 350	15 May 1883
848	People	Fine, Joff	Obtaining goods by false pretenses	3: 351	16 May 1883
849	Miller, James R. & Miller, Mary J.	Miller, Zerilda; Miller, Armelia M.; Miller, Rachel	Partition	3: 352	19 May 1883
850	Irwin, Thomas N.	McPeak, Harmon; Quigley, Laura; Sutton, Cornelia; Neff, Susan; Blakely, Martin L.; Blakeley, Eugene; Blakeley, Unity; Blakeley, John A.; Bond, J. F.	To quiet title	3: 353	19 May 1883
851	People	Kizer, Abe	Grand larceny	3: 354	21 May 1883
852	People	Kizer, Abe	Grand larceny	3: 355	21 May 1883
853	People	Wood, Ben S.	Assault with intent to commit murder	3: 356	21 May 1883
854	Koenig, Frank	Koenig, Ellen	Divorce	3: 357	21 May 1883
855	Monahan, Patrick, Sr.	Melone, Peter	Appeal	3: 358	21 May 1883
856	Ord, Augustias	Kahn, Moise & Moritz, Miche	At law	3: 359	22 May 1883
857	Dempsey, Patrick	Lannan, Patrick	Injunction	3: 360	24 May 1883
858	Hopkins, S. J.	Little, John D.; Little, Joe H.; Little, H. W.	Assumpsit	3: 361	28 May 1883
859	Bishop, Martha		Writ of habeas corpus	3: 362	28 May 1883
859½	Savings Bank of Santa Rosa	Orr, John	Foreclosure	3: 362	20 Jun 1883
860	Case, Adelaide L.	Brush, G. M. (Adm. Est. A. J. Winslow); Winslow, E. C. (Mrs.); Winslow, John Doe; Winslow, Jane Doe; Doe, John; Roe, Richard	Foreclosure	4: 1	2 Jun 1883

179

Suit #	Plaintiffs	Defendants	Cause of Suit	Register of Actions Volume: page(s)	Action Date
861	Walker, John	Whitehouse, W. B.	Attachment	4: 2	8 Jun 1883
862	McKeadney, Kate	McKeadney, Hugh	Divorce	4: 3	9 Jun 1883
863	Weeks, Rosetta L.	Mitthell, G. F.	Ejectment	4: 4	14 Jun 1883
864	Vanderhoof, M. V.	Gillett, E. F.	Attachment	4: 5	16 Jun 1883
865	Hinz, August & Landt, Paul	Gillett, E. F.	Attachment	4: 6	20 Jun 1883
866	Bray, Reuben	Bray, M. E.	Divorce	4: 7	20 Jun 1883
867	People	Worth, Charles	Assault to murder	4: 8	25 Jun 1883
868	Plumley, M. W.		Application for writ of habeas corpus	4: 9	25 Jun 1883
869	Sherman, Leander S. & Clay, Charles C. (dba Sherman, Clay & Co.)	Rue, James B. & Dimmick, F. M.	Complaint on bond	4: 10, 117	25 Jun 1883
870	Gillett, E. F.		Insolvency	4: 11, 42	26 Jun 1883
871	Ridgway, Jeremiah & Ridgway, Joseph	Davis, E. L.	Assumpsit	4: 12	29 Jun 1883
872	Santa Rosa Bank	Plummer, H. W. & Watson, J. A.	Assumpsit & Attachment	4: 13	6 Jul 1883
873	Plumley, M. W. (ex parte)		Writ of review	4: 14	2 Jul 1883
874	Savage, G. N.		Insolvency	4: 15, 163	7 Jul 1883
875	Dodge, A. C.	Dodge, S. F.	Divorce	4: 16	9 Jul 1883
876	Black, Joseph	Santa Rosa Alden Fruit Preserving Company; Stanley, William B.; Thompson, G. W.; McCrea, William; Doe, John; Roe, Richard; Fen, James	Foreclosure	4: 17	9 Jul 1883
877	O'Connor, Daniel	Mayer, L. W. & Mayer, J. S.	Unlawful detainer	4: 18	13 Jul 1883
878	Mosely, A. P.	Torrence, S. H.		4: 19	13 Jul 1883
879	Brooks, Henry C.	Brooks, Emma S.; Brooks, Emma S. (Adm. Est. Thomas J. Brooks); Brooks, Ernest K. (a minor); Brooks, Frederick A. (a minor)	Equity	4: 20	21 Jul 1883

Suit #	Plaintiffs	Defendants	Cause of Suit	Register of Actions Volume: page(s)	Action Date
880	People	Frehe, Michael	Attempt to commit burglary	4: 21	23 Jul 1883
881	Mason, W. C.	San Francisco & North Pacific Rail Road Co.	Damages	4: 22	23 Jul 1883
882	Bohan, Miles	Anderson, Andrew	Unlawful detainer	4: 23	26 Jul 1883
883	Peugh, Jennie	Haggard, Vianna & Haggard, Ida Mable	Equity-partition	4: 24	27 Jul 1883
884	Franchi, C.	Lehn, Charles		4: 25	30 Jul 1883
885	People	Grider, Theodore & Donovan, B.	Grand larceny	4: 26	6 Aug 1883
886	People	Burt, Russell	Embezzlement	4: 27	6 Aug 1883
887	Cummings, Anna M.	Cummings, Thomas; Cummings, Catherine; Cummings, Michael; Boyle, Owen	Equity	4: 28	6 Aug 1883
888	Jenkins, Eliza	McNamara, Bernard	Foreclosure	4: 29	7 Aug 1883
889	Sullivan, James	Brandon, William	Appeal	4: 30	7 Aug 1883
890	People	Aiken Bros.	At law	4: 31	8 Aug 1883
891	Schloss, S.	Gaberel, George W. & Gaberel, Mattie	Attachment	4: 32	10 Aug 1883
892	Williams, Robert B.	Slusser, Levi S. B.	Damages	4: 33	7 Aug 1883
893	Gaberel, G. W.		Insolvency	4: 34, 121	13 Aug 1883
894	Wood, Rosa L.	Wood, J. L.	Divorce	4: 35	13 Aug 1883
895	Shearer, John (Road overseer of Vallejo Road District)	Miller, C. S.	Nuisance	4: 36, 186	14 Aug 1883
896	Grace Church of Petaluma		Application to mortgage property	4: 37	15 Aug 1883
897	Clark, James P.	Herman, J. F.	Injunction	4: 38	17 Aug 1883
898	Forsyth, Caroline	Howe, Edwin A. & Howe, Ann Frances	Foreclosure	4: 39	20 Aug 1883
899	Frazier, Mary A.	Callahan, Daniel T.	Foreclosure	4: 40	22 Aug 1883

Suit #	Plaintiffs	Defendants	Cause of Suit	Register of Actions Volume: page(s)	Action Date
900	Ingham, Andrew H.; Litchfield, Durant; Gardner, John W.; Stiles, Rueben T.; Starratt, Handley; Williams, John A.; Thompson, Hannah J.; Meyer, Eleanor W.; Kauffman, Frank; Lindemood, Israel; Coon, Mary; Coon, James; Saxton, W. R.; McKenzie, James; McChristian, James; Seeley, David; Pierine, Valentine; Gautier, Eudoxie	Howell, L. V.; Callaghan, Walter; Howell, Margaret; Howell, L. V., Jr.; Howell, Albina	Equity	4: 41, 120	22 Aug 1883
901	Sanford, J. L.	Reynolds, W. B. & Ragsdale, J. W.		4: 43	27 Aug 1883
902	Redmond, P.		Insolvency	4: 44	27 Aug 1883
903	Leiby, Fannie K.	Leiby, George	Divorce	4: 45	28 Aug 1883
904	Wells, E.		Insolvency	4: 46, 113	29 Aug 1883
905	Colton, Ellen M.	Stanford, Leland; Huntington, C. P.; Crocker, Charles; Wells Fargo & Co.	Equity	4: 47, 98-99, 189, 364-366	29 Aug 1883
906	Yow, Ah	Juilliard, L. W.	Appeal	4: 48	3 Sep 1883
907	Presby, Elizabeth	Presby, Elijah	Divorce	4: 49	3 Sep 1883
908	Low, Elizabeth; Dittemore, Flavilla; Low, William Wallace; Low, Frank E.; Low, Martin L.; Low, Ellen N.	Low, Harriet A.	Equity	4: 50	5 Sep 1883
909	Foster, Margaret C.	Stearns, F. R.	Appeal	4: 51	11 Sep 1883
910	People	Donnelly, Frank	Burglary	4: 53	17 Sep 1883
911	Rains, Gallant	Rains, W. P.	Specific performance of agreement	4: 54	19 Sep 1883
912	Cook, Charles	Higgins, Alfred, Sr.	Appeal	4: 55	20 Sep 1883
913	Greiner, Frederick	Bradwick, Albert & Bradwick, Mary Roe		4: 56	20 Sep 1883
914	People	Warren, Frank	Murder	4: 57	21 Sep 1883
915	Burris, David	Young, Maria E.	Foreclosure	4: 58	22 Sep 1883
916	Shaw, James A.	Skillman, Theodore	Appeal	4: 59	24 Sep 1883
917	Brooks, Henry C.	Brooks, Emma S.; Brooks, Emma S. (Adm. Est. Thomas J. Brooks); Brooks, Ernest K. (a minor); Brooks, Frederick A. (a minor); Cooper, Sidney R.	Partition	4: 60	27 Sep 1883

182

Suit #	Plaintiffs	Defendants	Cause of Suit	Register of Actions Volume: page(s)	Action Date
918	Cereghino, A.	Tachella, Pietro	Assumpsit	4: 61	28 Sep 1883
919	Cereghino, A.	Tachella, Pietro & Reghitto, David	Assumpsit	4: 62	28 Sep 1883
920	People	Donnelly, Frank	Assault with intent to commit rape	4: 63	2 Oct 1883
921	Petaluma, City of	Van Doren, J. S.; Brainard, H. P.; Purrington, Joseph	Equity	4: 65	4 Oct 1883
922	Mealy, Jane	Kearny, D. H.	Assumpsit	4: 66	6 Oct 1883
923	Stoner, Sarah E.	Stoner, Zachariah R.	Divorce	4: 67	6 Oct 1883
924	Gaillard, Josephine	Milon, Alphonse	Foreclosure	4: 68	5 Oct 1883
925	Carrillo, Mary Ettie	Carrillo, Frank J.	Divorce	4: 69	9 Oct 1883
926	Hitchcock, Hollis	Bloom, Jonas	At law	4: 70	9 Oct 1883
927	Minges, Peter	Heisel, Paul	At law	4: 71	9 Oct 1883
928	Taggart, John, Jr.	Byrne, M.	Appeal	4: 72	10 Oct 1883
929	Young, Charles & St. Clair, George (dba Young & St. Clair)	Roberts, J. W.	Appeal	4: 73	13 Oct 1883
930	Pimm, Jacob	Conner, John	Appeal	4: 74	13 Oct 1883
931	Keller, Susie	Keller, John	Divorce	4: 75	13 Oct 1883
932	Gipson, John	Sullivan, T. J.	Appeal	4: 76	13 Oct 1883
933	Perkins, J. J.	McPherson, A. W.; Heeser, William; Mann, R. F.; Haskell, G. W.; Heeser, Augustus; Wing, W. H.; Steiger, W. H.; Hendy, George	Equity	4: 77, 184	16 Oct 1883
934	Goldstein, H.	Whychoff, G. H.	Appeal	4: 78	17 Oct 1883
935	Heisel, Ellen	Heisel, Paul	Divorce	4: 79	19 Oct 1883
936	People	Fine, Joff	Obtaining goods by false pretenses	4: 80	22 Oct 1883
937	People	Sam, Ah & Ling, Ah	Gambling	4: 81	22 Oct 1883
938	Stedman, George W.		Insolvency	4: 82	22 Oct 1883

183

Suit #	Plaintiffs	Defendants	Cause of Suit	Register of Actions Volume: page(s)	Action Date
939	Jackson, Frances F.; Jackson, Timothy L.; Jackson, Sherry; Brown, Olivia M.; Jackson, Frank; Brown, Martha Ann	Dodson, Elizabeth	Partition	4:83	24 Oct 1883
940	Kulberg, Andrew	Wheeler, Edward	Appeal	4:84	29 Oct 1883
941	Wheeler, Edward	Bliss, W. D. & Kulberg, Andrew	Equity	4:85	29 Oct 1883
942	Willits, W. H.	Callahan, Daniel T.	Injunction	4:86	5 Nov 1883
943	Crisp, John B.; Downing, Mary F.; Smith, Lucinda J.; Smith, Lucinda J. (Executrix Will Isaac P. Smith)	Murphy, Wyman	Damages	4:87, 164	10 Nov 1883
944	People	Brumfield, Byrd	Grand larceny	4:88	12 Nov 1883
945	Wickersham, I. G.; Zartman, William; Lippitt, E. S.	Walsh, M.; Poehlman, C.; Denman, E.; Ayres, William; Decker, H. (Trustees of the City of Petaluma) & Henry, A. (Treasurer of the City of Petaluma)		4:89	12 Nov 1883
946	Gauger, Bertha	Gauger, William	Divorce	4:90	12 Nov 1883
947	Coogen, Bridget	Quinlan, John & Quinlan, Lydia	Foreclosure	4:91	14 Nov 1883
948	People	Towne, Charles & Hoag, James W.	Libel	4:92	19 Nov 1883
949	Panella, G.	Jones, C. E.		4:93	21 Nov 1883
950	People	Sharp, John	Grand larceny	4:94	23 Nov 1883
951	Joyce, Martin	Johnson, William R.	Assumpsit	4:95	23 Nov 1883
952	Storni, Giacomina	Storni, Peter	Divorce	4:96	27 Nov 1883
953	Lim, Lee	Jewell, J. R.	At law	4:97	30 Nov 1883
954	Schute, Anthony	Stegman, William	Attachment	4:100	3 Dec 1883
955	Griffith, G.	Lightner, J. S. & St. John, A. (dba Lightner & St. John)	Equity	4:101	5 Dec 1883
956	Hager, George D.	Russell, William H.; Russell, Amelia; Coughran, Wiley	Foreclosure	4:102	6 Dec 1883
957	Fairbanks, J. K.	Winslow, George & Winslow, Emma I.	Equity	4:103	7 Dec 1883
958	Hager, George D.	Russell, William H.; Russell, Amelia; Wright, Emma A.	Grand larceny	4:104	8 Dec 1883
959	People	Taggart, Henry	Foreclosure	4:105	10 Dec 1883
960	Cox, Charles B.	Smith, John K. & Santa Rosa Bank	Divorce	4:106	11 Dec 1883
961	Martin, Eliza Jane	Martin, Nathaniel E.	Appeal	4:107	12 Dec 1883
962	Burrus, G. W.	Sonoma, County of	Divorce	4:108	12 Dec 1883
963	McMillan, Sarah Jane	McMillan, Wilson		4:109	15 Dec 1883

Suit #	Plaintiffs	Defendants	Cause of Suit	Register of Actions Volume: page(s)	Action Date
964	Quackenbush, Russell M.	Quackenbush, Mary	Divorce	4: 110	15 Dec 1883
965	Sharp, William	Sonoma Valley Bank	At law	4: 111	21 Dec 1883
966	People	Hubsch, A. J.	Assault with a deadly weapon	4: 112	24 Dec 1883
967	Meyer, Anton	Reiss, Jacques	Foreclosure	4: 114	24 Dec 1883
968	Epperson, J.	Truitt, R. K.	Appeal	4: 115	26 Dec 1883
969	Miller, George T.	Dolan, Peter	Foreclosure	4: 116	26 Dec 1883
970	Archambeau, Peter T.	Englehart, James	At law	4: 118	29 Dec 1883
971	Sherman, Clay & Co.	Rue, James B. & Dimmick, F. M.		4: 119, 207	29 Dec 1883
972	Hamlin, N. C.		Insolvency	4: 122	9 Jan 1884
973	Mutz, Henry	Carter, L. & Carter, Mary Frances	Assumpsit	4: 123	12 Jan 1884
974	Kennedy, George		Obtaining goods by false pretenses	4: 124	17 Jan 1884
975	People	Brannan, James	Assault with a deadly weapon	4: 125	17 Jan 1884
976	Kerr, Hester Ann	Kerr, Robert	Divorce	4: 126	18 Jan 1884
977	Neyce, J. H.	Swett, F. H. & Crane, E. T. (dba Swett & Crane)	Appeal	4: 127	18 Jan 1884
978	Wegener, Ed	Craig, O. W.	Appeal	4: 128	19 Jan 1884
979	Congelton, George		Application for writ of habeas corpus	4: 129	19 Jan 1884
980	People	Hubsch, A. J.	Murder	4: 130	24 Jan 1884
981	People	Yung, Ah & King, Ah	Gaming	4: 131	24 Jan 1884
982	Tomasini, Julian	Price, Joseph K.	Foreclosure	4: 132	25 Jan 1884
983	Daniels, Henry	Cox, J. C.	Foreclosure	4: 133	25 Jan 1884
984	Connolly, M. W.	Lambert, C. L.	Appeal	4: 135	28 Jan 1884
985	People	Logan, John	Burglary	4: 136	28 Jan 1884

Suit #	Plaintiffs	Defendants	Cause of Suit	Register of Actions Volume: page(s)	Action Date
986	Barnes, Aaron	Davis, W. W.	At law	3: 137	2 Feb 1884
987	People	Barron, William	Assault to murder	4: 138	4 Feb 1884
988	Society of the Seventh Day Adventist Church of Healdsburg		Application to sell real estate	4: 139	5 Feb 1884
989	Bray, L. J.	Bray, E. J.	Divorce	4: 140	7 Feb 1884
990	People	Suie, Ah	Petit larceny	4: 141	11 Feb 1884
991	Neblett, Edward		Insolvency	4: 142	11 Feb 1884
992	Paine, David	Robinson, William; Adams, Hiram; Coolbroth, Samuel; Woodard, M. W.		4: 143	11 Feb 1884
993	Willits, W. H.	Van Voast, W. H.	Assumpsit	4: 144	12 Feb 1884
994	Petaluma, City of	Bank of Sonoma County		4: 145	13 Feb 1884
995	McGee, James H.	Zimmerman, John M.	Attachment	4: 146	15 Feb 1884
996	Dougherty, Ben G.	Dougherty, John & Parsons, Joseph (dba Dougherty & Parsons)	Attachment	4: 147	16 Feb 1884
997	Peckinpah, T. E.		Insolvency	4: 148	18 Feb 1884
998	Grove, Elmira	Grove, David	Divorce	4: 149	21 Feb 1884
999	Williams, C. B.	Tharp, J. B.		4: 150	25 Feb 1884
1000	Daniels, Henry	Cox, Jesse C. & Harmon, S. H.	Foreclosure	4: 151	29 Feb 1884
1001	Shirley, Almira C.	Shirley, J. Q.	Divorce	4: 152	4 Mar 1884
1002	Tivnen, John	Monahan, Patrick	At law	4: 153	6 Mar 1884
1003	Canepa, L.; Canepa, G.; Canepa, D.	Piffero, Benedetto	Equity	4: 154	12 Mar 1884
1004	Adamson, Isaac Newton	Adamson, Belle	Divorce	4: 155	13 Mar 1884
1005	Smith, Lucinda J. (Executrix Will Isaac P. Smith); Yates, C. H.; Smith, Lucinda J.	Murphy, Wyman	Damages	4: 156	15 Mar 1884
1006	Honriet, L.	Conner, E. P.	Promissory note	4: 157	17 Mar 1884
1007	Chamblin, J. L.	Shirley, J. Q.	Promissory note	4: 158	17 Mar 1884
1008	Forsyth, Rebecca A.	McGeorge, Robert	Damages	4: 159	17 Mar 1884

Suit #	Plaintiffs	Defendants	Cause of Suit	Register of Actions Volume: page(s)	Action Date
1009	Allsopp, John F.	Forbes, Alexander; Forbes, Ellen; Pinto, Jose Antonio; Barron, Guillermo; Barron, Dolores; Barron de Luzarraga, Antonia Maria Georgina; Barron, Eustaquio Francisco; Barron, Francisco Carlos; Escandon y Barron, Pablo; Escandon y Barron, Manuel; Escandon y Barron, Eustquio; Estandon y Barron, Carlota; Escandon y Barron, Maria; Escandon y Barron, Guadalupe		4: 160	18 Mar 1884
1010	Cronin, P.	Partee, B. F. & Partee, George		4: 161	19 Mar 1884
1011	Ursuline Community		Application to mortgage property	4: 162	20 Mar 1884
1012	Ingham, Andrew H.	Ingham, Malinda J.	Divorce	4: 165	26 Mar 1884
1013	Joyce, Martin		Insolvency	4: 166	28 Mar 1884
1014	Clark, Ida F.	Clark, George C.; Clark, Almer; Temple, Conrad	Equity	4: 167, 202	1 Apr 1884
1015	Savings Bank of Santa Rosa	McMinn, John & McMinn, Joseph	Assumpsit	4: 168	2 Apr 1884
1016	Sam, Ah	Ahn, Mah	Appeal	4: 169	4 Apr 1884
1017	Sonoma, County of	Roney, J. M.		4: 170	5 Apr 1884
1018	Sonoma, County of	Aikin, William & Aikin, Henry		4: 171	5 Apr 1884
1019	Ella, Mrs.	Layton, G. Richard	Attachment	4: 172	8 Apr 1884
1020	Burris, William & Burris, Elizabeth	Fitch, Mary A. & Fitch, Wallace B.		4: 173, 290, 356, 362	9 Apr 1884
1021	Savings Bank of Santa Rosa	Thompson, Thomas L. & Thompson, Marion S.		4: 174	31 Mar 1884
1022	Farmers and Mechanics Bank of Healdsburg	Quitzow, Aug	Attachment	4: 175	21 Apr 1884
1023	Landsborough, Thomas S. (Trust)		Appointment of trustee	4: 176	23 Apr 1884
1024	Monahan, Patrick, Jr.	Malone, P.	Equity-to abate nuisance	4: 177	25 Apr 1884
1025	Pickett, William	Esser, H. & Cooper, J.	Ejectment	4: 178, 358	25 Apr 1884

Suit #	Plaintiffs	Defendants	Cause of Suit	Register of Actions Volume: page(s)	Action Date
1026	Cole, M. A.	King, George F.		4: 179	28 Apr 1884
1027	Grangers Business Association	Pritchett, J. H.	Attachment	4: 180	2 May 1884
1028	People	Olsen, Bernard	Burglary	4: 181	10 May 1884
1029	Warner, Rebecca J.	Warner, Edward H.	Divorce	4: 182	10 May 1884
1030	Kearns, James	Russ, H.	Appeal	4: 183	13 May 1884
1031	Phillips, Fannie E.	Phillips, Millard F.	Divorce	4: 185	20 May 1884
1032	Hogan, Thomas	Hogan, Alice	Divorce	4: 187	23 May 1884
1033	Bank of Sonoma County	Hechheimer, Lee & Fine, J. M.	At law & attachment	4: 188	23 May 1884
1034	Kirch, Henry	Young, Henry; Groshong, Celia; Hershberger, Emily; Hershberger, Charles; Hershberger, Frank; Hershberger, Jeremiah; McCracken, Jasper; McCracken, George F.; McCracken, Emma; Miller, Daniel E.; Groshong, H. F.	To quiet title	4: 190	27 May 1884
1035	Heath, Barbara M.	Heath, Henry A.	Divorce	4: 191	28 May 1884
1036	Benham, Lucius T. & Benham, Raymond S.	Lannan, P.	Attachment	4: 192	29 May 1884
1037	Ward, John W.	Hassett, John D.	Appeal	4: 193	7 Jun 1884
1038	Whitman, H. H. & Wayman, John V.	Napa Wood Company	To quiet title	4: 194	11 Jun 1884
1039	Kissack, Andrew	Newsome, George F.; Kissack, Delmar Max; Kissack, Lewin D.	To quiet title	4: 195	13 Jun 1884
1040	Cronin, P.	Partee, B. F. & Taboas, F. C.	Assumpsit	4: 196	14 Jun 1884
1041	Denman, E.	Walsh, M.	Equity	4: 197	16 Jun 1884
1042	Stephens, William	Wohler, Ann M. G. & Molero, Amelia	To quiet title	4: 198	18 Jun 1884
1043	Santa Rosa Bank	Crowley, Cornelius & Hewitt, H. T.	Foreclosure	4: 199	18 Jun 1884
1044	Velasco, Maria Loretto	Velasco, Ysidro	Divorce	4: 200	20 Jun 1884

Suit #	Plaintiffs	Defendants	Cause of Suit	Register of Actions Volume: page(s)	Action Date
1045	Rugg, William H.	Fairbanks, H. F.; Wilsey, Henry; Spaulding, Mary; Rugg, Fannie A.; Haney, Ella J.; Sproul, Lena; Tayler, Cordelia; Tayler, Medora A.; Tayler, Paul Chester; Tayler, John Franklin; Tayler, Ernest M.; Gill, George Q. (Guardian); Wilsey, Frankie Jane; Wilsey, Henry Martin; Wilsey, Hayes; Wilsey, Mary Elizabeth; Wilsey, Sarah M. (Guardian)	At law	4: 201, 302	17 Jun 1884
1046	Fowler, Mary Jane; Johnston, Ida; Kastich, Josephine; Robinson, Agnes	Murray, Patrick		4: 203	23 Jun 1884
1047	Howe, Abbie E.	Howe, Charles W.	Divorce	4: 204	24 Jun 1884
1048	Mutz, Henry	Carter, Lander & Carter, Mary Frances		4: 205	28 Jun 1884
1049	Allen, Elizabeth		Application for writ of habeas corpus	4: 206	26 Jun 1884
1050	People (ex rel. Denman, E.; Farrell, William; Humphries, Charles)	Walsh, M.; Nay, L. G.; Polk, Charles E.		4: 208	30 Jun 1884
1051	Sonoma, County of	Irwin, N. C.		4: 209	3 Jul 1884
1052	Smith, Dexter	Juilliard, C. F.		4: 210	5 Jul 1884
1053	Mount Jackson Quicksilver Mining Company	Liverpool & London & Globe Insurance Co.		4: 211	5 Jul 1884
1053½	Hecker, Henry & Hecker, Peter	Tharp, J. W.	Appeal	4: 206	7 Jul 1884
1054	Helen, Lady		Application for writ of habeas corpus	4: 212	9 Jul 1884
1055	Saul, Annie A.	Saul, Rodman M.	Divorce	4: 213	14 Jul 1884
1056	Knapp, A. H. & McAllister, John	Johnson, Richard		4: 214	15 Jul 1884
1057	Canepa, L. & Canepa, G.	Peffero, Benedetto		4: 215	16 Jul 1884
1058	Griffin, Ida S.	Griffin, Perry L.	Divorce	4: 216	16 Jul 1884
1059	People	McClemmy, John	Burglary	4: 217	18 Jul 1884
1060	People	Dinussi, Antonio	Assault to murder	4: 218	18 Jul 1884

Suit #	Plaintiffs	Defendants	Cause of Suit	Register of Actions Volume: page(s)	Action Date
1061	Gill, Fannie E.	Gill, Marvin	Divorce	4: 219	23 Jul 1884
1062	Carter, A. E.		Insolvency	4: 220	26 Jul 1884
1063	Carriger, Nicholas	Harvey, Keturah J. & Zimmerman, G. H.		4: 221	28 Jul 1884
1064	Kimble, Jerry W.		Insolvency	4: 222	29 Jul 1884
1065	People	Goheen, Gray	Grand larceny	4: 223	29 Jul 1884
1066	People	Goheen, Gray	Grand larceny	4: 224	29 Jul 1884
1067	People	Arnold, William	Assault to murder	4: 225	4 Aug 1884
1068	People	Timperly, Nickolas	Assault to murder	4: 226	4 Aug 1884
1069	People	Staley, Isaac	Assault to murder	4: 227	4 Aug 1884
1070	First Presbyterian Church of Petaluma		Application to sell real estate	4: 228	28 Jul 1884
1071	French, Charles F.		Insolvency	4: 229	18 Aug 1884
1072	Weyl, Henry	Tan, W. A.	Appeal	4: 230	16 Aug 1884
1073	Savings Bank of Santa Rosa	McCaughey, James	Promissory note	4: 231	21 Aug 1884
1074	Ellison, Charles E.	McLeane, Ina B. & McLeane, George M.	Equity	4: 232	21 Aug 1884
1075	Conzelman, William E. (Executor Last Will Gottlieb Conzelman)	Hoen, Berthold; Hoen, Mary; Hoen, Ernest; Savings Bank of Santa Rosa	Foreclosure	4: 233, 361	21 Aug 1884
1076	Bank of Sonoma County	Coniff, John; Coniff, Bridget; Mathews, L. P. (Miss)	Ejectment	4: 234	22 Aug 1884
1077	Erickson, Conrad	Sickles, J. E.	Damages	4: 235	23 Aug 1884
1078	Harlan, J. J.	Jacobi, John	At law & attachment	4: 236	23 Aug 1884
1079	Cooper, Sidney R. & Chamberlain, David (Executors Est. William McK. Cooper)	Douglass, W. A.	Promissory note	4: 237	25 Aug 1884
1080	People	Arnold, William	Assault to murder	4: 238	25 Aug 1884

Suit #	Plaintiffs	Defendants	Cause of Suit	Register of Actions Volume: page(s)	Action Date
1081	Sacramento Bank	Kearney, John; Kearney, Elizabeth D.; Coleman, W. P.; Hamilton, Ed R.; Meyer, William		4: 239	25 Aug 1884
1082	Walls, David	Claassen, Jens Peter	Ejectment	4: 240	27 Aug 1884
1083	Nathanson, Martin M.; Nathanson, Dora L.; Nathanson, R. E.; Nathanson, Arthur E.	Ferera, Louis	Unlawful detainer	4: 241	27 Aug 1884
1084	Doe, Loring B. & Kimball, George H. (dba Doe, Kimball & Co.)	Mersereau, H. P.	At law & attachment	4: 242	30 Aug 1884
1085	People	Gould, George F.	Embezzlement	4: 243	1 Sep 1884
1086	People	Smith, Henry	Burglary	4: 244	1 Sep 1884
1087	Hinshaw, W. P.	Cannon, J. C.	Appeal	4: 245	1 Sep 1884
1088	California Farmers Mutual Fire Insurance Association	White, W. H.	Appeal	4: 246	1 Sep 1884
1089	Harris, R. A.	Harris, L. S. J.	Divorce	4: 247	6 Sep 1884
1090	Reed, Michael	Roberts, Charles & Nissen, E. P.	Ejectment	4: 248, 353	8 Sep 1884
1091	Bank of Healdsburg	Hitchcock, Hollis	Partition	4: 249	10 Sep 1884
1092	Tatum, Henry L. & Bowen, J. J.	Ludolff, Henry; Doe, John; Roe, Richard	Foreclosure of mechanics's lien	4: 250	10 Sep 1884
1093	Mutz, Henry	Carter, Lander & Carter Mary Frances		4: 251	11 Sep 1884
1094	Cooper, S. R.	Houser, S. R.	Foreclosure	4: 252	12 Sep 1884
1095	Order of Mutual Companions	Griest, Eliza; Cook, Israel (Executor Est. Peter Griest); Young, Rebecca; Young, John; Cook, Israel (Mrs.); Cook, Israel; Brumfield, Priscilla; Black, Allie; Black, -; Griest, Agnes; Griest, Artie	Equity	4: 253	12 Sep 1884
1096	People	Lorentino, Antonio	Murder	4: 254	15 Sep 1884
1097	People	Corbaley, Melvin S.	Forgery	4: 255	23 Sep 1884
1098	Grissim, Lizzie V.	Grissim, W. H.	Divorce	4: 256	24 Sep 1884
1099	Kamp, N.	Franklin, D. B. & Franklin, Winnie	Ejectment	4: 257	26 Sep 1884
1100	Strode, C. E.	Sylvester, D. W.	Ejectment	4: 258	29 Sep 1884
1101	Rogers, H. G. & McMackin, James	Sparks, G. W. & Schockin, S.		4: 259	29 Sep 1884
1102	People	Corbaley, Melvin S.	Forgery	4: 260	29 Sep 1884

Suit #	Plaintiffs	Defendants	Cause of Suit	Register of Actions Volume: page(s)	Action Date
1103	People	Sear (An Indian)	Assault to murder	4: 261	29 Sep 1884
1104	Bryan, C. L.		Insolvency	4: 262	30 Sep 1884
1105	Magee, Richard	Partee, B. F.	Attachment	4: 263	30 Sep 1884
1106	Fountian, Minervia A.	Fountian, Thomas T.	Divorce	4: 264	1 Oct 1884
1107	Goldfish, B.; Cohn, S.; Wilson, William	Benjamin, A.	Attachment	4: 265	3 Oct 1884
1108	Kearns, James	Russ, H.	Ejectment	4: 266	7 Oct 1884
1109	Dorman, Jane	Dorman, James	Divorce	4: 267	8 Oct 1884
1110	Kron, Elizabeth & Schmidt, Mary	Williams, Joseph		4: 268, 359	8 Oct 1884
1111	Harden, Bridget F.	Harden, William H.	Divorce	4: 269	8 Oct 1884
1112	Bazzoni, Ellen	Bazzoni, Louis	Divorce	4: 270	10 Oct 1884
1113	White, J. H.	Bihler, William; White, N.; Casey, J.	Ejectment	4: 271	13 Oct 1884
1114	People	Smith, Joseph	Robbery	4: 272	13 Oct 1884
1115	People	Sear (An Indian, alias Sear, Gabrial)	Assault to murder	4: 273	13 Oct 1884
1116	People	Wells, John	Grand larceny	4: 274	13 Oct 1884
1117	People	Friedell, George	Grand larceny	4: 275	13 Oct 1884
1118	Shainwald, Herman	Callender, J. A.	Assumpsit	4: 276	24 Oct 1884
1119	DeWolf, Maria E.	Calpella Gravel Mining Company; Wheaton, J. B.; North, Eusebia R.	Equity	4: 277	29 Oct 1884
1120	Ward, H. J.		Insolvency	4: 278	1 Nov 1884
1121	Hill, William	Michelssen, Edward; Brown, B. W.; Roth, D. (dba Michelssen, Brown & Co.)		4: 279, 354	3 Nov 1884
1122	Ridgway, Jeremiah & Ridgway, Joseph W.	Emerson, P. N. & Emerson, S. R.	Assumpsit	4: 280	6 Nov 1884
1123	Faught, John H.	Mason, Matthew & McChristian, Patrick	Foreclosure	4: 281	7 Nov 1884
1124	Wehrspon, August	Lewis, R. E.	Ejectment	4: 282	10 Nov 1884
1125	Burrough, Alfred & Winters, Charles	Webster, Perry; Webster, Joseph L.; Webster, Adrian; McKeand, Anna (formerly Webster, Anna); Webster, Jane Roe (Heirs at law of Joseph Webster, dec'd)	To quiet title	4: 283	10 Nov 1884
1126	Nowell, Hattie	Nowell, Frank C.	Divorce	4: 284	10 Nov 1884

192

Suit #	Plaintiffs	Defendants	Cause of Suit	Register of Actions Volume: page(s)	Action Date
1127	Lunsford, R. B.	Van Vorst, John; Folks, John; Westcoat, Oliver	Ejectment	4: 285	11 Nov 1884
1128	Shorey, F. A.	Mayfield, G. W. & Decoe, T. C.	Foreclosure of mechanics's lien	4: 286	13 Nov 1884
1129	Santa Rosa Bank	Juilliard, C. F.; Stanley, W. B.; Neblett, E.	Renewal of judgment	4: 287	14 Nov 1884
1130	Wilson, John R.	Wetmore, Frederick R.; Wetmore, Georgiana A.; Garnett, A. G.; Joy, E. F.	Foreclosure	4: 288	14 Nov 1884
1131	Wayman, John V.	Ward, Francis M.	Assumpsit	4: 291	26 Nov 1884
1132	First Presbyterian Church of Fulton		Application to sell real estate	4: 292	26 Nov 1884
1133	Smith, Frank	Roberts, J. W.	Dissolution of co-partnership	4: 293, 311	26 Nov 1884
1134	Hofler, V. F.	Hofler, W. W.	Divorce	4: 294	28 Nov 1884
1135	Nevins, E. M.	Hedges, W. H.	Appeal	4: 295	8 Dec 1884
1136	Creighton, Thomas		Insolvency	4: 296	11 Dec 1884
1137	Aredeau, J.	Jackson, A.	Foreclosure	4: 297	11 Dec 1884
1138	Metzger, Joseph E. & Metzger, Albert V. (dba Metzger Bros.)	Adler, David	At law	4: 298	12 Dec 1884
1139	Shiveley, David C.		Involuntary insolvency	4: 299	13 Dec 1884
1140	Fox, John T.	Hopper, Ellen S. & Hopper, Isaiah D.	Equity-to annul marriage	4: 300	15 Dec 1884
1141	Patten, R. R.	Patten, Mary C. G.	Divorce	4: 301	16 Dec 1884
1142	Ridgway, Jeremiah	Zimmerman, J. M.	Attachment	4: 303	22 Dec 1884
1143	Martin, Joseph P.	Drake, R. S.	Attachment	4: 304	23 Dec 1884
1144	Taboas, M. M.	Hinkston, John G.	Attachment	4: 305, 355	24 Dec 1884
1145	Schmidlapp Live Oak Distillery Co.	Prewett, E.	Appeal	4: 306	29 Dec 1884
1146	Tunzi, Domenico	Tunzi, Geiessippi	Equity	4: 307	31 Dec 1884

Suit #	Plaintiffs	Defendants	Cause of Suit	Register of Actions Volume: page(s)	Action Date
1147	Roberts, D.	Dolce, C.	Appeal	4: 308	5 Jan 1885
1148	Mayer, August	Patterson, James H. & Von Rotz, Joseph	At law	4: 309	7 Jan 1885
1149	Stone, Nathan J.	Houser, Sylvester R.	Attachment	4: 310	8 Jan 1885
1150	Santa Rosa Bank	Houser, S. R.	Attachment	4: 312	10 Jan 1885
1151	Keser, L., Jr.	Houser, S. R.	Attachment	4: 313	12 Jan 1885
1152	Schloss, S.	Brizzalaar, Louis	Attachment	4: 314	12 Jan 1885
1153	Edwards, Helen R.	Edwards, Benjamin	Divorce	4: 315	12 Jan 1885
1154	People	Tong, Ah	Burglary	4: 316	9 Jan 1885
1155	Rossi, Peter	Glynn, F. B.	Appeal	4: 317	15 Jan 1885
1156	O'Reilly, Martin	Hinkston, John	Assumpsit	4: 318, 360	16 Jan 1885
1157	Weyl, Henry	Sonoma Valley Rail Road Co. & Donahue, Peter	Damages	4: 319	19 Jan 1885
1158	Gaffney, Miles	Murray, Annie	Slander	4: 320	20 Jan 1885
1159	Keen, A. H.	Thayer, F. L.	Attachment	4: 321	22 Jan 1885
1160	Goldfish, B.; Wilson, William; Cohn, S. (dba Goldfish, Wilson & Co.)	Watson, J. A.	Attachment	4: 322	24 Jan 1885
1161	People	Larson, John	Murder	4: 323	24 Jan 1885
1162	People	Brown, James	Burglary	4: 324	24 Jan 1885
1163	People	Donahue, Thomas (informed against as Thomas Donohue)	Grand larceny	4: 325	24 Jan 1885
1164	Donahue, Thomas		Application for writ of habeas corpus	4: 326	24 Jan 1885
1165	People	Quong, Sam	Attempt at bribery	4: 327	24 Jan 1885
1166	Morris, Miles	Hoen, B.	Appeal	4: 328	26 Jan 1885
1167	Graves, W. S.	McCluskey, W.	Appeal	4: 329	26 Jan 1885
1168	Hays, Mary T.; Krager, Isabella G.; Mann, Thomas D.; Mann, Edward H. (infant by his guardian Mary T. Hays)	Steiger, Edward	Equity	4: 330	29 Jan 1885

Suit #	Plaintiffs	Defendants	Cause of Suit	Register of Actions Volume: page(s)	Action Date
1169	Main, Charles & Winchester, E. H. (dab Main & Winchester)	Burgtorf, C. W.	Attachment	4: 331	30 Jan 1885
1170	Klute, Anna C. (Adm. Est. Henry Klute)	Frehe, Louis & Frehe, H. F.	Assumpsit	4: 332	31 Jan 1885
1171	Farmers and Mechanics Bank of Healdsburg	Grangers Business Association	Attachment	4: 333	31 Jan 1885
1172	Curtiss, Maria Louise	Curtiss, Francis E.	Divorce	4: 334, 336	2 Feb 1885
1173	Strode, John	Gater, James E.	Appeal	4: 335	30 Jan 1885
1174	Dinwiddie, J. L.	Griess, George; Griess, Catherine; Dortmond, Henry	Partition	4: 337	2 Feb 1885
1175	Richardson, Thomas H.		Insolvency	4: 338	2 Feb 1885
1176	Warner, James & McReynolds, James		Application to be released from bond	4: 339	3 Feb 1885
1177	Drake, R. S.		Insolvency	4: 340, 357	3 Feb 1885
1178	Hastings, Alice & Hastings, Edith	Carter, R. W. & Carter, Mary	To quiet title	4: 341	3 Feb 1885
1179	Proletti, Joseph	Calkins, J. A. & Durkee, L. O.	Foreclosure	4: 342	5 Feb 1885
1180	Fyfe, Julia C.	Fyfe, David K.	Divorce	4: 343	5 Feb 1885
1181	Hovey, Theodore	Hovey, Ada A.	Divorce	4: 344	7 Feb 1885
1182	Hutchings, Mary H.	Hutchings, Thomas	Divorce	4: 345	9 Feb 1885
1183	Grangers Business Association of Healdsburg		Involuntary insolvency	4: 346, 351-352	7 Feb 1885
1184	Bank of Healdsburg	Hitchcock, Hollis	Partition	4: 347; 7: 232	9 Feb 1885
1185	Charles, Vernetta	Charles, George W.	Divorce	4: 348	12 Feb 1885
1186	Patterson, James H.		Insolvency	4: 349	13 Feb 1885
1186½	Paul, H. C.	Wetmore, Frederick R.; Wetmore, Georgiana; Gurnett, A. G.; Joy, E. F.; Wilson, John R.	Foreclosure of mechanics's lien	4: 350	14 Feb 1885
1187	Kron, Elisabeth & Schmitt, Mary	Williams, Bridget; Williams, Albert; Williams, Sophia	Partition	5: 1, 233, 351	16 Feb 1885
1188	Liveroni, Catherine	Liveroni, Manuel	Divorce	5: 2	17 Feb 1885
1189	Hurney, J. F.	Roberts, J. W.	Appeal	5: 3	4 Feb 1885
1190	Reed, John	Mock, Wesley	Appeal	5: 4	14 Feb 1885
1191	Bank of Sonoma County	Bishop, T. C. (Tax collector of Sonoma County)	Injunction	5: 5	24 Feb 1885

Suit #	Plaintiffs	Defendants	Cause of Suit	Register of Actions Volume: page(s)	Action Date
1192	Neeley, T. L.	Alexander, Henry	To remove obstruction	5: 6	24 Feb 1885
1193	King, N. (Adm. Est. William S. Brown)	Skillman, Theodore		5: 7	24 Feb 1885
1194	Hutchinson, Samuel	Vance, John B.; Preston, J. M.; Palmer, J. M.	Foreclosure	5: 8	25 Feb 1885
1195	Carriger, Nicholas	McMackin, James	Ejectment	5: 9	25 Feb 1885
1196	Nowell, Charles	Prindle, Nellie L.; Prindle, Marion Ella; Prindle, Fred	To quiet title	5: 10	25 Feb 1885
1197	Brown, Hannah		Application for writ of habeas corpus	5: 11	27 Feb 1885
1198	People	Howe, Henry	Grand larceny	5: 12	2 Mar 1885
1199	Muma, Aditha	Muma, Peter	Divorce	5: 13	28 Feb 1885
1200	Day, A. L.	Nosler, H. E.	Attachment	5: 14	5 Mar 1885
1201	Carroll, James H.	Gautier, E. V.; Gautier, Leopold; Gautier, Marie; Gautier, Marguerite; Gautier, Lambert; Gautier, Leonore; Gautier, Julienne; Gautier, Edouard; Gautier, Leonidas	To quiet title	5: 15	5 Mar 1885
1202	Townsend, Horace R.	Tomlinson, John	Damages	5: 16	6 Mar 1885
1203	Forsyth, Robert	West, John	Partition	5: 17	10 Mar 1885
1204	Haskell, Emma A.	Park, George W.	Foreclosure	5: 18	14 Mar 1885
1205	Melder, P. A.	Melder, G. M.	Divorce	5: 19	14 Mar 1885

196

Suit #	Plaintiffs	Defendants	Cause of Suit	Register of Actions Volume: page(s)	Action Date
1206	Beets, Louisa; Drummond, Milly A.; Shelton, Parmelia; Farmer, Elizabeth; Agnew, Letha Jane; Harris, Henry R.; Sneed, Thomas J.; Cook, Ann E.; Moffitt, Sarah F.; Sharp, Samuel O.; Houchins, Lucinda J.; Withers, Mary E.; Clewe, F.; Lyon, Prudence; Raney, John; Raney, Sarah; Lyon, A. J.; Singleterry, Lillie; Lays, Richard; Lyon, Robert; Lyon, John H.; Tuggles, Eliza Ann; Cannon, Mattie A.; Fowler, Susan M.; Shattuck, Parallee; Sneed, Peter S.; Sharp, Matt H.; Sharp, Rebecca C.; Richey, Virginia E.; Cummins, Linia A.; Brooks, Nancy E.; Lyon, Sarah A.; Hill, Louisa; Raney, Thomas; Lewis, Mary; Lyon, William; Lyon, Charles; Lays, Jane; Sneed, Richard	Chart, Obed; Rurbke, H.; Dresel, Julius	Ejectment	5: 20, 168, 352	16 Mar 1885
1207	More, Samuel (dba Samuel More & Co.)	Dolan, Peter	Appeal	5: 21	14 Mar 1885
1208	Boreland, R. A. (Mrs.), wife of L. Boreland	Bell, J. S. (Constable) & Truitt, R. K.	Appeal	5: 22	14 Mar 1885
1209	Leavenworth, T. M.	Johnson, George C.	Ejectment	5: 23	18 Mar 1885
1210	People	Key, Harry	Burglary	5: 24	17 Mar 1885
1211	Boreland, L.	McCluskey, William (Constable of Mendocino Township)	Replevin	5: 25	19 Mar 1885
1212	Weise, Lisette	Weise, Christian & Weise, George Frederick	Divorce	5: 26	19 Mar 1885
1213	Sparrow, E. D.	Rhoads, Alphonso A. H.	Ejectment	5: 27	19 Mar 1885
1214	Lougee, Frank W.	McCune, Alexander & McCune, Ada (Executors Est. J. N. McCune); McCune, Ada; McCune, Laura Georgina (minor); McCune, Alexander Charles (minor); McCune, James Nelson (minor); McCune, Ada Wakelee (minor)	To quiet title	5: 28	20 Mar 1885
1215	Zimmerman, George	Perinoni, G.	Attachment	5: 29	20 Mar 1885
1216	McDermott, Charles F.	Simpson, John	Foreclosure	5: 30	21 Mar 1885
1217	People	Hall, Frank	Assault with intent to murder	5: 31	9 Mar 1885

197

Suit #	Plaintiffs	Defendants	Cause of Suit	Register of Actions Volume: page(s)	Action Date
1218	Busman, A.	King, G.	Appeal	5: 32	23 Mar 1885
1219	Sutliff, Henry	Doe, L. B.; Mott, Charles W.; Kimball, George H.	Foreclosure	5: 33	23 Mar 1885
1220	Gregory, T. J.		Application for writ of habeas corpus	5: 34	23 Mar 1885
1221	Hobson, A. D.	Hassett, A.	Assumpsit	5: 35	26 Mar 1885
1222	Schulte, H. A.	Holmes, Lydia N. & Holmes, John W.	Foreclosure	5: 36	28 Mar 1885
1223	Slayton, C. W.	Slayton, Margaret	Divorce	5: 37	31 Mar 1885
1224	People	Lee, Quong	Appeal	5: 38	4 Apr 1885
1225	People	Newby, H. C.	Murder	5: 39	7 Apr 1885
1226	People	Gregory, Thomas	Assault with a deadly weapon	5: 40	8 Apr 1885
1227	Savings Bank of Santa Rosa	Wright, Sampson B. & Wright, Fannie L.	Foreclosure	5: 41	14 Apr 1885
1228	Davidson, Sarah J.	Davidson, Alex T.	Divorce	5: 42	16 Apr 1885
1229	Grissim, Lizzie V.	Grissim, William H.	Divorce	5: 43	16 Apr 1885
1230	Greer, Jane E.	Order of Mutual Companions		5: 44	16 Apr 1885
1231	Caldwell, F. M.	Caldwell, Mary L.	Divorce	5: 45	17 Apr 1885
1232	People	Sue, Ah	Burglary	5: 46	17 Apr 1885
1233	Plumly, Mardon W.	Quatman, J. H.		5: 47	16 Apr 1885
1234	Bank of Healdsburg	Bailhache, John N. & Bailhache, Josephine		5: 48	21 Apr 1885
1235	Petaluma, City of		Contest in municipal election	5: 49	27 Apr 1885
1236	Springer, Jason & Salsbury, W. H. (dba Jason Springer & Co.)	Brown, H. K.		5: 50	27 Apr 1885
1237	Dinwiddie, J. L.	Watson, G.	Promissory note	5: 51	28 Apr 1885
1238	People	Joe, Ah	Burglary	5: 52	27 Apr 1885
1239	People	Pattini, Louis	Burglary	5: 53	27 Apr 1885

Suit #	Plaintiffs	Defendants	Cause of Suit	Register of Actions Volume: page(s)	Action Date
1240	People	Bazoni, Louis & Demartini, Frank	Robbery	5: 54	4 May 1885
1241	People	Demartini, Mary & Monfredino, A.	Robbery	5: 55	4 May 1885
1242	People	Sick, Lee	Embezzlement	5: 56	4 May 1885
1243	Hall, Clarence C.	Hall, Alice C.	Divorce	5: 57	4 May 1885
1244	Wetmore, Henry D.	Wetmore, Georgiana A. & Wetmore, F. R.	Attachment	5: 58	4 May 1885
1245	Savings Bank of Santa Rosa	Smith, John K. & Wright, W. S. M.	Assumpsit	5: 59	7 May 1885
1246	People	Collins, John	Assault with a deadly weapon	5: 60	11 May 1885
1247	Bledsoe, Linn	Torrence, Shubal H. & Keran, James N.		5: 61	12 May 1885
1248	Congrove, Lucy A.	Congrove, Jonathan	Divorce	5: 62	18 May 1885
1249	Savings Bank of Santa Rosa	Wright, W. S. M. & Brown, W. B.	Assumpsit	5: 63	20 May 1885
1250	Cohen, Abraham	Mego, Toney	Injunction	5: 64	25 May 1885
1251	Smith, Mary E.	Smith, T. F.	Divorce	5: 65	25 May 1885
1252	Doss, Joel A.	Doss, May Bell	Divorce	5: 66	25 May 1885
1253	Conklin, Annie	Conklin, Charles	Divorce	5: 67	26 May 1885
1254	Swank, J. W.	Kelsey, B.	To quiet title	5: 68	27 May 1885
1255	Kier, H.	Berry, Nancy G.; Berry, William D.; Berry, E. W.; Berry, W. L.	Foreclosure	5: 69	29 May 1885
1256	King, N. (Adm. with Will annexed Est. A. H. L. Dias) & Dias, Rosa (surviving widow)	Dias, Alzina G. (Adm. Est. I. L. Dias); Freeman, W. D.; Bailey, Robert (her bondsmen)		5: 70, 171	29 May 1885
1257	Fisher, Ebenezer	Dawson, H. C.	Attachment	5: 71	3 Jun 1885
1258	Herrmann, Siegmund (dba Herrmann & Co.)	Sullivan, P. J.	Attachment	5: 72	8 Jun 1885
1259	McQuade, John	McCaughey, James	Injunction	5: 73	8 Jun 1885
1260	Healdsburg College	Bishop, T. C.	Claim & delivery	5: 74	8 Jun 1885
1261	McCune, S.	Burke, J. H.	Dissolution of co-partnership	5: 75	9 Jun 1885
1262	Taylor, John	Tuck, Charles E.; Davis, C. L. (Mrs.); Davis, L. T.	Foreclosure	5: 76	10 Jun 1885

Suit #	Plaintiffs	Defendants	Cause of Suit	Register of Actions Volume: page(s)	Action Date
1263	Schwartz, Henry & Smith, John	Stuart, Mrs. Charles D. (Mrs.); Stuart, Jane Doe; Stuart, Jane Roe; Stuart, John Roe	Ejectment	5 : 77	10 Jun 1885
1264	Schwartz, Henry & Smith, John	Justi, Charles & Justi, Marie	Ejectment	5 : 78	10 Jun 1885
1265	Schwartz, Henry & Smith, John	Warfield, K. F. & Warfield, John Doe	Ejectment	5 : 79	10 Jun 1885
1266	Schwartz, Henry & Smith, John	Gibson, John & Gibson, Jane Doe	Ejectment	5 : 80	10 Jun 1885
1267	Schwartz, Henry & Smith, John	Thelan, John J. & Thelan, Jane Doe	Ejectment	5 : 81	10 Jun 1885
1268	Schwartz, Henry & Smith, John	Williams, Bridget; Williams, Sophia; Williams, Albert	Ejectment	5 : 82	10 Jun 1885
1269	Schwartz, Henry & Smith, John	Krone, Elizabeth; Schmitt, George; Schmitt, Mary; Williams, Bridget; Williams, Sophia; Williams, Alfred	Ejectment	5 : 83	10 Jun 1885
1270	Schwartz, Henry & Smith, John	McHeamy, James	Ejectment	5 : 84	10 Jun 1885
1271	Schwartz, Henry & Smith, John	Tarrant, H. F.	Ejectment	5 : 85	10 Jun 1885
1272	Leavenworth, Thaddeus M.	Warfield, Kate; Stuart, Ellen M.; Stuart, Charles D.; Justi, Marie; Tarrant, John Doe; Goodfellow, W. S.; Gibson, John; Doe, John; Roe, Richard; Stiles, John; Stiles, Peter; Mokes, John; Mokes, Peter	Ejectment	5: 86, 186, 214	11 Jun 1885
1273	Dodge, Leonard; Nelson, Alfred; Galvin, M. J. C.	Williams, Bridget K.; Williams, Albert; Williams, Sophia A.; Williams, Joseph; Kron, Elizabeth; Schmitt, Mary; LeRoy, Theodore; Peterson, Errick; Thelan, John J.; Justi, C.; Tarrant, H. F.; Warfield, Kate; Stuart, Ellen M.; Pickett, Mary E.; Stuart, Charles D.; Stargroom, Emily; Stargroom, Marc L., her husband; Stuart, Antoinette R.; Sessions, Ida; Sessions, George W., her husband; Stuart, Isabel; Leavenworth, T. M.; Doe, John; Doe, Henry; Doe, Peter; Doe, Mary; Roe, Richard; Roe, Charles; Roe, Jane; Roe, Sarah	Ejectment	5: 87	11 Jun 1885
1274	Murray, W. E.	Burroughs, Alfred & Sprengel, Christian	Foreclosure	5: 88	12 Jun 1885
1275	Schmidt, V.	Trewholtz, E. M.	Damages	5: 89	15 Jun 1885
1276	Lancel, A. & Lancel, E.		Application for writ of habeas corpus	5: 90	9 Jun 1885

200

Suit #	Plaintiffs	Defendants	Cause of Suit	Register of Actions Volume: page(s)	Action Date
1277	Zartman, William & Zartman, W. H. (dba W. Zartman & Co.); Fine, J. M.; Hasbrouck, H. B. H.; Bauer, J. W.; Burgtorf, C. W.; Hammel, H. H.; Shorr, A. J.; Laurence, James A.; Spotswood, Andrew; Edelman, G. W.; Davidson, James; Maynard, Frank T.; Rhodehaver, J. P.	Hardin, William Jefferson	Appeal	5: 91, 243	15 Jun 1885
1278	Marsteinstein, Jacob A.	Pruett, E.	Appeal	5: 92	15 Jun 1885
1279	Goldfish, B.; Wilson, William; Cohn, S. (dba Wilson, Goldfish & Co.)	Lowell, J. P.	Attachment	5: 93	16 Jun 1885
1280	Eagan, George		Appeal	5: 94	16 Jun 1885
1281	Chamberlain, David C.	Tarwater, Martin & Savings Bank of Santa Rosa	Foreclosure	5: 95	17 Jun 1885
1282	Rued, J. C.	Aulich, Charles G. & Aulich, Mary J.	Foreclosure	5: 96	19 Jun 1885
1283	Wilson, William	Lowell, J. P. & Lowell, Alphia	Foreclosure	5: 97	16 Jun 1885
1284	Ruffino, L. J. & Bianchi, C. D. (dba Ruffino & Bianchi)	Lightner, John S. & St. John, A. C. (dba Lightner & St. John)	Attachment	5: 98	16 Jun 1885
1285	Happy, Abe		Application for writ of habeas corpus	5: 99	20 Jun 1885
1286	Murray, W. E.	Burrough, Alfred; Sprengel, Christian; Henninger, Joseph G.	Foreclosure	5: 100	22 Jun 1885
1287	Lingenfelter, William J.	Espey, John	Appeal	5: 101	19 Jun 1885
1288	Kron, Elizabeth & Schmitt, Mary	Williams, Bridget (Executrix Last Will Joseph A. Williams)		5: 102, 338	24 Jun 1885
1289	Goldfish, B.; Wilson, William; Cohn, S. (dba Goldfish, Wilson & Co.)	McClelland, Buchanan & McClelland, Elizabeth B.	Attachment	5: 103	27 Jun 1885
1290	Wilson, William	McClelland, Buchanan & McClelland, Elizabeth B.	Foreclosure	5: 104	29 Jun 1885
1291	Frank, George P. & Frank, Frederick A. (dba Frank Bros.)	Lowell, J. P.	Attachment	5: 105	1 Jul 1885
1292	Swett, F. H.	Crane, E. T.		5: 106	1 Jul 1885

Suit #	Plaintiffs	Defendants	Cause of Suit	Register of Actions Volume: page(s)	Action Date
1293	Burnett, Matt		Application for writ of habeas corpus	5: 107	2 Jul 1885
1294	People	Lancel, Anselmo & Lancel, Isaiah	Assault to commit murder	5: 108	7 Jul 1885
1295	Van Doren, W. L.	Order of Mutual Companions	Attachment	5: 109	7 Jul 1885
1296	Cooper, H. H.	Order of Mutual Companions	Attachment	5: 110, 333	8 Jul 1885
1297	Grove, Elmira	Grove, David; Grove, W. H.; Grove, L. G.; Grove, C. C.; Hopper, M. F.; Grove, S. L.		5: 111	8 Jul 1885
1298	Allen, S. I.		Application to be released from bond	5: 112	10 Jul 1885
1299	Beckner, W. S.	Beckner, Mary M.	Divorce	5: 113	10 Jul 1885
1300	Murphy, Rufus	Starrett, John & Gliddon, William A. (dba Starrett & Gliddon); Beaver, Henry		5: 114	10 Jul 1885
1301	Copsey, D. M.	Clark, M. C.	Appeal	5: 115	9 Jul 1885
1302	Metzger Bros.	Rambo, J. H.	Appeal	5: 116	11 Jul 1885
1303	Hoffman, K. W.	Schloss, S.	Appeal	5: 117	11 Jul 1885
1304	Keser, Louis, Jr.	Houser, S. R.; Santa Rosa Bank; Stone, Nathan J.	Foreclosure	5: 118	11 Jul 1885
1305	Joe, Ah	Allen, O. B.	Attachment	5: 119	20 Jul 1885
1306	Wilson, William	Hudson, Alvin P.; Hudson, Bettie; Hudson, Mattie F.; Hudson, Lena	Partition	5: 120	20 Jul 1885
1307	Bermel, Ernestine (Executrix Last Will Est. J. G. Bermel)	Truitt, R. K.	Appeal	5: 121	26 Jun 1885
1308	People	Sanches, Ramon	Assault with a deadly weapon	5: 122	20 Jul 1885
1309	Noonan, P. H. & Towey, P. (dba Noonan & Towey)	Gardella, C. L.	Attachment	5: 123	23 Jul 1885

Suit #	Plaintiffs	Defendants	Cause of Suit	Register of Actions Volume: page(s)	Action Date
1310	People	Peal, W. J.	Obtaining money by false pretense	5: 124	27 Jul 1885
1311	Thayer, F. L.	Justices Court of Redwood Township & Florence, M. (Justice)	Writ of prohibition	5: 125	9 Jul 1885
1312	Roney, J. M.	Burrough, Alfred	Appeal	5: 126	3 Aug 1885
1313	Gardella, C. L.		Insolvency	5: 127, 155	3 Aug 1885
1314	Heffron, A. H.		Insolvency	5: 128	3 Aug 1885
1315	Order of Mutual Companions		Petition to sell real estate	5: 129	3 Aug 1885
1316	Levy, M.		Insolvency	5: 130	1 Aug 1885
1317	Ward, John W.	Hindson, Frank	Unlawful detainer	5: 131	7 Aug 1885
1318	Samuels, James	Order of Mutual Companions		5: 132	10 Aug 1885
1319	Bartlett, Mary J.	Hasbrouck, Augustus	Foreclosure	5: 133	10 Aug 1885
1320	Foster, Margaret Porteous	Foster, Henry C.	Divorce	5: 134	10 Aug 1885
1321	Benbow, E. M.		Insolvency	5 : 135, 293	12 Aug 1885
1322	Taylor, W. F.	Heffron, Sarah & Heffron, A. H.	Foreclosure	5: 136	15 Aug 1885
1323	Bowman, John & Bowman, Zilpha	Order of Mutual Companions	Attachment	5: 137	17 Aug 1885
1324	Winters, Dennis & Winters, Ellen	Graves, George W.	Damages	5: 138, 191, 334	17 Aug 1885
1325	People	Doe, John		5: 139	17 Aug 1885
1326	Daly, Fannie N.	Daly, Thomas B.	Divorce	5: 140	14 Aug 1885
1327	Bussman, Anton	King, George	Appeal	5: 141	21 Mar 1885
1328	People	Joe, Ah	Petit larceny	5: 142	7 Aug 1885
1329	People	Koop, J. C.	Grand larceny	5: 143	7 Aug 1885
1330	Stone, J. S. & Weaver, C. W. (dba Stone & Weaver)	Sonoma, County of	Appeal	5: 144	10 Aug 1885
1331	People	Houser, S. R.	Embezzlement	5: 145	14 Aug 1885
1332	People	Houser, S. R.	Embezzlement	5: 146	14 Aug 1885
1333	Order of Mutual Companions		Involuntary insolvency	5: 147, 202-203, 307	22 Aug 1885

Suit #	Plaintiffs	Defendants	Cause of Suit	Register of Actions Volume: page(s)	Action Date
1334	Levy, M.		Involuntary insolvency	5: 148	22 Aug 1885
1335	Ridgway, Joseph W.; Ridgway, Jeremiah; Todd, Judith A. (Executors & Executrix Est. Jeremiah Ridgway)	Morrison, Oscar		5: 149	24 Aug 1885
1336	Hood, Eliza Ann	Thompson, Charles P. (Adm. with Will annexed Est. John McCracken); McCracken, Anna P., Sr.; McCracken, Mary Jenkin; McCracken, William D.; McCracken, John Henry; McCracken, Anna P., Jr.; McCracken, Charlotte M.; McCracken, Mary J.; Hood, William		5: 150	24 Aug 1885
1337	Callaway, Sarah	Callaway, David B.	Divorce	5: 151	26 Aug 1885
1338	Case, A. B.	Fritsch, John; Ellsworth, Lee; Weston, H. L.; Temple, C.; Order of Mutual Companions; Morrow, George P.; Hewlett, Frederick; Whitney, Calvin E. (Executors) & Whitney, Susan D. (Executrix Last Will A. P. Whitney)	Accounting	5: 152	27 Aug 1885
1339	Favor, John	Cook, Israel (Executor Last Will & Testament Peter Griest)	Foreclosure	5: 153	27 Aug 1885
1340	Wheeler, Jacob	Duncan, Florence B. & Duncan, S. M., Jr.	Foreclosure	5: 154	1 Sep 1885
1341	Creelman, L.	Creelman, F.	Divorce	5: 157	3 Sep 1885
1342	Meyer, Samuel		Involuntary insolvency	5: 158	7 Sep 1885
1343	Stevens, François	Stevens, Charles Louis	Contract	5: 159	11 Sep 1885
1344	Brown, Catherine A.	Brown, William M.	Divorce	5: 160	11 Sep 1885
1345	Cox, C. B.	Gardella, C. L.; Hoag, O. H.; DeMartin, Charles; Rhegetti, Bartolemo; Foppiano, Gaitano	Foreclosure	5: 161	16 Sep 1885
1346	DeNise, R. C.	Lewis, H.	Claim & delivery	5: 162	18 Sep 1885
1347	DeNise, R. C.	Lewis, H. & Smith, C. W.	Claim & delivery	5: 163	19 Sep 1885

204

Suit #	Plaintiffs	Defendants	Cause of Suit	Register of Actions Volume: page(s)	Action Date
1348	Eden, Edward (Pub. Adm. Marin County & Adm. Est. Martha Aikin)	Aikin, Matthew		5: 164	13 Aug 1885
1349	Tilgner, Franz Ferdinand	Kreuz, Frank P.; Kreuz, Catherine; Tilgner, Ferdinand Joseph Hugo		5: 165	23 Sep 1885
1350	McNear, George P.	Alexander, Lawrence	Attachment	5: 166	26 Sep 1885
1351	Burke, George P.	Frazier, Mary A.; Willits, W. H.; Bane, D. C.; Doe, John; Roe, Richard; Coe, Cornelius; Jones, Thomas; Smith, Robert; White, Samuel	Ejectment	5: 167	1 Oct 1885
1352	Grogan, A. B.; Page, Henry; Page, Charles; Page, Wilfred (Executors Last Will & Est. Thomas S. Page)	Lichon, A. E.	Attachment	5: 169	3 Oct 1885
1353	Bryan, Elizabeth (Executrix Last Will Thomas Bryan)	Bryan, Thomas W.; Bryan, Frederick J.; Muller, Mary J.; Muller, John, her husband; Bryan, Kate A.; Bryan, Anne E.; Bryan, Rosina; Bryan, William F.; Bryan, Joseph P.; Bryan, John L. (heirs at law and devisees of Thomas Bryan)	Equity	5: 170	3 Oct 1885
1354	Ludwig, T. J.		Insolvency	5: 172	8 Oct 1885
1355	African Methodist Episcopal Church of Petaluma, Trustees of		Application to sell real estate	5: 173	5 Oct 1885
1356	Solley, Emely Marcella	Solley, Stephen J.	Divorce	5: 174	7 Oct 1885
1357	Lacey, B. T. & Parke, L. C. (dba Berry & Place Machine Co.)	Ludwig, Thomas J.		5: 175	7 Oct 1885
1358	Rubke, H.	McMackin, James	Appeal	5: 176	22 Sep 1885
1359	Holloway, Lester		Application for writ of habeas corpus	5: 177	6 Oct 1885
1360	People	Hinkston, John G.	Assault with a deadly weapon	5: 178	5 Oct 1885
1361	Gregory, Joseph	Franks, C. & Pomeroy, George		5: 179	9 Oct 1885
1362	Curtis, Richard H.	Morris, Joseph		5: 180	10 Oct 1885

205

Suit #	Plaintiffs	Defendants	Cause of Suit	Register of Actions Volume: page(s)	Action Date
1363	Lauterne, Ferdinand	Lauterne, M. A.	Divorce	5: 181	10 Oct 1885
1364	Gow, Ong		Application for writ of habeas corpus	5: 182	14 Oct 1885
1365	Bishop, T. C. (Sheriff)	Sonoma, County of	Appeal	5: 183	3 Oct 1885
1366	German, William W.		Voluntary insolvency	5: 184	22 Oct 1885
1367	Schloss, S.	Brown, R. B.	Foreclosure	5: 185	24 Oct 1885
1368	Morrison, J. J. & Curtis, J. D. (dba Morrison & Curtis)	Hoag, O. H.	Appeal	5: 187	22 Oct 1885
1369	Inderstroth, Theodore	Bishop, T. C. (Sheriff); Aylett, Alice D. (Executrix Last Will C. T. Botts); Oakland Quicksilver Mining Co.	To quiet title	5: 188	24 Oct 1885
1370	People	Rickliff, Clinton	Grand larceny	5: 189	26 Oct 1885
1371	Myers, Edgar N.	Myers, Sarah Ellen	Divorce	5: 190	31 Oct 1885
1372	People	Jackson, John B.	Grand larceny	5: 192	4 Nov 1885
1373	Hotchkiss, W. J.	Hemenway, M. L.		5: 193	4 Nov 1885
1374	Norton, L. A.	Briggs, J. T. & Richey, John		5: 194	5 Nov 1885
1375	Bliven, James I. & Mitchell, D. C. (Co-partners)	Sullivan, P. J.		5: 195	7 Nov 1885
1376	Dickson, John	Fine, Emily; Norsworthy, John M.; Niblock, James	Damages	5: 196	11 Nov 1885
1377	Hefner, Philip	Urton, W. L. & Urton, Sarah	Ejectment	5: 197	11 Nov 1885
1378	McCarthy, E. R.	Mutual Relief Association of Petaluma	Damages	5: 198, 354	12 Nov 1885
1379	Society of the Seventh Day Adventist Church of Healdsburg		Petition to sell real estate	5: 199	12 Nov 1885
1380	Sheppard, Eli T. & Lewton, Lewis	Reed, William B.	Injunction	5: 200, 346	13 Nov 1885
1381	Barry, John P.	Barry, Margaret	Divorce	5: 201	16 Nov 1885
1382	Plunket, John	Sawyer, Lucy H.; Wiley, H.; Kelsey, B.	Foreclosure	5: 204	24 Nov 1885
1383	Rackliff, Eugene L.	Rackliff, W. G.; Rackliff, Ella C.; Allen, W. T.	Equity	5: 205	25 Nov 1885
1384	Rackliff, W. G.	Rackliff, Ella C.; Rackliff, Eugene L.; Allen, W. T.	Equity	5: 206	25 Nov 1885
1385	Rackliff, Ella C.	Rackliff, Eugene L.; Rackliff, W. G.; Allen, W. T.	Equity	5: 207	25 Nov 1885
1386	English, John F.	Peters, John T.	Foreclosure	5: 208	27 Nov 1885
1387	People	Stone, James (Informed against as Bell, Charles)	Burglary	5: 209	16 Nov 1885

Suit #	Plaintiffs	Defendants	Cause of Suit	Register of Actions Volume: page(s)	Action Date
1388	Bishop, T. C. (Assignee of the Order of Mutual Companions, an insolvent debtor)	Faulkner, M.	Mandamus	5: 210	30 Nov 1885
1389	Sargent, R. C.	Hatfield, Alice M. & Smith, Frank	Foreclosure	5: 211	1 Dec 1885
1390	Wheeler, D. R.	Neyce, J. H.	Unlawful detainer	5: 212	2 Dec 1885
1391	Peters, John T.		Insolvency	5: 213, 244	2 Dec 1885
1392	Jordan, J. L.	Hammond, A. C. & Frost, C. W.	Promissory note	5: 214	2 Dec 1885
1393	King, N. (Adm. Est. Giulio Velleggia)	Sartori, P. G.	Promissory note	5: 215	4 Dec 1885
1394	McChristian, Patrick	Home Mutual Insurance Company of California		5: 216	8 Dec 1885
1395	Sonoma, County of	Downs, Vernon	Action to condemn right of way	5: 217	10 Dec 1885
1396	Micheli, Charles	Griess, George	Rent	5: 218	11 Dec 1885
1397	Grimes, John	Cheeney, Jonathan	Appeal	5: 219	7 Dec 1885
1398	Truitt, Sarah E.	Truitt, John R.	Divorce	5: 220	14 Dec 1885
1399	Campbell, Joseph H.	Harris, Thomas S.; Tunzi, Dominico; Tunzi, Giuseppi; Lunardini, E.; Besagno, Benditto	Foreclosure	5: 221	15 Dec 1885
1400	People	Forget, Frank & Allen, George	Appeal	5: 222	30 Nov 1885
1401	People	Etheridge, Parmily L.	Arson	5: 223	21 Dec 1885
1402	Freehill, Thomas	Meyer, Sam & Hawley, George T.	Foreclosure	5: 224	26 Dec 1885
1403	Adler, David	Metzger, Joseph E. & Metzger, Albert V. (dba Metzger Bros.)		5: 225	29 Dec 1885
1404	People	Loy, Wong	Offering a bribe	5: 226	31 Dec 1885
1405	Carrillo, F.		Application for writ of habeas corpus	5: 227	2 Jan 1886

Suit #	Plaintiffs	Defendants	Cause of Suit	Register of Actions Volume: page(s)	Action Date
1406	People	Joe, Ah	Subornation of perjury	5: 228	2 Jan 1886
1407	People	Carrillo, Frank	Grand larceny	5: 229	4 Jan 1886
1408	Robbins, Leander	Walk, J. J. & Walk, H. L.	Ejectment	5: 230	4 Jan 1886
1409	Clanton, D. C.	Metzger, J. E.; Metzger, A. V.; Metzger, E. B. (dba Metzger Bros.)	Appeal	5: 231	14 Dec 1885
1410	People	Robinson, P. F.	Resisting a public officer	5: 232	6 Jan 1886
1411	Hudson, W. T.	Hudson, J.	Divorce	5: 234	12 Jan 1886
1412	Cronin, Patrick	Palmer, John A.; McDermott, William; Holm, Jacob F. (Adm. Est. John P. Holm)	Attachment	5: 235	13 Jan 1886
1413	Totten, Samuel & Norton, W. H.	Sichel, Michael	Claim & delivery	5: 236, 345	14 Jan 1886
1414	Norton, W. H. & Totten, Samuel	Sichel, Michael		5: 237	14 Jan 1886
1415	French, George & Lock, George	Morrow, James H.; Morrow, Jane Doe, his wife; Graham, Albert W.	Foreclosure	5: 238	14 Jan 1886
1416	Palmer, John A.		Insolvency	5: 239, 347	14 Jan 1886
1417	People	Rickliff, Peter H. & Roney, J. M.		5: 240	15 Jan 1886
1418	Brush, G. M.		Insolvency	5: 241, 350	16 Jan 1886
1419	Hopper, Thomas	Seawell, D. R.; Seawell, James B.; Seawell, D. H.	Foreclosure	5: 242	16 Jan 1886
1420	Haubrick, Peter	Muller, Frank	Attachment	5: 245	19 Jan 1886
1421	Santa Rosa Bank	Minor, B. M.; Minor, Fidus; Schintz, J. H.	Foreclosure	5:246	20 Jan 1886
1422	Ellison, John B.; Ellison, William P.; Ellison, Rodman B. (dba John B. Ellison & Sons)	McArthur, D.		5: 247	22 Jan 1886
1423	People	Benetti, John Paul (Informed against as Burnetti, Peter)	Murder	5: 248	18 Jan 1886
1424	People	Johnson, Andrew Bernard (Informed against as Johnson, Andrew)	Murder	5: 249	25 Jan 1886
1425	Leavenworth, T. M.	Thelan, John J.; Koster, John L.; Hamilton, James P.	Foreclosure	5: 250	30 Jan 1886
1425½	Myers, S.	Prows, S. W. & Prows, Bettie	Assumpsit	5: 251	2 Feb 1886

Suit #	Plaintiffs	Defendants	Cause of Suit	Register of Actions Volume: page(s)	Action Date
1426	Prows, S. W.		Voluntary insolvency	5: 252	8 Feb 1886
1427	Powers, Frank	Powers, Jennie	Divorce	5: 253	9 Feb 1886
1428	Conrad, Jane	Conrad, Charles	Divorce	5: 254	9 Feb 1886
1429	Williams, Mary A.	Williams, Charles H.	Divorce	5: 255	9 Feb 1886
1430	Wright, Isaac	Ellis, William	Claim & delivery	5: 256	13 Feb 1886
1431	French, Ellen M.	French, William L.	Divorce	5: 257	15 Feb 1886
1432	Byrne, M.	Thompson, John	Appeal	5: 258	5 Dec 1885
1433	People	Young, J. S.	Appeal	5: 259	1 Feb 1886
1434	Norton, L. A.	Briggs, J. T. & Richey, John		5: 260	18 Feb 1886
1435	Barnes, Aaron	Neal, James M. & Neal, Esther E.	Foreclosure	5: 261	18 Feb 1886
1436	Kee, Kon		Application for writ of habeas corpus	5: 262	20 Feb 1886
1437	Graham, Mary Isabel	Graham, Joseph M.	Divorce	5: 263	23 Feb 1886
1438	Shedd, Mary R. J.	Shedd, Charles & Shedd, Clarence	Partition	5: 264	23 Feb 1886
1439	Morrisey, Kate	Barry, John	Damages	5: 265	23 Feb 1886
1440	Loucks, Mort		Application for writ of habeas corpus	5: 266	24 Feb 1886
1441	Wickersham, I. G.	Ross, D. L. B. & Bihler, William	Assumpsit	5: 267	27 Feb 1886
1442	People	Tai, Ah (alias Duck, Ong Tai & Suang, Ang Ah)	Murder	5: 268	27 Jan 1886
1443	Montgomery, A.	Nourse, George E.; Nourse, Laura A.; Cralle, L. J.; Rex, William	Foreclosure	5: 269	3 Mar 1886
1444	Itin, John	Estep, Sarah R. (Executrix Last Will & Testament Joseph H. Estep)		5: 270	1 Mar 1886
1445	Metcalf, C. E.		Involuntary insolvency	5: 271	1 Mar 1886

Suit #	Plaintiffs	Defendants	Cause of Suit	Register of Actions Volume: page(s)	Action Date
1446	McLaughlin, William		Application for writ of habeas corpus	5: 272	1 Mar 1886
1447	Throop, Rachel C.		Divorce	5: 273	2 Mar 1886
1448	Santa Rosa, City of	Boyce, A. J.	Delinquent tax	5: 274	3 Mar 1886
1449	Santa Rosa, City of	Allen, J.	Delinquent tax	5: 275	3 Mar 1886
1450	Santa Rosa, City of	Gentzell, G.	Delinquent tax	5: 276	4 Mar 1886
1451	Santa Rosa, City of	Garbornni, F.	Delinquent tax	5: 277	4 Mar 1886
1452	Santa Rosa, City of	Cacello, J. G.	Delinquent tax	5: 278	4 Mar 1886
1453	Santa Rosa, City of	Gore, A. J. & Laik, Ellen V.	Delinquent tax	5: 279	4 Mar 1886
1454	Santa Rosa, City of	Manning, John	Delinquent tax	5: 280	5 Mar 1886
1455	Santa Rosa, City of	Low, N. A. (Mrs.)	Delinquent tax	5: 281	5 Mar 1886
1456	Santa Rosa, City of	Jacques, J. F.	Delinquent tax	5: 282	5 Mar 1886
1457	Brush, William T.	Dixon, E. F.		5: 283	5 Mar 1886
1458	Hopkins, S. J	Bishop, John J.; Bishop, Martha; O'Reilly, Martin	Foreclosure of mechanic's lien	5: 284	5 Mar 1886
1459	Pieratt, Gerald	Pieratt, James	Divorce	5: 285	6 Mar 1886
1460	Santa Rosa Bank	Farmer, C. C. & McConnell, William E. (Executors Est. Elijah T. Farmer); Farmer, Rebekah W.; Farmer, Charles R.; Farmer, Henry Thomas; Fox, Sarah Angeline; Farmer, Lillie Bell; Farmer, Frances May		5: 286	6 Mar 1886
1461	People (ex rel. Zartman, William; Denman, E.; Decker, H.; Farrell, William; McNear, J. A.; Spotswood, A.)	Walsh, M; Ayers, William; Lewis, W. A.; Nay, L. G.; Winans, J. L.		5: 287	9 Mar 1886
1462	People	Eagan, George L.	Obtaining money by false pretense	5: 288	15 Feb 1886
1463	People	Loucks, Mort	Robbery	5: 289	24 Feb 1886
1464	People	Simoni, Giovanni	Buggery	5: 290	8 Mar 1886
1465	Santa Rosa, City of	Olmstead, O. A.	Delinquent tax	5: 291	11 Mar 1886

210

Suit #	Plaintiffs	Defendants	Cause of Suit	Register of Actions Volume: page(s)	Action Date
1466	Santa Rosa, City of	Renieri, Mechi & Guidotti, F.	Delinquent tax	5: 292	11 Mar 1886
1467	Trescony, Alberto	Hopper, Thomas	Damages	5: 294	16 Mar 1886
1468	Poehlman, Martin & Poehlman, Conrad	Johnson, Sanborn	Foreclosure	5: 295	22 Mar 1886
1469	Faessler, Robert	Barker, John; Payne, William; Blazer, John S.; Bank of Healdsburg	Foreclosure	5: 296	22 Mar 1886
1470	Janssen, F. A.		Voluntary insolvency	5: 297	23 Mar 1886
1471	Winter, Thomas P.	Winter, Anne	Divorce	5: 298, 349, 355	27 Mar 1886
1472	First Presbyterian Church of Petaluma		Petition to mortgage property	5: 299	26 Mar 1886
1473	Liveroni, John	Sheppard, E. T.		5: 300	29 Mar 1886
1474	Smith, Charles A.	Martinelli, L.	Appeal	5: 301	22 Mar 1886
1475	Caldwell, George O. & Schmidli, Joseph (dba Caldwell & Schmidli)		Voluntary insolvency	5: 302	30 Mar 1886
1476	Santa Rosa, City of	Noonan, George P.	To remove obstruction	5: 303	31 Mar 1886
1477	Hawkins, L. J.	Dawson, H. C.; Fowler, J.; Fowler, Jane Doe	Foreclosure	5: 304	31 Mar 1886
1478	Taggart, John	Burnett, Matt; O'Flaherty, Ann; O'Flaherty, Ann (Adm. Est. Patrick O'Flaherty); O'Flaherty, Mary; O'Flaherty, Patrick E.		5: 305, 348	1 Apr 1886
1479	Hamlin, T. T.	Geary, T. J.		5: 306	2 Apr 1886
1480	Donahue, James M.; Donahue, Annie; Von Schroder, Mary Ellen (Executors Est. Peter Donahue)	Vallejo, Mariano G.; Vallejo, Benicia F., his wife; Doe, John; Roe, Richard; Hen, Mary; Fen, Carrie	Foreclosure	5: 308	7 Apr 1886
1481	People	Mathison, George	Assault with a deadly weapon with intent to commit murder	5: 309	7 Apr 1886

211

Suit #	Plaintiffs	Defendants	Cause of Suit	Register of Actions Volume: page(s)	Action Date
1482	Farmers and Mechanics Bank of Healdsburg	Keyes, H. M. & Keyes, S. E.	Foreclosure	5: 310	8 Apr 1886
1483	Watriss, Martha C.; Watriss, Franklin; Watriss, George; Watriss, Emma	Queen, W. D. & Reed, William B.	Ejectment	5: 311, 358	8 Apr 1886
1484	Watriss, Martha C.	Reed, E. S.	Ejectment	5: 312, 357	8 Apr 1886
1485	People	Grieves, Samuel H.	Assault with a deadly weapon	5: 313	14 Apr 1886
1486	Ashley, C.	Camm, William	Appeal	5: 314	26 Apr 1886
1487	Taylor, William	Mills, W. J.; Johnson, John; Graeff, John M.	Foreclosure of mortgage	5: 315	27 Apr 1886
1488	Walker, Louisa	Walker, Joseph	Divorce	5: 316	4 May 1886
1489	Stephens, William	Conklin, Charles & Conklin, Annie	Foreclosure of mortgage	5: 317	5 May 1886
1490	Fredericks, George	Schrack, George	Foreclosure of mortgage	5: 318	8 May 1886
1491	Shaw, Elias	Shaw, Melissa	Divorce	5: 319	8 May 1886
1492	Miller, George T.	Rawson, G. C.; Vaughn, E. K.; Foster, Joseph	Foreclosure of mortgage	5: 320, 356	8 May 1886
1493	Hussey, Edward	O'Leary, Thomas; O'Leary, Bridget, his wife; Meeker, M. C.; Meeker, A. P.; Doe, John; Roe, Richard; Snow, Susanna	Foreclosure of mortgage	5: 321	12 May 1886
1494	Crigler, Laura A.	Crigler, Lloyd A.	Divorce	5: 322	14 May 1886
1495	Meyer, S.	Fogerty, Michael & Fogerty, John		5: 323	14 May 1886
1496	Newby, Carrie	Newby, H. C.	Divorce	5: 324	17 May 1886
1497	Beeson, Isaac R.		Voluntary insolvency	5: 325	17 May 1886
1498	Parks, D. H.	Parks, O. B.	Assumpsit	5: 326	18 May 1886
1499	Truell, George		Voluntary insolvency	5: 327, 353	19 May 1886
1500	Baron, A.	Daly, James R.		5: 328	22 May 1886

Suit #	Plaintiffs	Defendants	Cause of Suit	Register of Actions Volume: page(s)	Action Date
1501	Skellenger, S. R.	Skellenger, D. A.	Divorce	5: 329	24 May 1886
1502	Meyer, Lorentz	Meyer, Elizabeth & Meyer, Catharine Bertha; Meyer, William Jacob; Meyer, Caroline Louise; Meyer, Lorentz, Jr.; Meyer, Margareta Salamona (minors) & Kauffmann, Phillip L. (Guardian of minors)	To quiet title	5: 330	28 May 1886
1503	De Forest, W. F. & De Forest, Margaret	Kinkead, C. I.	Unlawful detainer	5: 331	1 Jun 1886
1504	Sperry & Co.	Percival Milling Co.	Injunction	5: 332	1 Jun 1886
1505	Henshaw, W. P.	Cannon, J. P.; Hoag, O. H.; Roney, J. M.	Appeal	5: 335	22 May 1886
1506	Sutherland, Frank B.	Barton, Francis A.; Barton, Emily J., his wife; Nowell, Charles W.	Foreclosure	5: 336	4 Jun 1886
1507	Chamberlain, David	Trosper, Thomas G. W.	Foreclosure	5: 337	10 Jun 1886
1508	Coffey, Henry	Savings Bank of Santa Rosa	To cancel contract	5: 339	15 Jun 1886
1509	Pridham, Charles H.	Quitzow, Augustus		5: 340	15 Jun 1886
1510	Richardson, Maria H.	Richardson, Nathan W.	To quiet title	5: 341	16 Jun 1886
1511	Dassel, Helen	Dassel, W. H.	Divorce	5: 342	16 Jun 1886
1512	Moore, A. P. (Assignee of C. E. Metcalf, insolvent)	Harris, Thomas M. & Hoag, O. H.	To set aside judgment	5: 343	18 Jun 1886
1513	Richardson, H. A.	Anderson, John; Sturdevant, Edward; Johnson, Robert	Injunction	5: 344	22 Jun 1886
1514	Abraham, Casper	Hixon, William H.		6: 1	26 Jun 1886
1515	Hopper, Thomas	Holmes, Henderson P.	Foreclosure	6: 2	28 Jun 1886
1516	Thompson, Charles T.	Akin, Mat		6: 3	1 Jul 1886
1516½	Warner, Caroline W.	Warner, James	Divorce	6: 4	2 Jul 1886
1517	Hobbs, Caroline	Hobbs, Elijah Moses	Divorce	6: 5	3 Jul 1886
1518	Hudson, John N.	Sanderson, J. L.; Doe, John; Roe, Richard (dba J. L. Sanderson & Co.)		6: 6	8 Jul 1886
1519	Lewis, Gilford Howard	Lunibus, John; Morris, T. D.; Morris, James B.; Goess, G. A.; Hartman, Jane Doe; Cheney, Thomas H.; Cheney, Thomas; Hooper, George F.	Ejectment	6: 7	12 Jul 1886

Suit #	Plaintiffs	Defendants	Cause of Suit	Register of Actions Volume: page(s)	Action Date
1520	Hill, William	Cooper, Henry H. & Cooper, B. M.		6: 8	15 Jul 1886
1521	Kendall, John	Wright, Isaac; Mederias, A. J.; Doe, John; Roe, Richard		6: 9	16 Jul 1886
1522	Carles, James H.		Voluntary insolvency	6: 10	19 Jul 1886
1523	Boyes, H. E.	Leavenworth, T. M. & Schetter, Otto		6: 11	21 Jul 1886
1524	Farmers and Mechanics Bank of Healdsburg	Soules, L. O.; Soules, Albert; Russell, W. F.; Alexander, Mary A.	Foreclosure	6: 12	22 Jul 1886
1525	Wickersham, I. G.	Norton, William H. & Naughton, John F.		6: 13	26 Jul 1886
1526	Irwin, Alfred	Farmer, C. C. & McConnell, W. E. (Executors Will & Est. Elijah T. Farmer); Farmer, Rebekah W.; Farmer, Charles R.; Fox, Sarah Angeline; Farmer, Henry Thomas; Farmer, Lillie Belle; Farmer, Frances May	To quiet title	6: 14	28 Jul 1886
1527	Stofen, Peter N.	Infanger, Anton	Assumpsit	6: 15	28 Jul 1886
1528	Gater, J. E	Gater, Mary Jane	Divorce	6: 16	30 Jul 1886
1529	Reed, Ellen	Reed, James	Divorce	6: 17	31 Jul 1886
1530	Kron, Elizabeth & Schmitt, Mary	Williams, Bridget K.	Equity	6: 18	3 Aug 1886
1531	Maher, James	Bihler, William		6: 19	5 Aug 1886
1532	Torrance, S. H.	Sicotte, F.	Ejectment	6: 20	6 Aug 1886
1533	Shaw, Isaac E.	Hall, Isaac R.		6: 21	6 Aug 1886
1534	Wiley, Harriet	Sawyer, Lucy H.; Plunkett, John; Kelsey, B.; Haight, Robert	Foreclosure of mortgage	6: 22	9 Aug 1886
1535	People	Gow, Ah	Felony	6: 23	7 Aug 1886
1536	Gibbs, J. D.	Ranard, J. H.	Damages	6: 24, 129	14 Aug 1886
1537	Beaver, Henry	Starrett, John & Gliddon, William (dba Starrett & Gliddon)	Accounting	6: 25	14 Aug 1886
1538	Gwinn, John E.	Walsh, Michael; Nay, L. G.; Ayers, William; Lewis, William; Winans, J. L. (Board of Trustees of the City of Petaluma) & Maynard, F. T.; Singley, James; Edelman, G. W.; Hedges, N. M.; Campbell, James (Board of Education of the City of Petaluma)	Injunction	6: 26	14 Aug 1886

Suit #	Plaintiffs	Defendants	Cause of Suit	Register of Actions Volume: page(s)	Action Date
1539	People	Wilson, George & Cole, Charles	Robbery	6: 27	17 Aug 1886
1540	Henderson, H. W.	Henderson, Mary	Divorce	6: 28	21 Aug 1886
1541	Mann, Lulu B.	Mann, Robert J.	Divorce	6: 29	23 Aug 1886
1542	Peugh, Jennie	Butcher, Squire		6: 30	28 Aug 1886
1543	Haas, Rosa	Haas, Herman	Divorce	6: 31	7 Sep 1886
1544	Algren, John & Algren, Annie, his wife	Blomfield, H.		6: 32	8 Sep 1886
1545	Sonoma Valley Bank	King, Joseph L. & King, Flora Ellen	Foreclosure	6: 33	11 Sep 1886
1546	Boothby, Caroline	Boothby, B. F.	Divorce	6: 34	14 Sep 1886
1547	People (ex rel. John E. Gwinn)	Petaluma, City of; Walsh, Michael; Nay, L. G.; Ayers, William; Lewis, William; Winans, J. L. (Board of Trustees of the City of Petaluma) & Maynard, F. T.; Singley, James; Edelman, G. W.; Hedges, N. M.; Campbell, Joseph (Board of Education of the City of Petaluma); Camm, William; Phillips, A. G.	Injunction	6: 35	13 Sep 1886
1548	People	Albee, A. B.	Grand larceny	6: 36	8 Sep 1886
1549	Jacobs, Brit		Application for writ of habeas corpus	6: 37	10 Sep 1886
1550	Carrillo, Andrew		Application for writ of habeas corpus	6: 38	10 Sep 1886
1551	Winter, Thomas P.	Hopkins, Peter (Sheriff of San Francisco) & Winter, Anne		6: 39	14 Sep 1886
1552	Cooper, H. H.	Thompson, A. W.	At law	6: 40	18 Sep 1886
1553	Trosper, Thomas G. W.	Bail, Adolph	At law	6: 41	22 Sep 1886
1554	People	Van Doren, John S.	Embezzlement	6: 42	8 Sep 1886
1555	People	Van Doren, John S.	Embezzlement	6: 43	8 Sep 1886
1556	People	Van Doren, John S.		6: 44	8 Sep 1886
1557	People	Rains, Jasper O'Farrell	Rape	6: 45	8 Sep 1886
1558	Walker, John L.	Walker, Louise C.	Divorce	6: 46	24 Sep 1886

Suit #	Plaintiffs	Defendants	Cause of Suit	Register of Actions Volume: page(s)	Action Date
1559	Hendrickson, A.	Sponogle, J. C.	To set aside deed	6: 47	27 Sep 1886
1560	Cloverdale Banking and Commercial Company	Staley, Isaac & Scott, Sylvester (dba Scott & Staley)	Assumpsit	6: 48	27 Sep 1886
1561	Cloverdale Banking and Commercial Company	Scott, Sylvester	Assumpsit	6: 49	27 Sep 1886
1562	Santa Rosa, City of	Santa Rosa Street Rail Road Company	Nuisance	6: 50	27 Sep 1886
1563	People (ex rel. John E. Gwinn)	Maynard, F. T.; Singley, James; Edelman, G. W.; Hedges, N. M.; Campbell, Joseph (Board of Education of the City of Petaluma); Camm, William; Phillips, A. G.; Scott, J. D.; Doe, John; Roe, Richard	Injunction	6: 51, 102	30 Sep 1886
1564	Adams, Joshua	Scott, Sylvester & Staley, Isaac (dba Scott & Staley)	Assumpsit	6: 52	30 Sep 1886
1565	Scollay, Oceana	Lancel, Anselme H.; Lancel, Eugene Henri; Doe, John; Roe, Richard; Fenn, John; Fenn, Richard	Foreclosure	6: 53	1 Oct 1886
1566	Wheelock, Daniel	Scott, Sylvester & Staley, Isaac	Assumpsit	6: 54	1 Oct 1886
1567	Chopard, Louis	Cannon, J. P.	Appeal	6: 55	20 Sep 1886
1568	Hobbs, Caroline	Hobbs, Elijah Moses	Divorce	6: 56	30 Sep 1886
1569	Healey, Julia H.	Tarwater, Martin W.	Foreclosure	6: 57	4 Oct 1886
1570	Lockwood, William	Totten, Samuel	Appeal	6: 58	5 Oct 1886
1571	Lockwood, William	Norton, William H.	Appeal	6: 59	5 Oct 1886
1572	Perry, William	Lean, Antoine	Appeal	6: 60	6 Oct 1886
1573	Scott, Sylvester & Staley, Isaac (dba Scott & Staley)		Involuntary insolvency	6: 61, 163, 339	8 Oct 1886
1574	Sonoma, County of	Gottig, Lawrence & Roeding, F.		6: 62	8 Oct 1886
1575	Mattei, G. (Adm. Est. Santina Mattei)	Respini, Michael	At law	6: 63, 106	8 Oct 1886
1576	Rains, Anna	Carrie, J. A. (Adm. with Will annexed Est. Gallant Rains)		6: 64	11 Oct 1886
1577	McNear, George P.	Sullivan, James		6: 65	11 Oct 1886
1578	Perry, William	Leal, Antoine	Attachment	6: 66	13 Oct 1886
1579	Ty, Ah & Yeat, Ah		Application for writ of habeas corpus	6: 67	13 Oct 1886

216

Suit #	Plaintiffs	Defendants	Cause of Suit	Register of Actions Volume: page(s)	Action Date
1580	Meyer, Anton	Mitcheli, Charles; Griess, George; Wickersheimer, August	Foreclosure of mortgage	6: 68	14 Oct 1886
1581	Sullivan, James G.	Bishop, T. C.	Claim & delivery	6: 69	15 Oct 1886
1582	Joyce, M.		Application for writ of habeas corpus	6: 70	18 Oct 1886
1583	Sonoma, County of	Haehl, Conrad & Hermann, Barbory	To condemn right of way	6: 71	22 Oct 1886
1584	Gage, J. S.	Gage, Emma	Divorce	6: 72	11 Oct 1886
1585	Rien, George E. & Rien, Nellie J. (Minors by guardian T. D. Hoskins); Rien, J. M.; Rien, S. W.	Hitchcock, Hollis	Ejectment	6: 73	23 Oct 1886
1586	Hicks, E. S.		Voluntary insolvency	6: 74, 128	26 Oct 1886
1587	Hood, George (Adm. with Will annexed Est. Charles J. Hanneth)	McKean, Hugh	Ejectment	6: 75	27 Oct 1886
1588	Casey, L. J. & Minehan, M.	Walker, D. W.	At law	6: 76	27 Oct 1886
1589	McClellan, James E.	Seymour, L. B.		6: 77	28 Oct 1886
1590	West, Mary	King, N. (Adm. Est. James Notti)		6: 78	6 Oct 1886
1591	People	Green, Morris	Grand larceny	6: 79	22 Oct 1886
1592	Norton, L. A.	Briggs, J. T. & Richey, John		6: 80	3 Nov 1886
1593	Kier, H.	Yarbrough, Crockett D.	Foreclosure of mortgage	6: 81	9 Nov 1886
1594	Page, Henry; Page, Charles; Page, Wilfred (Executors Last Will Est. Thomas S. Page)	Clarke, James; Clarke, W. H.; Clarke, J. T.; Clarke, James, Jr.		6: 82	16 Nov 1886
1595	Naughton, John F.	Moore, A. P.	Election contest	6: 83	19 Nov 1886
1596	Italian Swiss Agricultural Colony	Sparrow, Edward, D.; Venaia, Michele F.; Doe, John	Foreclosure of mortgage	6: 84	20 Nov 1886
1597	People	Gilfoyle, John	Grand larceny	6: 85	26 Oct 1886

217

Suit #	Plaintiffs	Defendants	Cause of Suit	Register of Actions Volume: page(s)	Action Date
1598	People	Joyce, Martin	Grand larceny	6: 86	8 Nov 1886
1599	Hosler, William H.		Voluntary insolvency	6: 87	27 Nov 1886
1600	People	Bailiff, John	Murder	6: 88	24 Nov 1886
1601	People	Reed, W. A.	Murder	6: 89	24 Nov 1886
1602	People	Van Doren, John S.	Embezzlement	6: 90	29 Nov 1886
1603	People	Van Doren, John S.	Embezzlement	6: 91	29 Nov 1886
1604	People	Van Doren, John S.	Embezzlement	6: 92	29 Nov 1886
1605	Coomes, Edmund	Coomes, Albert M.	To cancel instruments	6: 93	1 Dec 1886
1606	Purrington, T. F.	Neustadt, Walter & Ellis, Mary	To set aside deed	6: 94	1 Dec 1886
1607	Hall, A. B.	Hall, Effie E.	Divorce	6: 95	6 Dec 1886
1608	Rodgers, W. H.	Sozer, Manuel	Rent	6: 96	6 Dec 1886
1609	McChristian, Patrick	Hicks, Edward S.; Hicks, Etta M.; Whitney, A. L.; Whitney, C. E.; Moore, A. P.	Foreclosure of mortgage	6: 97	6 Dec 1886
1610	Dianda, D.	McNamara, B.	Appeal	6: 98	6 Dec 1886
1611	Ferrari, Innocenti	San Francisco and North Pacific Rail Road Company	Damages	6: 99	7 Dec 1886
1612	Cooper, S. V.	Bishop, T. C. (Sheriff of Sonoma County)	To restrain writ of execution	6: 100	7 Dec 1886
1613	Souza, Manuel		Voluntary insolvency	6: 101	8 Dec 1886
1614	Wickersham, I. G.	Rowe, Orena	Foreclosure of mortgage	6: 103	9 Dec 1886
1615	McCarthy, E. R.	Rogers, E.		6: 104	15 Dec 1886
1616	Cloverdale, Town of	McElarney, Frank	Appeal	6: 105	15 Dec 1886
1617	Walters, Soloman	Beeson, William S.	Assumpsit	6: 106	23 Dec 1886
1618	Tunzi, Ellen	Hedges, W. H.	Claim & delivery	6: 107	27 Dec 1886

218

Suit #	Plaintiffs	Defendants	Cause of Suit	Register of Actions Volume: page(s)	Action Date
1619	Casassa, Domenico; Gardella, Catherine; Liveroni, Augusti; Domica, Luigi	Cavagnaro, Giovanni	Equity	6: 108	30 Dec 1886
1620	Colson, Louisa	Colson, Nicholas	Divorce	6: 109	31 Dec 1886
1621	People	Cleary, John	Burglary	6: 110	21 Dec 1886
1622	People	Sellers, William	Grand larceny	6: 111	21 Dec 1886
1623	Wood, Frank		Application for writ of habeas corpus	6: 112	1 Jan 1887
1624	Perry, William	Rafael, M. E.	Appeal	6: 113	4 Jan 1887
1625	Rafael, M. E.	Bishop, T. C.	Replevin	6: 114	7 Jan 1887
1626	Wood, Frank		Application for writ of habeas corpus	6: 115	8 Jan 1887
1627	Carpenter, L. F. (Executor Last Will Patrick Moore)	Sullivan, James & Sullivan, Mary, his wife	Foreclosure of mortgage	6: 116	10 Jan 1887
1628	Brumfield, George; Brumfield, Charles; Strong, Jennie	Brumfield, Summers		6: 117	10 Jan 1887
1629	Guerne, George E. & Murphy, Rufus (dba Guerne & Murphy)	Armstrong, J. B. & Brown, Albert (dba Armstrong & Brown)	Assumpsit	6: 118	12 Jan 1887
1630	Hanify, John R.	Dei, G. Ph. (aka Dey, G. P.) & Dei, Ella Wooten (aka Dey, Ella Wooten); Sonoma Valley Bank; Doe, John; Roe, Richard	Foreclosure of mechanic's lien	6: 119	12 Jan 1887
1631	Myer, Samuel	Skaggs, Wilson W. & Butcher, Squire	Contract	6: 120	14 Jan 1887
1632	Hobart, Mary A.	Black, Fannie B.	To quiet title	6: 121	15 Jan 1887
1633	Hall, L. J.	Beach, H. S.	Foreclosure of mortgage	6: 122	18 Jan 1887
1634	McCone, Robert	McGinty, James	Assumpsit	6: 123	19 Jan 1887
1635	Sherry, John	Scown, Adolph G. & Faggiano, J. B.		6: 124	19 Jan 1887
1636	Cohn, S.	Hardesty, Charles W.; Hardesty, Catherine A.; Cralle, L. J.	Foreclosure of mortgage	6: 125	19 Jan 1887

219

Suit #	Plaintiffs	Defendants	Cause of Suit	Register of Actions Volume: page(s)	Action Date
1637	Ward, J. A. & Coen, James	Hovenden, Thomas; Bunster, Arthur; Chalfant, E.; Witham, Charles H.		6: 126	20 Jan 1887
1638	Coomes, Edmund	Perazzo, G.	Injunction	6: 127	24 Jan 1887
1639	Bogart, Julia R.	Bogart, Charles H.	Divorce	6: 130	1 Feb 1887
1640	People	Wood, Frank	Murder	6: 131	3 Feb 1887
1641	People	Daniels, Charles M.	Grand larceny	6: 132	3 Feb 1887
1642	Mitchell, Samuel J. (Assignee of Henry Goldstein)	Colgan, E. P.	Conversion	6: 133	5 Feb 1887
1643	French, John H.		Voluntary insolvency	6: 134	5 Feb 1887
1644	Van Doren, J. S.	Bank of Sonoma County & Denman, E.	Conversion	6: 135	11 Feb 1887
1645	Colson, Louisa	Colson, Nicholas & Colson, John	To cancel deed	6: 136	14 Feb 1887
1646	Goldfish, B.; Wilson, William; Cohn, S. (dba Goldfish, Wilson & Co.)	Watson, J. A.	Ejectment	6: 137	14 Feb 1887
1647	Knapp, A. H.	McMillan, H.	Appeal	6: 138	12 Feb 1887
1648	Knapp, A. H.	Parks, D. H., Jr. & Parks, Abraham H.	Appeal	6: 139	12 Feb 1887
1649	People	Van Doren, John S.	Embezzlement	6: 140	16 Feb 1887
1650	Leavenworth, T. M.	Thelan, John J.; Koster, John L.; Hamilton, James P.	Foreclosure	6: 141	17 Feb 1887
1651	Parker, E. C.	Parker, Minnie B.	Divorce	6: 142	17 Feb 1887
1652	Carroll, P. (Bond of Kenneally, Elizabeth [Adm. Est James Kenneally])		Application for release of surety	6: 143	17 Feb 1887
1653	Kean, J. B.	Kean, Serena A.	To quiet title	6: 144	21 Feb 1887
1654	Goldstein, Henry		Voluntary insolvency	6: 145, 254	21 Feb 1887
1655	Parks, D. H.	Mauzy, S. H.	Attachment	6: 146	24 Feb 1887
1656	Van Doren, J. S.	Bank of Sonoma County; Denman, E.; Dutton, Warren	Claim & delivery	6: 147	25 Feb 1887
1657	Harris, A. I.	Thayer, Franklin L. & Keen, A. H.	Foreclosure of mortgage	6: 148	1 Mar 1887

220

Suit #	Plaintiffs	Defendants	Cause of Suit	Register of Actions Volume: page(s)	Action Date
1658	Guerne, George E. & Murphy, Rufus (dba Guerne & Murphy)	Armstrong, J. B. & Brown, Albert (dba Armstrong & Brown)	Attachment	6: 149	1 Mar 1887
1659	People	Spear, Charles	Burglary	6: 150	2 Mar 1887
1660	Manzy, S. H.		Involuntary insolvency	6: 151	3 Mar 1887
1661	Guerne, George E. & Murphy, Rufus	Armstrong, J. B. & Brown, Albert	To abate nuisances	6: 152, 364	7 Mar 1887
1662	Thelen, J. J.	Warfield, Kate F.	Account for labor	6: 153	7 Mar 1887
1663	Denny, Carrie	Denny, John P.	Divorce	6: 154	7 Mar 1887
1664	Woman's Relief Association		Application to change its corporate name	6: 155	7 Mar 1887
1665	People	Redden, Eugene	Felony	6: 156	25 Feb 1887
1666	Woods, James A.	Miller, C. S.; Miller, Charles; Miller, John	Appeal	6: 157	28 Feb 1887
1667	McCarthy, E. R. & Blume, Julius	Hedges, William H.	Appeal	6: 158	7 Mar 1887
1668	Lee, Joseph		Application for writ of habeas corpus	6: 159	14 Mar 1887
1669	West, John; West, Fred; West, Charles; West, John (Adm. Est. Charles West)	Lynch, Sarah P.	To quiet title	6: 160	15 Mar 1887
1670	Morrow, James	Morrow, Hattie B.	Divorce	6: 161	16 Mar 1887
1671	Carleton, Charles		Application for writ of habeas corpus	6: 162	17 Mar 1887
1672	De Vincenzi, Giovanni	Lunardini, G.	Promissory note	6: 164	22 Mar 1887
1673	People	Smith, Harry	Felony	6: 165	23 Mar 1887

221

Suit #	Plaintiffs	Defendants	Cause of Suit	Register of Actions Volume: page(s)	Action Date
1674	Gale, Otis	Inghram, Mary E. & Inghram, John M.	Foreclosure of mortgage	6: 166	26 Mar 1887
1675	Hill, William B.	Stuart, Edwin; Doe, John; Roe, Richard; Snow, Susana	Foreclosure of mortgage	6: 167	28 Mar 1887
1676	Castagnetto, Bartolomeo	Bacigalupo, Rosa (aka Bicigalupi, Rosi); Bacigalupo, John (aka Bicigalupi, John); Bacigalupo, Natale (aka Bicigalupi, Natola); Bacigalupo, Louis (aka Bicigalupi, Louis) & Bicigalupi, Rosi (aka Bacigalupo, Rosa, Adm. Est. Louis Bicigalupi (aka Luigi Bacigalupo))	Foreclosure of mortgage	6: 168	28 Mar 1887
1677	Big Bottom Rail Road Company	Guerne, George E. & Murphy, Rufus (dba Guerne & Murphy); Thompson, L.; Savings Bank of Santa Rosa	To condemn right of way	6: 169, 245	30 Mar 1887
1678	Beeson, William S.		Voluntary insolvency	6: 170	30 Mar 1887
1679	Dudley, Nellie	Dudley, Charles	Divorce	6: 171	1 Apr 1887
1680	Sanders, Inda	Sanders, John	Divorce	6: 172	1 Apr 1887
1681	Fong, Ah & Hoe, Ah		Application for writ of habeas corpus	6: 173	1 Apr 1887
1682	Goldfish, B.; Wilson, William; Cohn, S. (dba Goldfish, Wilson & Co.)	McMinn, John	Assumpsit	6: 174	4 Apr 1887
1683	Connolly, M. W.	Francisco, D.	Ejectment	6: 175	5 Apr 1887
1684	Clanton, David C.	Ruffner, William & Lee, Robert	Libel	6: 176	5 Apr 1887
1685	Clanton, David C.	Ellis, Wilson R.	Libel	6: 177	5 Apr 1887
1686	Jacobs, M.		Voluntary insolvency	6: 178	5 Apr 1887
1687	Pauli, Caroline J.; Pauli, Pauline M.; Pauli, A. F. (dba A. F. Pauli & Co.)		Involuntary insolvency	6: 179, 212, 371	6 Apr 1887
1688	Jones, John H.	Jones, Martha	To set aside deed	6: 180	6 Apr 1887
1689	Thompson, A. C.	Lightner, J. S.	Assumpsit	6: 181	7 Apr 1887

Suit #	Plaintiffs	Defendants	Cause of Suit	Register of Actions Volume: page(s)	Action Date
1690	Bank of Sonoma County	Scott, Sylvester; Scott, Malinda, his wife; Staley, Isaac; Heald, Rachel; Adams, Joshua; Wheelock, David; Cloverdale Banking & Commercial Co.; Carrie, J. A. (Assignee)	Foreclosure of mortgage	6: 182, 253	8 Apr 1887
1691	Thelen, John J.		Voluntary insolvency	6: 183	8 Apr 1887
1692	Carleton, Charles		Application for writ of habeas corpus	6: 184	8 Apr 1887
1693	Shafter, P. J.	Edwards, Ben	Attachment	6: 185	19 Apr 1887
1694	Hoen, Mary A. (Executrix Est. Berthold Hoen)	Savings Bank of Santa Rosa	Conversion	6: 186	22 Apr 1887
1695	King, William & King, Mary E.	North Pacific Coast Railroad Co.	Damages	6: 187	25 Apr 1887
1696	People	Leard, Alfred	Grand larceny	6: 188	25 Apr 1887
1697	Baumgarten, Joseph; Fisher, Godfrey; Brown, W. L. (dba J. Baumgarten & Co.)	Hettrich, Charles		6: 189	2 May 1887
1698	Davidson, Sarah J.	Davidson, Alexander T.	Divorce	6: 190, 365	7 May 1887
1699	Long, L. F.; Reed, John S.; Donohoe, J. H.	Ludwig, Mary (Mrs.); Hagmeyer, Gottlieb; Goetzleman, John; Burney, E. (Mrs.); Heald, J. G.; Elliott, John; Ellis, A. M. (Mrs.); Cooley, Charles H.; Kuhfuss, Herman; Mowbray, Jane (Mrs.)	Arbitration	6: 191	4 May 1887
1700	People	Baters, Tom (an Indian)	Assault to murder	6: 192	6 May 1887
1701	People	Baker, Joseph	Assault to murder	6: 193	6 May 1887
1702	People	Cash, J. F.	Forgery	6: 194	6 May 1887
1703	Gaver, A. P.	Brown, J. H.	Assumpsit	6: 195	9 May 1887
1704	Tomblinson, Samuel	Wehrspon, August	Slander	6: 196	9 May 1887
1705	Brumfield, George P.	Brumfield, Summers	To quiet title	6: 197	13 May 1887
1706	People	Neville, John	Burglary	6: 198	13 May 1887
1707	People	Guilfoyle, Frank	Grand larceny	6: 199	14 May 1887

223

Suit #	Plaintiffs	Defendants	Cause of Suit	Register of Actions Volume: page(s)	Action Date
1708	Bazoni, Louis		Application for writ of habeas corpus	6: 200	13 May 1887
1709	Falietti, Luigi		Application for writ of habeas corpus	6: 201	10 May 1887
1710	Muther, Frank	Muther, Fannie M.	Divorce	6: 202, 236	14 May 1887
1711	Van Allen, William	Eames, Margaret	Foreclosure of mortgage	6: 203	16 May 1887
1712	Piffero, Virginia	Piffero, Benedetto	Divorce	6: 204	20 May 1887
1713	Walters, Solomon	Richardson, Holena E.; Richardson, L. B.; Richardson, J. H.	Foreclosure of mortgage	6: 205	21 May 1887
1714	Haehl, Conrad	Bond, George & Bond, Albert	At law	6: 206	23 May 1887
1715	Basone, Ellen	Basone, Louis	Divorce	6: 207	24 May 1887
1716	Kessing, C.	Kessing, J. F.	Appeal	6: 208	11 May 1887
1717	McCormack, William M.	McRossie, James & McRossie, Jane, his wife	Foreclosure of mortgage	6: 209	25 May 1887
1718	Singer Manufacturing Company	Vance, James M. & Taylor, W. H.	Foreclosure of mortgage	6: 210	25 May 1887
1719	Oates, James W. & Jones, C. J. (Executors Will Thomas J. Jones)	Hemenway, M. L.	Ejectment	6: 211	26 May 1887
1720	Donahue, James		Application for writ of habeas corpus	6: 213	24 May 1887
1721	Daw, A. W.		Application for writ of mandate against Sonoma County	6: 214	11 Jun 1887

Suit #	Plaintiffs	Defendants	Cause of Suit	Register of Actions Volume: page(s)	Action Date
1722	Wright, Fannie L.	Wright, Sampson B.	Divorce	6: 215	11 Jun 1887
1723	Campbell, S. A. (Mrs.)	Campbell, George S.	Divorce	6: 216	13 Jun 1887
1724	Anderson, John	Richardson, H. A.	Ejectment	6: 217, 374	13 Jun 1887
1725	Peterson, Mary	Free, Thomas H.	To compel delivery of deed	6: 218	13 Jun 1887
1726	Norton, L. A.	Briggs, J. T. & Richey, John	Contract	6: 219	15 Jun 1887
1727	Leiding, C. F.	Harding, Edwin H.; Harding, Reka; Robinson, J. R.; Robinson, Laura A.; Lachman, H.	Foreclosure of mortgage	6: 220	15 Jun 1887
1728	Christieson, James B.	Lancel, Anselme H.	Assumpsit	6: 221	22 Jun 1887
1729	Peterson, Edward		Application for writ of habeas corpus	6: 222	22 Jun 1887
1730	Williams, C. B.	Overton, A. P.	Foreclosure of mechanic's lien	6: 223	22 Jun 1887
1731	Williams, C. B.	Overton, A. P. & Doyle, M.	Foreclosure of mechanic's lien	6: 224	22 Jun 1887
1732	Ross, Frank C.	Laughlin, C. W.; Shaw, E. H.; Geer, C. V.; Groom, M. W.; Laughlin, L.	Damages	6: 225	24 Jun 1887
1733	Duncan, Ada M.	Duncan, F. L.	Divorce	6: 226	25 Jun 1887
1734	Cronin, Patrick	Carty, Charles	Dissolution of co-partnership	6: 227, 368, 377	25 Jun 1887
1735	Favour, John	Bermel, Ernestine (Executrix Last Will Est. J. G. Bermel); Thompson, Amelie L.; Bermel, Pauline; Bermel, Ernestine; Rowland, William; Wilson, H. M.	Foreclosure of mortgage	6: 228	30 Jun 1887
1736	Roberts, Charles	Reed, Michael & Reed, Bridget	Foreclosure of mortgage	6: 229	30 Jun 1887
1737	Farmers and Mechanics Bank of Healdsburg	Sewell, James B. & Sewell, J. W.	Assumpsit	6: 230	2 Jul 1887

Suit #	Plaintiffs	Defendants	Cause of Suit	Register of Actions Volume: page(s)	Action Date
1738	Wedemeyer, Elizabeth	Wedemeyer, Frederick William	Divorce	6: 231	8 Jul 1887
1739	Archer, A. C. & Paddock, E. S.	Frazier, Alexander	Settlement of co-partnership	6: 232	12 Jul 1887
1740	Johnson, Robert C.	Burnham, Edward A.	Damages	6: 233	12 Jul 1887
1741	Farmers and Mechanics Bank of Healdsburg	Keyes, H. M. & Keyes, M. M.	Assumpsit	6: 234	9 Jul 1887
1742	Phillips, A. G.	Haskins, Robert & Haskins, Mary	Trover	6: 235	12 Jul 1887
1743	Nichols, Thomas	Frasier, M. J. & Misner, D. R. (Partners)	Appeal	6: 237	5 Jul 1887
1744	Wheeler, Jacob	Hoag, O. H.	Foreclosure of mortgage	6: 238	15 Jul 1887
1745	Congleton, Agnes L.	Congleton, George W.	Divorce	6: 239	20 Jul 1887
1746	Carrie, Joseph A. (Assignee Est. Scott & Staley, co-partners, composed of Scott, Sylvester & Staley, Isaac, insolvent debtors)	Cloverdale Banking & Commercial Company	Damages	6: 240, 375	22 Jul 1887
1747	Case, A. B.	Coburn, W. R.	Assumpsit	6: 241	26 Jul 1887
1748	Menihan, Michael	Rush, John; Thompson, W. A.; Howell, Morris; Howell, Eleanor M.	Foreclosure of mortgage	6: 242	26 Jul 1887
1749	Goldfish, B.; Cohn, S.; Wilson, William (dba Goldfish, Wilson & Co.)	Benjamin, A.	Assumpsit	6: 243	26 Jul 1887
1750	Schmitt, George	Ketelsen, Ocke & Burk, Julius	Attachment	6: 244	27 Jul 1887
1751	Farmers and Mechanics Bank of Healdsburg	Alexander, Charles; Alexander, Lawrence; Benjamin, George; Bledsoe, A. C.; Bledsoe, Linn; Bledsoe, Sophie; Bledsoe, Sally; Bouton, A.; Dow, George W.; Gladden, W. N.; Hassett, Aaron; Jacobs, G. H.; Jones, Charles; Lewis, R. E.; McClish, J. L.; McClish, John N.; Moore, C. P.; McClendon, W. J.; Stapp, I. N.; Stites, A. H.; Wright, B. F.; Wiedersheim, H.; Wisecarver, J. R.; Young, George; Kraft, E. H.; Nalley, A. B.; Barnes, E. H.; Hamilton, Emmor; Burnes, Thomas; Allen, W. T.; Proctor, Ira	At law	6: 246, 328	29 Jul 1887

226

Suit #	Plaintiffs	Defendants	Cause of Suit	Register of Actions Volume: page(s)	Action Date
1752	Savings Bank of Santa Rosa	Gleason, P. H.; Philips, Walter; Kelly, J. W.	Promissory note	6: 247	4 Aug 1887
1753	People	Bryant, John	Rape	6: 248	18 Jul 1887
1754	Petaluma Savings Bank	Thomson, F. M. (Adm. Est. J. P. Thomson) & Thomson, F. M.	Assumpsit	6: 249	8 Aug 1887
1755	Spaulding, Laura B.	Spaulding, Kimball D.	Divorce	6: 250	10 Aug 1887
1756	Hall, E. G.	Van Alen, William	Foreclosure of mechanic's lien	6: 251	10 Aug 1887
1757	Potter, C. H.		Application for writ of habeas corpus	6: 252	11 Aug 1887
1758	Meyer, Samuel	Raffee, Angello	Appeal	6: 255	22 Jun 1887
1759	Nay, S. A.	Winans, J. L.	Attachment	6: 256	13 Aug 1887
1759½	Wickersham, I. G.	Baldwin, J. T.	Assumpsit	6: 257	13 Aug 1887
1760	Ebers, Abbie A.	Ebers, Henry F.	Divorce	6: 258	16 Aug 1887
1761	Hutchings, Martha E.	Hutchings, Thomas R.	Divorce	6: 259	16 Aug 1887
1762	Santa Rosa & Carquinez Rail Road Co.	Tate, Frank	Condemnation for right of way	6: 260	18 Aug 1887
1763	Santa Rosa & Carquinez Rail Road Co.	McMackin, James & Kizer, A. N.	Condemnation for right of way	6: 261	18 Aug 1887
1764	Santa Rosa & Carquinez Rail Road Co.	Nordwell, O. W.		6: 262	18 Aug 1887
1765	Santa Rosa & Carquinez Rail Road Co.	Clark, R.	Condemnation for right of way	6: 263	19 Aug 1887
1766	Santa Rosa & Carquinez Rail Road Co.	Thierkoff, Frank G.; Thierkoff, M. A.; Sullivan, T. J.	Condemnation for right of way	6: 264	19 Aug 1887

Suit #	Plaintiffs	Defendants	Cause of Suit	Register of Actions Volume: page(s)	Action Date
1767	Santa Rosa & Carquinez Rail Road Co.	Gibson, John; Gibson, Ann Eliza; Humbolt Savings & Loan Society; Leavenworth, T. M.	Condemnation for right of way	6: 265	19 Aug 1887
1768	Santa Rosa & Carquinez Rail Road Co.	Tarrant, H. F.; Tarrant, Sophie Adele; Santa Rosa Bank	Condemnation for right of way	6: 266	19 Aug 1887
1769	Santa Rosa & Carquinez Rail Road Co.	Clarke, J. & Clarke, Charlotte F.	Condemnation for right of way	6: 267	19 Aug 1887
1770	Santa Rosa & Carquinez Rail Road Co.	Hudson, Alvin P.; Hudson, Bettie; Hudson, Mattie & Hudson, Lena (minors); McConnell, William E.	Condemnation for right of way	6: 268	20 Aug 1887
1771	Santa Rosa & Carquinez Rail Road Co.	Farmer, Rebekah W.; Fox, Sarah Angeline; Farmer, Charles Rollins; Farmer, Henry Thomas; Farmer, Francis May; Farmer, Lillie Belle & Farmer, C. C. (Trustee)		6: 269	20 Aug 1887
1772	Santa Rosa & Carquinez Rail Road Co.	Flint, Eugene; Campbell, Barbara; Flint, Purdy; McDonald, Emma; Cooper, Jennette; Harris, Granville; Cooper, Thomas S.; Cooper, John R. & Cooper, Thomas S. & Cooper, John R. (Executors Will Est. Sarah E. Harris)	Condemnation for right of way	6: 270	20 Aug 1887
1773	Santa Rosa & Carquinez Rail Road Co.	Brown, O. W., Jr. & Nordwell, O. W.	Condemnation for right of way	6: 271	20 Aug 1887
1774	Santa Rosa & Carquinez Rail Road Co.	Sonoma County Land & Improvement Co.; Decker, Peter E.; Jewett, J. H.; Jewett, M. M.	Condemnation for right of way	6: 272	31 Aug 1887
1775	Santa Rosa & Carquinez Rail Road Co.	Sonoma County Land & Improvement Co.; Decker, Peter E.; Jewett, J. H.; Jewett, M. M.	Condemnation for right of way	6: 273	31 Aug 1887

228

Suit #	Plaintiffs	Defendants	Cause of Suit	Register of Actions Volume: page(s)	Action Date
1776	Santa Rosa & Carquinez Rail Road Co.	Sonoma County Land & Improvement Co.; Decker, Peter E.; Jewett, J. H.; Jewett, M. M.	Condemnation for right of way	6: 274	31 Aug 1887
1777	Santa Rosa & Carquinez Rail Road Co.	Sonoma County Land & Improvement Co.; Decker, Peter E.; Jewett, J. H.; Jewett, M. M.	Condemnation for right of way	6: 275	31 Aug 1887
1778	Haskins, T. J. & Cadwell, J. A. (dba Haskins & Cadwell)		Involuntary insolvency	6: 276, 334; 9: 296	29 Aug 1887
1779	Kiser, Anton	McNeil, Elizabeth Ann Kennedy (Adm. Est. James Kennedy)	Equity	6: 277	29 Aug 1887
1780	People	Elliott, N. J.	Misdemeanor	6: 278	29 Aug 1887
1781	Schillingman, William	Tharp, J. W.	Assumpsit	6: 279	31 Aug 1887
1782	Devoto, David	Hardt, Henry William	Assumpsit	6: 280	2 Sep 1887
1783	Jones, John H.	Maguiness, Thomas	Assumpsit	6: 281	2 Sep 1887
1784	People	Bryant, John	Assault with intent to commit rape	6: 282	12 Aug 1887
1785	People	McCook, John	Murder	6: 283	12 Aug 1887
1786	Titus, I. S., Jr.		Voluntary insolvency	6: 284, 372	3 Sep 1887
1787	Cleary, Mike		Application for writ of habeas corpus	6: 285	5 Sep 1887
1788	McVay, Lucinda	McVay, James A. J.	Divorce	6: 286	6 Sep 1887
1789	Bohlin, Frank A.	Haehl, Conrad	Appeal	6: 287	6 Sep 1887
1790	Bank of Sonoma County	Turri, G. & Gambetta, G.	Assumpsit	6: 288	8 Sep 1887
1791	Ellsworth, L. G. & Ellsworth, H. L. (dba Ellsworth & Son)	Gummer, James	Assumpsit	6: 289	10 Sep 1887
1792	Waldier, Katie R.	Waldier, Charles	Divorce	6: 290	12 Sep 1887

229

Suit #	Plaintiffs	Defendants	Cause of Suit	Register of Actions Volume: page(s)	Action Date
1793	Glynn, Ellen	Hard, Estella A. & Hard, David T., her husband	Unlawful detainer	6: 291	12 Sep 1887
1794	Ivancovich, George	Case, A. B.	Appeal	6: 292	12 Sep 1887
1795	Manfredini, P.	Piffero, Benedetto & Piffero, Virginia	Appeal	6: 293	14 Sep 1887
1796	People	Rains, Jasper O'Farrell	Rape	6: 294	12 Aug 1887
1797	People	Behmer, Dan	Receiving bribe	6: 295	15 Sep 1887
1798	Millett, A. R.		Application for writ of habeas corpus	6: 296	15 Sep 1887
1799	Nanyoks, Annie M.	Hedges, W. H.; Tempel, C.; Lawrence, H. E.		6: 297	15 Sep 1887
1800	Hard, David T. & Hard, Estelle A., his wife	Glynn, Ellen	Injunction	6: 298	15 Sep 1887
1801	Shepherd, J. Avery	Tupper, George A. (Adm. Est. Evelyn Manro Shepherd)	To quiet title	6: 299	19 Sep 1887
1802	Handy, Philo & Johnson, D. T.	Yates, Charles H.	Injunction	6: 300	27 Sep 1887
1803	Santa Rosa & Carquinez Rail Road Co.	Furbee, T. J. & Buckland, C. J.	Condemnation	6: 301	28 Sep 1887
1804	Fernandez, Bernardo (Adm. Est. Francisco Silva)	McNear, George P.		6: 302	28 Sep 1887
1805	Black, Emma F. C.	Gurnett, A. G.; Hobart, Mary A.; Doe, John	Ejectment	6: 303; 7: 225	30 Sep 1887
1806	Pacific Benefit Association	Robertson, John T. & Whitson, Frank	Equity	6: 304	30 Sep 1887
1807	People	Behmer, Dan	Felony	6: 305	15 Sep 1887
1808	Gleason, Patrick H.		Voluntary insolvency	6: 306	3 Oct 1887
1809	Bailiff, John	Riley, P.	Appeal	6: 307	3 Oct 1887
1810	Hinz, A. & Landt, P. (dba Hinz & Landt)	Stewart, K. M. (Mrs.)	Appeal	6: 308	5 Oct 1887
1811	Snelson, John	Long, Isaac	Appeal	6: 309	3 Oct 1887
1812	Bliss, Alexander & Bliss, Ellen Louise (Executrix Last Will W. D. Bliss)	Allen, John		6: 310	7 Oct 1887
1813	Parsons, Isaac	Ludwig, Thomas J. & Hopper, Thomas	Foreclosure of mortgage	6: 311	7 Oct 1887

Suit #	Plaintiffs	Defendants	Cause of Suit	Register of Actions Volume: page(s)	Action Date
1814	Mitchell, C. E.		Application for writ of mandate against Town of Cloverdale	6: 312	7 Oct 1887
1815	Heilbron, August; Heilbron, Adolph; Clayburgh, Simon; Poly, Isaac; Clayburgh, Celia	Clarke, Charlotte F. (Guardian of Jeremiah Clarke) & Clarke, Charlotte F.	To compel conveyance	6: 313	10 Oct 1887
1816	Hinkston, Greenbury	O'Reilly, Martin; Overton, A. P.; Geary, Thomas J.; Hinkston, John	To compel conveyance	6: 314	10 Oct 1887
1817	Buscelle, James R.	Bihler, W.	At law	6: 315	10 Oct 1887
1818	Bank of Sonoma County	Kendall, John; Kendall, Maria K.; Kendall, Charles Elmer	Foreclosure of mortgage	6: 316	14 Oct 1887
1819	Stewart, K. M.		Involuntary insolvency	6: 317	15 Oct 1887
1820	Ingram, S. D.	Noethig, William		6: 318	17 Oct 1887
1821	Rennie, William	Hartman, Maggie V. (Adm. Est. Adolph Hartman); Hartman, Maggie V.; Hartman, Frederick; Hartman, Bertha; Hartman, Alice Maud; Hartman, Robert Charles; Hartman, Jennie H.	To quiet title	6: 319	22 Oct 1887
1822	Quinn, Margret	Quinn, John	Divorce	6: 320	24 Oct 1887
1823	Hopkins, S. J. & Perry, A. F.	Perry, James A. & Dryden, C. C.		6: 321	24 Oct 1887
1824	Hardt, Henry William		Voluntary insolvency	6: 322	24 Oct 1887
1825	Schocken, S.	Hard, David T.; Hard, Estella A.; Ames, Mary E.	Foreclosure of mortgage	6: 323	26 Oct 1887
1826	Spencer, Byron M.; Merriam, Nathan; Nason, Abner W.	Gray, Elizabeth; Wilson, J. H.; Wilson, Susan; Wilson, Nellie	To quiet title	6: 324	27 Oct 1887
1827	Manfredini, Pietro	Giovannini, Daniele	Libel	6: 325	27 Oct 1887
1828	Gossage, Rachel A. (Adm. Est. Jerome B. Gossage)	Carpenter, Calvin D.; Canfield, W. D.; Canfield, Sally Ann	Assumpsit	6: 326	28 Oct 1887

Suit #	Plaintiffs	Defendants	Cause of Suit	Register of Actions Volume: page(s)	Action Date
1829	Fitzpatrick, Andrew	Galagher, John	Injunction	6: 327, 376	28 Oct 1887
1830	Hardin, J. A.; Carr, J. D.; Brown, W. B.; Hershey, D. N.; Davis, M.; Wiles, J. M.	Pacific Methodist College, President & Board of Trustees of	Foreclosure	6: 329	31 Oct 1887
1831	Santa Rosa & Carquinez Rail Road Co.	Pierce, Henry	Condemnation for right of way	6: 330	7 Nov 1887
1832	Doyle, M.	Aiken, H. S.	Assumpsit	6: 331	10 Nov 1887
1833	Sonoma Valley Bank	Stofen, John J. & Stofen, Peter N.	Foreclosure of mortgage	6: 332	10 Nov 1887
1834	Cannon, R. D.		Application for writ of habeas corpus	6: 333	11 Nov 1887
1835	People	Owens, George	Misdemeanor	6: 335	12 Nov 1887
1836	People	Giles, Grant & Orris, William	Burglary	6: 336	12 Nov 1887
1837	Bernhard, Isaac & Bernhard, Jacob (dba Bernhard & Son)	Bryan, Elizabeth	Petition for appointment of appraisers	6: 337	14 Nov 1887
1838	Holmes, Edward	Holmes, William; Duval, Lucy; Main, Medora; Holmes, Frederick A.; Witham, Josephine	Partition	6: 338	14 Nov 1887
1839	Glynn, F. B.	Paul, H. C.	Account	6: 339	17 Nov 1887
1840	Bazoni, Louis		Application for writ of habeas corpus	6: 340	21 Nov 1887
1841	Perry, William	Bishop, T. C.	At law	6: 341	21 Nov 1887
1842	O'Reilly, Martin	James Clark & Sons	Account	6: 342; 7: 210	21 Nov 1887
1843	Dickson, William M.		Voluntary insolvency	6: 343	21 Nov 1887
1844	McDonogh, Thomas		Voluntary insolvency	6: 344	28 Nov 1887

232

Suit #	Plaintiffs	Defendants	Cause of Suit	Register of Actions Volume: page(s)	Action Date
1845	Schierhold, Herman & Wohlers, Theodor (dba Schierhold & Wohlers)		Voluntary insolvency	6: 345	29 Nov 1887
1846	Savings Bank of Santa Rosa	Bailiff, J. & Reed, J. H.		6: 346	30 Nov 1887
1847	Fairbanks, Levina	Fairbanks, Frank & Fairbanks, Mary	Divorce	6: 347	2 Dec 1887
1848	Colgan, E. P. (Sheriff of Sonoma County)	Sonoma, County of	Appeal	6: 348	30 Nov 1887
1849	Tighe, Thomas W. (Constable of Santa Rosa Township)	Sonoma, County of	Appeal	6: 349	30 Nov 1887
1850	People	Mendosa, S. & Walsh, David	Burglary	6: 350	1 Dec 1887
1851	People	Morrow, Robert F.	Felony	6: 351	5 Dec 1887
1852	Lodge, J. D.	Newby, H. C.; Newby, Carrie; Hassett, Sarah E. (Adm. Est. John D. Hassett)	Foreclosure	6: 352	5 Dec 1887
1853	Elliott, N. J.		Application for writ of habeas corpus	6: 353	6 Dec 1887
1854	Wilson, John	Wilson, Emma Jane	Divorce	6: 354	9 Dec 1887
1855	Hornick, John	Bishop, T. C. (ex officio Sheriff of Sonoma County)	Appeal	6: 355	12 Dec 1887
1856	Tunzi, Giuseppi		Voluntary insolvency	6: 356	12 Dec 1887
1857	Allen, John		Voluntary insolvency	6: 357	14 Dec 1887
1858	Morrow, E. E.	Barnes, H. L. & Frazee, C. DeWitt	Foreclosure of mechanic's lien	6: 358, 373	14 Dec 1887
1859	Berka, F.	Barnes, H. L. & Frazee, C. DeWitt	Foreclosure of mechanic's lien	6: 359	17 Dec 1887
1860	Kroncke, H.; Ludwig, T. J.; Berka, F. (dba Santa Rosa Planing Mill & Building Co.)	Frazee, C. D. & Barnes, H. L.	Foreclosure of mechanic's lien	6: 360	17 Dec 1887
1861	Lambert, W. S.	Lambert, Caroline V.; Lavell, Jane; Gibson, Emma; Lambert, R. F.; Lambert, C. E.; Lambert, George L.	Partition	6: 361	19 Dec 1887

Suit #	Plaintiffs	Defendants	Cause of Suit	Register of Actions Volume: page(s)	Action Date
1862	Baldwin, John T.		Voluntary insolvency	6: 362	19 Dec 1887
1863	Torliatt, Peter	Merian, Louis	Equity	6: 363	29 Dec 1887
1864	Farmer, Charles R.	Fox, Sarah Angeline; Farmer, Henry Thomas; Farmer, Francis May; Farmer, Lillie Bell; Farmer, C. C. (Trustee)	Partition	6: 366	27 Dec 1887
1865	People	Brander, F.	Misdemeanor	6: 367	27 Dec 1887
1866	Chauvet, J.	Hill, William McPherson	Injunction	7: 1	3 Jan 1888
1867	Rogers, Ethan L.		Application for writ of habeas corpus	7: 2	3 Jan 1888
1868	Lord, Eva I.	Lord, Charles A.	Divorce	7: 3	4 Jan 1888
1869	Pfister, Conrad	Tupper, G. A. & Tupper, Harriet E.	Lien	7: 4	5 Jan 1888
1870	Baxter, T. P. & Grenn, Paul F. (dba Baxter & Green)	Barnes, H. L. & Frazee, C. D.	Foreclosure of material man's lien	7: 5	7 Jan 1888
1871	Robertson, Albert		Application for writ of habeas corpus	7: 6	9 Jan 1888
1872	Coolbroth, S. W. & Coolbroth, Hattie, his wife	Williams, George H.	Damages	7: 7	11 Jan 1888
1873	Philips, Edward	Day, Edwin	Damages	7: 8	12 Jan 1888
1874	People	Robertson, Albert B.	Assault with a deadly weapon with intent to murder	7: 9	13 Jan 1888
1875	Edwards, Ben	Shafter, P. J.	Appeal	6: 369	19 Dec 1887
1876	Blume, Julius	Colgan, E. P.	Appeal	6: 370	19 Dec 1887
1877	Santa Rosa & Carquinez Rail Road Co.	Doyle, M.	Condemnation for right of way	7: 10	16 Jan 1888

234

Suit #	Plaintiffs	Defendants	Cause of Suit	Register of Actions Volume: page(s)	Action Date
1878	Tucker, Morgan G.	Tucker, Mary E.	Divorce	7:11	18 Jan 1888
1879	Wright, Fannie L.	Wright, Sampson B.	Divorce	7:12	18 Jan 1888
1880	Stuart, Anabel McGaughey (Executrix Est. Absalom B. Stuart)	Simmons, John R. & Simmons, Elizabeth	Foreclosure of mortgage	7:13	21 Jan 1888
1881	Tucker, Morgan G.	Carrie, J. A.; Mitchell, C. E.; Goetzelman, John; Hoadley, J. F., Jr.; Leitch, John; Casey, L. J.; Markell, R. S.	Damages	7:14	26 Jan 1888
1882	Wellman, William B. & Wellman, Ruth A. (Executors Last Will & Testament Bela Wellman)	Tilley, William J. (Executor Last Will & Testament J. H. Whitman); Doe, Jane; Roe, Richard; Yellow, John	Foreclosure of mortgage	7:15	28 Jan 1888
1883	Kellogg, C. W.	Colgan, E. P. (Sheriff of Sonoma County)	At law	7:16, 305	30 Jan 1888
1884	Lippitt, E. S.	Bradbury, Mrs. & Starke & Edwards	Ejectment	7:17	31 Jan 1888
1885	McGarvey, R.	Lilienthal, J. Leo & Lilienthal, E. R. (dba Lilienthal & Co.)		7:18	4 Feb 1888
1886	Methodist Episcopal Church South, Trustees of		Application to sell real estate	7:19	6 Feb 1888
1887	Kennady, D.	Clark, A.	Appeal	7:20	6 Feb 1888
1888	Tuomey, Catharine	Tuomey, B.	Divorce	7:21	9 Feb 1888
1889	Casarotti, M.	North Pacific Coast Railroad Company	Appeal	7:22	11 Feb 1888
1890	Merchant, Joel	Colgan, E. P. (Sheriff of Sonoma County)	Appeal	7:23	11 Feb 1888
1891	Skaggs, A.	Wickersham, Fred A.	Appeal	7:24	11 Feb 1888
1892	Bloomer, William & Bloomer, Elizabeth	Central California Land Exchange	Cancellation of contract	7:25	13 Feb 1888
1893	Sonoma, County of	Barry, Julia	Condemnation for road way	7:26	15 Feb 1888
1894	Hopkins, S. J.	Hall, George; Hall, Carrie E.; McNear, George P.; McNear, John A.; Petaluma Savings Bank	Foreclosure of mechanic's lien	7:27	15 Feb 1888
1895	People	Juan, Louie (an Indian)	Murder	7:28	15 Feb 1888
1896	Chamberlain, David	Trosper, Thomas	Correction of mortgage	7:29	16 Feb 1888

235

Suit #	Plaintiffs	Defendants	Cause of Suit	Register of Actions Volume: page(s)	Action Date
1897	Wellman, William B. & Wellman, Ruth A. (Executors Last Will & Testament Bela Wellman)	Tilley, William J. (Executor Last Will & Testament Joseph H. Whitman); Doe, Jane; Roe, Richard; Yellow, John	Foreclosure of mortgage	7: 30	17 Feb 1888
1898	Park, George W.	Frazee, D. C. & Barnes, -	Foreclosure of mechanic's lien	7: 31	20 Feb 1888
1899	McNear, George P.	Mecartny, A.	To quiet title	7: 32	20 Feb 1888
1900	Rule, Elizabeth & Rule, Charles H. S.	Rule Mill Lumber, Wood & Tan-bark Association	At law	7: 33	23 Feb 1888
1901	Mead, Sarah J.	Mead, William E.	Divorce	7: 34	23 Feb 1888
1902	Hall, J. E.; Hall, O. M., his wife; Hall, J. E. (Adm. Estates Winnie Wright Hall & Olive Edna Hall); Robertson, Sarah Jessie & Robertson, James Calhoun (minors by their guardian William A. Robertson)	DeTurk, Isaac	Injunction	7: 35	27 Feb 1888
1903	Stormes, Mattie	Stormes, S. H.	Divorce	7: 36	28 Feb 1888
1904	Hall, J. E.; Hall, O. M., his wife; Hall, J. E. (Adm. Estates Winnie Wright Hall & Olive Edna Hall); Robertson, Sarah Jessie & Robertson, James Calhoun (minors by their guardian William A. Robertson)	Santa Rosa, City of	Injunction	7: 37, 109	5 Mar 1888
1905	Perry, John R.	Morrow, E. E.; Berka, F.; Santa Rosa Planing Mill & Building Co.; Glynn, F. B.; Park, George W.; Baxter & Green; Bell, S. S.; Latson, F. P.; Wilson Bros.; Frazee, C. D.; Barnes, H. L.	Foreclosure of mechanic's lien	7: 38	5 Mar 1888
1906	Casassa, Domenico	Gardella, C. L.; Gardella, Caterna; Gardella, Lorenzo	Assumpsit	7: 39	6 Mar 1888
1907	Morey, Almeda		Application for writ of prohibition	7: 40	6 Mar 1888
1908	Santa Rosa Manufacturing Company		Dissolution	7: 41	8 Mar 1888
1909	Miller, George T.	McMillen, Henry	Injunction	7: 42	8 Mar 1888
1910	Tomblinson, John	Cassassi, D.	Appeal	7: 43	27 Feb 1888

236

Suit #	Plaintiffs	Defendants	Cause of Suit	Register of Actions Volume: page(s)	Action Date
1911	Cooper, John D.	Hardt, Henry W.; Hardt, Augusta; Raschen, John Frederick; Colgan, E. P. (Assignee Est. Henry W. Hardt, insolvent debtor)	Foreclosure of mortgage	7:44	14 Mar 1888
1912	Donegan, Joseph		Application for writ of habeas corpus	7:45	14 Mar 1888
1913	Wheeler, Jacob	Frazer, G. W.	Contract	7:46	16 Mar 1888
1914	Perrin, E. B.; Thornton, George F.; Cheape, George C.	Coffey, Henry		7:47	16 Mar 1888
1915	Solomon, Arthur	Grosse, Guy E.	To cancel instruments & damages	7:48	17 Mar 1888
1916	Heeser, August	Heeser, William	At law	7:49	21 Mar 1888
1917	Bank of Healdsburg	Givens, R. R.	Foreclosure of mortgage	7:50	23 Mar 1888
1918	Percival Milling Company		Application to change its corporate name	7:51	26 Mar 1888
1919	Santa Rosa Water Works Company	Colwell, Charles Y.	Injunction	7:52	26 Mar 1888
1920	People	Carr, James	Resisting a public officer	7:53	28 Mar 1888
1921	People	Philips, H. (alias Philips, E.)	Misdemeanor	7:54	28 Mar 1888
1922	Clover, Amanda	Norton, W. M.	To renew judgment	7:55	28 Mar 1888
1923	Fritsch, John	Finch, Ziba & Finch, R.	Assumpsit	7:56	31 Mar 1888
1924	Benson, Josiah H.	Bryan, Elizabeth; Bryan, Thomas W.; Bryan, Frederick J.; Muller, Mary; Muller, John, her husband; Bryan, Kate; King, N.; Bernhard, I.	Foreclosure of mortgage	7:57	2 Apr 1888
1925	Lowe, Jennie Elizabeth	Lowe, George Frederick	Divorce	7:58	2 Apr 1888

237

Suit #	Plaintiffs	Defendants	Cause of Suit	Register of Actions Volume: page(s)	Action Date
1926	Campbell, Eliza Ann (Adm. Est. Joseph H. Campbell)	Moulton, William M. & Moulton, Kate D.	To renew judgment	7: 59	2 Apr 1888
1927	Perinoni, Filippo		Voluntary insolvency	7: 60	3 Apr 1888
1928	Murray, Georgiana & Lyndup, P.	Decker, Phoebe M. (Adm. Est. Henry Decker)	Equity	7: 61	4 Apr 1888
1929	King, George F.	Chandler, W. R.	Appeal	7: 62	27 Mar 1888
1930	Ward, Charles H.		Insolvency	7: 63	16 Apr 1888
1931	Kennedy, George H.	Kennedy, Nancy A.	Divorce	7: 64	20 Apr 1888
1932	Hill, William	Colgan, E. P.	Conversion	7: 65	27 Apr 1888
1933	Merchant, Fred H.	Case, A. B. & Dougherty, S. K.	Claim & delivery	7: 66	27 Apr 1888
1934	Wilsey, H.	Helman, H. H. & Helman, William	Promissory note	7: 67	6 Apr 1888
1935	Romine, Mary	Cralle, L. J. & Hirschler, Ed.	Promissory note	7: 68, 187	10 Apr 1888
1936	Page, C. A.	Cannon, R. B.	Appeal	7: 69	30 Apr 1888
1937	Norton, W. H.	Morgan, G. W. & Morgan, W. C.	Appeal	7: 70	30 Apr 1888
1938	Totten, Samuel	Morgan, G. W. & Morgan, W. C.	Appeal	7: 71	30 Apr 1888
1939	Whitney, C. L.	Gardner, H. & Gardner, Clement	Appeal	7: 72	1 May 1888
1940	Ogilvie, John	Brown, William S.	Attachment	7: 73	1 May 1888
1941	McNear, George P.	Claassen, J. P.	Ejectment	7: 74	4 May 1888
1942	Sonoma, County of	Welch, Matilda	Condemnation for right of way	7: 75	11 May 1888
1943	Ridgway, Joseph W.	O'Rear, W. E. & White, J. M.		7: 76	12 May 1888
1944	Merchant, Joel		Voluntary insolvency	7: 77	14 May 1888
1945	Breen, Mary E.	Breen, James H.	Divorce	7: 78	16 May 1888
1946	Martin, Ezekiel	Martin, Mary	Divorce	7: 79	19 May 1888
1947	Sonoma Valley Improvement Company	Clark, Jeremiah	To quiet title	7: 80	21 May 1888

238

Suit #	Plaintiffs	Defendants	Cause of Suit	Register of Actions Volume: page(s)	Action Date
1948	Demetz, Annie J.	Demetz, Henry	Divorce	7: 81	22 May 1888
1949	Fox, Lucretia T.	Meinzer, Antoine	Equity	7: 82	22 May 1888
1950	People	Frey, Joseph	Murder	7: 83	21 May 1888
1951	People	Starger, Andrew	Grand larceny	7: 84	21 May 1888
1952	Furlong, James; Goodman, L. S.; Byrne, Thomas	North Pacific Coast Rail Road Company	Damages	7: 85	25 May 1888
1953	Knowles, D. C.	North Pacific Coast Rail Road Company	Damages	7: 86	25 May 1888
1954	Gardella, C. L. & Gardella, Caterina	Casassa, Domenico	Equity	7: 87, 204; 8: 182	25 May 1888
1955	Cannon, B. H.	Cannon, Charles H.	Divorce	7: 88	28 May 1888
1956	Sterger, Andrew (By R. M. Swain)		Application for writ of habeas corpus	7: 89	28 May 1888
1957	O'Reilly, Martin & Hinkston, Joseph	Hinkston, Greenbury	Partition	7: 90	28 May 1888
1958	Duffy, Mary E.	Duffy, Thomas	Divorce	7: 91	2 Jun 1888
1959	Lambert, Jennie King	Lambert, C. E.	Divorce	7: 92	4 Jun 1888
1960	Williams, C. B.	Woods, Isaac; Woods, John Doe; Vestal, Louis	Foreclosure of mechanic's lien	7: 93	4 Jun 1888
1961	Bulotti, V.	McDonell, Maggie (Mrs.) (widow of R. A. McDonell); McDonell, John; McDonell, Mary (daughter of Donald McDonell); McDonell, McDonell, Margery; McDonell, Bell; McDonell, Nancy; McDonell, Christy; McDonell, Alexander (son of Donald McDonell); Kennedy, Flora; Kennedy, Catharine; McDonell, Flora; McDonell, Maggie; McDonell, Mary J. (daughter of G. A. McDonell); McDonell, Alexander (son of G. A. McDonell); McDonell, Donald (son of G. A. McDonell)	Partition	7: 94, 184	6 Jun 1888
1962	Byington, Walter	Nichols, W. K.	Appeal	7: 95	7 Jun 1888
1963	Kelly, C. A.	Smith, W. S.	Appeal	7: 96	11 Jun 1888
1964	Dillon, Margaret G.	Dillon, M. C.	Divorce	7: 97	12 Jun 1888
1965	Cleary, Michael	Cleary, Bridget	Divorce	7: 98	13 Jun 1888

Suit #	Plaintiffs	Defendants	Cause of Suit	Register of Actions Volume: page(s)	Action Date
1966	Temple, Conrad	Phariss, P. H.	Promissory note	7:99	18 Jun 1888
1967	People	Thorn, Frank	Grand larceny	7:100	19 Jun 1888
1968	People	Samuels, James & Samuels, Jennie	Grand larceny	7:101	19 Jun 1888
1969	People	Leroy, Oscar	Counterfeiting	7:102	19 Jun 1888
1970	People	Starger, Andrew	Grand larceny	7:103	20 Jun 1888
1971	People	Coli, Michael	Murder	7:104	25 Jun 1888
1972	Zane, A. J.	Sponogle, F. M.	Appeal	7:105	25 Jun 1888
1973	Collins, F. M.	Fine, Emsley	Dissolution of co-partnership	7:106	28 Jun 1888
1974	Burling, George W.		Voluntary insolvency	7:107	5 Jul 1888
1975	Lambert, Jennie King	Lambert, C. E.	Divorce	7:108	6 Jul 1888
1976	Hall, J. E.; Hall, O. M., his wife; Hall, J. E. (Adm. Estates Winnie Wright Hall & Olive Edna Hall); Robertson, Sarah Jessie & Robertson, James Calhoun (minors by their guardian William A. Robertson)	Santa Rosa, City of	Injunction & damages	7:109	12 Jul 1888
1977	Decker, Phoebe M.	Decker, Henry (Estate of)	At law	7:110	14 Jul 1888
1978	Norton, L. A.	Berner, Robert; Wagele, Conrad; Feldmeyer, B. W.; Stamner, Julius Caesar; Schnicker, -	Ejectment	7:111	16 Jul 1888
1979	Schlicker, Frederick	Schmitt, George	At law	7:112	24 Jul 1888
1980	Ling, Ah		Application for writ of habeas corpus	7:113	28 Jul 1888
1981	Hong, Ah		Application for writ of habeas corpus	7:114	28 Jul 1888
1982	Toy, Ah; Sim, Ah; Sam, Ah; Lowe, Ah		Application for writ of habeas corpus	7:115	1 Aug 1888

Suit #	Plaintiffs	Defendants	Cause of Suit	Register of Actions Volume: page(s)	Action Date
1983	People	McElarney, Jim (an Indian) & Dick (an Indian)	Murder	7: 116	2 Aug 1888
1984	Patterson, William	Patterson, Mary	Divorce	7: 117	3 Aug 1888
1985	St. Clair, Nancy E. (Executrix Last Will & Testament Frank C. St. Clair)	McPherson, Early (a minor); Hall, L. J. (Guardian of Est. Early McPherson); Gird, Henry S. (Guardian of Person of Early McPherson)	At law	7: 118	4 Aug 1888
1986	Williams, Elizabeth	Williams, Frank	Divorce	7: 119	4 Aug 1888
1987	Lang, Ah		Application for writ of habeas corpus	7: 120	7 Aug 1888
1988	McPherson, Miller	McPherson, Colborn; McPherson, Lycurgus; McPherson, Ewell; McPherson, Early; McPherson, Annie; McPherson, Mary; Simmons, James Sylvester; McDaniel, Oliver; Gird, Henry S. (Guardian of Person & Est. Ewell McPherson, a minor); Gird, H. S. (Guardian of Person of Early McPherson, a minor); Hall, L. J. (Guardian of the Persons and Estates of Mary McPherson, Annie McPherson & James Sylvester Simmons, minors); Hall, L. J. (Guardian Est. Early McPherson, a minor)	Partition	7: 121, 186	9 Aug 1888
1989	Arizona Lumber Company	Meeker, M. C.; Meeker, A. P.; Buna, George		7: 122	9 Aug 1888
1990	Moore, Ellen; Moore, James E.; Morrow, Ellen C.; Moore, Charles; Moore, William; Moore, Anastasia; Joyce, Mary F.	Carpenter, Alice (Adm. Est. L. F. Carpenter); Carpenter, Alice; Durie, Frankie E.; Carpenter, Alice M.; Carpenter, S. E.	Equity	7: 123	13 Aug 1988
1991	Mitchell, Margaret A.	Mitchell, Linwood W.	Divorce	7: 124	17 Aug 1888
1992	Cronin, P.	Millerick, John	Assumpsit	7: 125	20 Aug 1888
1993	Cronin, P.	Millerick, M. & Millerick, John	Assumpsit	7: 126	20 Aug 1888
1994	Jamison, Anne Jane		Application for restoration to capacity	7: 127	17 Aug 1888

241

Suit #	Plaintiffs	Defendants	Cause of Suit	Register of Actions Volume: page(s)	Action Date
1995	Lang, Ah		Application for writ of habeas corpus	7: 128	24 Aug 1888
1996	Toon, Ah		Application for writ of habeas corpus	7: 129	24 Aug 1888
1997	Ross, James Edwin	Conway, John M. (Pastor of Roman Catholic Church of Santa Rosa); Noonan, George P.; Hyde, Patrick; Noonan, Patrick H.; Noonan, Alice & Noonan, Frank (minors)	To set aside deed	7: 130, 159, 281	29 Aug 1888
1998	Lynch, Ellen	Carr, Mary E. & Gwinn, John E.		7: 131	3 Sep 1888
1999	Jamison, Anne Jane	Jamison, William Jacob	Divorce	7: 132	4 Sep 1888
2000	Poehlman, Conrad (Trustee for creditors of Thomas Cadden)	Cadden, Thomas & Cadden, Catherine	Foreclosure of mortgage	7: 133	7 Sep 1888
2001	Hopper, Thomas	Kelly, Timothy	Foreclosure of mortgage	7: 134	5 Sep 1888
2002	Barker, C. A.	Kennedy, E. H.; Wetmore, W. P.; Knowles, W. A.; Moody, W. B. (dba Summit Mills); Wetmore, J. L.	Foreclosure of logger's lien	7: 135	12 Sep 1888
2003	Williams, George R.	Powers, David P. & Powers, Lottie, his wife	Foreclosure of mortgage	7: 136	12 Sep 1888
2004	Pfister, Conrad	McDonald, Mark L.	At law	7: 137	14 Sep 1888
2005	Tivnen, John (Pub. Adm. Sonoma County & Adm. Est. Pierce Ryan)	Stapleton, Patrick; Morrison, Thomas; Harris, Richard	At law	7: 138	15 Sep 1888
2006	Wright, Samson B.	Wright, Fannie L.	Divorce	7: 139	15 Sep 1888
2007	Byrne, Joseph (Surviving Executor Last Will & Testament Matthew Reed)	Reed, Michael & Reed, Bridget	Equity	7: 140	17 Sep 1888
2008	Hopper, Thomas	Holmes, Henderson P. & Holmes, Rebecca M.	Foreclosure of mortgage	7: 141	18 Sep 1888
2009	Metzger, Joseph E.		Voluntary insolvency	7: 142	18 Sep 1888

Suit #	Plaintiffs	Defendants	Cause of Suit	Register of Actions Volume: page(s)	Action Date
2010	Wood, Ben S.	Pieper, Leon	Appeal	7: 143	15 Sep 1888
2011	People	Algreen, John; Murphy, H. E.; Murphy, J. E.	Burglary	7: 144	18 Sep 1888
2012	Linebaugh, A.	Doss, J. W. & Doss, John R.	Assumpsit	7: 145	24 Sep 1888
2013	Casassa, D.	Gardella, C. L. & Gardella, Catarina	Injunction	7: 146	27 Sep 1888
2014	Green, William S.	Kennedy, George H.	To reform deed	7: 147	29 Sep 1888
2015	Leppo, D.	Ingham, A. H.		7: 148	1 Oct 1888
2016	Auradon, J.	Clark, A. N. & Mecartney, A.	Foreclosure of mortgage	7: 149	2 Oct 1888
2017	Marcy, J. G.	Sonoma Valley Land Company; Cady, M. K.; Cady, Gail, his wife	Foreclosure of mechanic's lien	7: 150	2 Oct 1888
2018	Wilson, W. P.	Sonoma Valley Land Company; Cady, M. K.; Cady, Gail, his wife	Foreclosure of mechanic's lien	7: 151	2 Oct 1888
2019	Savings Bank of Santa Rosa	Rutherford, R. H.	Foreclosure of mortgage	7: 152	2 Oct 1888
2020	Santa Rosa Gas Light Company		Dissolution	7: 153	3 Oct 1888
2021	Pfister, Conrad	McDonald, Mark L.		7: 154	3 Oct 1888
2022	People	Walsh, David & Mendosa, Cerilda	Arson	7: 155	27 Sep 1888
2023	People	Lee, Joe Wah	Appeal	7: 156	28 Sep 1888
2023½	Ingham, A. H.		Insolvency	7: 157	9 Oct 1888
2024	People	Stein, Henry	Burglary	7: 158	20 Oct 1888
2025	Cloverdale, Town of (by L. J. Casey, Marshall)	Mitchell, C. E.	Appeal	7: 160	13 Oct 1888
2026	People	Mehan, Daniel	Burglary	7: 161	29 Oct 1888
2027	Bank of Healdsburg	Hitchcock, Hollis		7: 162	3 Nov 1888
2028	Hall, J. E.	Santa Rosa Street Rail Road Company	Appeal	7: 163	1 Nov 1888
2029	Shea, Con	Sheward, D.; Harris, Jacob; Bishop, T. C.; Warner, James; Burger, C. H.	Attachment	7: 164	9 Oct 1888

243

Suit #	Plaintiffs	Defendants	Cause of Suit	Register of Actions Volume: page(s)	Action Date
2030	Gardner, John W.	Ames, Mary Ann; Ames, George; Ames, John F.; Ames, Isabella; Ames, Charles S.; Marshall, Lucy A.; Hubbell, Phoebe E.	To quiet title	7: 165	15 Oct 1888
2031	Laughlin, J. M.	Ingram, I. J.	Account	7: 166	20 Oct 1888
2032	Ramsey, Rebecca L.	Ramsey, William H.	Divorce	7: 167	23 Oct 1888
2033	Farmers and Mechanics Bank of Healdsburg	Keith, A. D.		7: 168	22 Oct 1888
2034	Murdock, L. A. (Adm. Est. L. J. Hawkins)	Hawkins, D. S.		7: 169	26 Oct 1888
2035	Newby, H. C.		Application for writ of habeas corpus	7: 170	27 Oct 1888
2036	Shetland, Edward		Application for writ of habeas corpus	7: 171	27 Oct 1888
2037	Pabst, Cora	Pabst, George	Divorce	7: 172	31 Oct 1888
2038	Dinwiddie, J. L.	Shores, Leander (Adm. Est. Henry R. Fowler)		7: 173	5 Nov 1888
2039	People	Mize, Fred & Mize, John	Assault to murder	7: 174, 221	5 Nov 1888
2040	People	Mize, John	Assault	7: 175	5 Nov 1888
2041	People	Mize, John	Assault with intent to commit murder	7: 176	5 Nov 1888
2042	Seawell, Joseph	Colgan, E. P.		7: 177	8 Nov 1888
2043	Eldred, Nancy E.	Hoffer, Charles A. (Adm.)	To quiet title	7: 178	8 Nov 1888
2044	Good, Walter C.	Thorne, Mary A.	Attachment	7: 179	10 Nov 1888
2045	Robbins, Abigail S.	Robbins, George H.	Divorce	7: 180	12 Nov 1888
2046	Williams, Benjamin F.	Ross, Frank		7: 181	13 Nov 1888
2047	Mason, Frank L.	Mason, Jennie F.	Divorce	7: 182	14 Nov 1888
2048	Savings Bank of Santa Rosa	Hoskins, T. D.; Thompson, Thomas L.; Baggett, N. P.; Harris, Jacob; Pressley, John G.		7: 183	15 Nov 1888

244

Suit #	Plaintiffs	Defendants	Cause of Suit	Register of Actions Volume: page(s)	Action Date
2049	People	Hall, Henry G.	Burglary	7: 185	17 Nov 1888
2050	Finley, Henry M.	Finley, Cynthia J.		7: 188	16 Nov 1888
2051	Good, Walter C.	Thorne, Mary A. (formerly Morey, Mary A.)		7: 189	26 Nov 1888
2052	People	Keegan, Timothy	Assault to murder	7: 190	3 Dec 1888
2053	People	Butner, Joseph & Wilson, Henry	Burglary	7: 191	6 Dec 1888
2054	People	Butner, Joseph & Wilson, Henry	Grand larceny	7: 192	6 Dec 1888
2055	Savings Bank of Santa Rosa	Holmes, H. P. & Warner, James	Promissory note	7: 193	30 Nov 1888
2056	Hansen, Susie	Hansen, A.	Divorce	7: 194	26 Nov 1888
2057	Dabner, Anton		Voluntary insolvency	7: 195	24 Nov 1888
2058	Piatt, George A.	Colgan, E. P. (Sheriff)		7: 196	1 Dec 1888
2059	McFarland, Margret	McFarland, John	Divorce	7: 197	3 Dec 1888
2060	People	Mitchell, C. E.	Appeal	7: 198	20 Nov 1888
2061	Sonoma County Stock Breeders' Association	Regan, James C.		7: 199	1 Dec 1888
2062	Piatt, J. P.		Voluntary insolvency	7: 200	10 Dec 1888
2063	Ducker, Sarah	Brooks, Rebecca & Brooks, Silas	Foreclosure of mortgage	7: 201	1 Dec 1888
2064	Elphick, Thomas A.	Elphick, Anna M.	Divorce	7: 202	12 Dec 1888
2065	Ross, James Edwin	Conway, John M.	Damages	7: 203	10 Dec 1888
2066	Barnett, J. D.	Davis, Preston	Promissory note	7: 204	11 Dec 1888
2067	Edwards, John L.; Young, John D.; Hodgson, David R.	Carlton, Rachel E. (formerly Vanlaningham, Rachel E.); Carlton, Lulu; Carlton, Fannie	To quiet title	7: 205	10 Dec 1888
2068	Sonoma Valley Bank	Weyl, Henry (Adm. Est. Attila Haraszthy); Haraszthy, Natalia; Haraszthy, Mariano J.; Haraszthy, Augustin (a minor); Haraszthy, Elenora (a minor); Haraszthy, Natalia (a minor)	Foreclosure of mortgage	7: 206	17 Dec 1888

Suit #	Plaintiffs	Defendants	Cause of Suit	Register of Actions Volume: page(s)	Action Date
2069	Cooley, Mary A.	Young, Charles H.		7: 207	17 Dec 1888
2070	Hill, William	Easter, George W.		7: 208	10 Dec 1888
2071	Timms, Ann	Smith, W. B.	Appeal	7: 209	20 Dec 1888
2072	People	Bennet, John	Burglary	7: 211	2 Jan 1889
2073	People	Bennet, John	Burglary	7: 212	2 Jan 1889
2074	Connell, John	Millerick, John	Promissory note	7: 213	27 Dec 1888
2075	Hitchcock, Hollis	Cerini, John		7: 214	3 Jan 1889
2076	Cunningham, John	Cunningham, Susanah	Divorce	7: 215	4 Jan 1889
2077	McNamara, James	Brown, H. C. (Adm.)		7: 216	5 Jan 1889
2078	Miller, John H. (by George F. Miller)		Application for writ of habeas corpus	7: 217	3 Jan 1889
2079	Weill, D. H.	Davis, Jennie	Promissory note	7: 218	10 Jan 1889
2080	Bank of Healdsburg	Mulligan, William & Mulligan, Margaret	Foreclosure of mortgage	7: 219	12 Jan 1889
2081	Anderson, Elizabeth	Burris, John F.	Foreclosure	7: 220	12 Jan 1889
2082	People	Todd, William S.	Burglary	7: 222	17 Jan 1889
2083	People	Todd, William S.	Arson	7: 223	17 Jan 1889
2084	Favour, John	Braman, J. J.	Foreclosure of mortgage	7: 224	18 Jan 1889
2085	Deal, - & Davis, - (dba Deal & Davis)		Involuntary insolvency	7: 226	26 Jan 1889
2086	Matthies, Lina	Tobin, Edward	Ejectment	7: 227	28 Jan 1889
2087	McCoy, Charles L.	Delanoy, Mary Frances & Delanoy, Fred. N.	Foreclosure of mortgage	7: 228	2 Feb 1889
2088	Ursuline Community		Application to mortgage real estate	7: 229	4 Feb 1889

Suit #	Plaintiffs	Defendants	Cause of Suit	Register of Actions Volume: page(s)	Action Date
2089	Savings Bank of Santa Rosa	Totton, Samuel	Foreclosure of mortgage	7: 230	4 Feb 1889
2090	Beckner, Lillie Ethel		Application for writ of habeas corpus	7: 231	9 Feb 1889
2091	Branch, George B.	Branch, Louise J.	Divorce	7: 233	12 Feb 1889
2092	Boyes, H. E. & Boyes, A. C., his wife	Maxwell, George H. & Verano Land Company		7: 234	14 Feb 1889
2093	Bailey, S. N.	Hicks, G. M.	Foreclosure of mortgage	7: 235	16 Feb 1889
2094	Bank of Healdsburg	Hall, E. G. & Ellis, L. G.	Promissory note	7: 236	16 Feb 1889
2095	Mutch, Isabella	Pipher, Philip	Foreclosure of mortgage	7: 237	20 Feb 1889
2096	Piatt, A.	Colgan, E. P.	Appeal	7: 238	21 Feb 1889
2097	Call, G. W.	North Coast Stage Company; Schroyer, A.; Quen, C.; Harmon, E. N.; Kruse, E.		7: 239	23 Feb 1889
2098	Barnes, Aaron	Goodrich, James H. & Glenn, Robert	Foreclosure of mortgage	7: 240	2 Mar 1889
2099	Santa Rosa Bank	Dillan, James & Dillan, M. C.	Foreclosure of mortgage	7: 241	5 Mar 1889
2100	Linebaugh, R. A.	Linebaugh, Emma	Divorce	7: 242	5 Mar 1889
2101	Sonoma, County of	Wehrspon, A.		7: 243	8 Mar 1889
2102	People	Genesi, Louis	Obtaining money by false pretenses	7: 244	4 Mar 1889
2103	Swygert, Sarah		Application for writ of habeas corpus	7: 245	4 Mar 1889
2104	Hogan, Alice F.	Hoag, O. H.	To quiet title	7: 246	11 Mar 1889

Suit #	Plaintiffs	Defendants	Cause of Suit	Register of Actions Volume: page(s)	Action Date
2105	Savings Bank of Santa Rosa	Thompson, Thomas L. & Thompson, Marion S.	Foreclosure of mortgage	7: 247	13 Mar 1889
2106	Ayers, David	Roux, Andrew F. & Roux, M. L.	Foreclosure of mortgage	7: 248	13 Mar 1889
2107	People	Mills, Richard	Robbery	7: 249	13 Mar 1889
2108	Holt, W. A. S.	Fish, F. L.; Brown, E.; Meeker, M. C.	Foreclosure of mechanic's lien	7: 250	18 Mar 1889
2109	Furbee, T. J.; Ripley, I. D.; Griffin, William; Ely, A. P. (dba Enterprise Planing Mill & Building Co.)	Fish, F. L.; Brown, E.; Meeker, M. C.	Foreclosure of mechanic's lien	7: 251	21 Mar 1889
2110	People	McCabe, A.	Gaming	7: 252	19 Mar 1889
2111	People	Sellers, Eugene	Grand larceny	7: 253	21 Mar 1889
2112	People	Gobie, John	Burglary	7: 254	25 Mar 1889
2113	People	Gobie, John	Burglary	7: 255	25 Mar 1889
2114	Fletcher, D. E. & Justin, Felix		Application for writ of habeas corpus	7: 256	23 Mar 1889
2115	Vandergrift, E. W.	McNamara, James J.; McNamara, Ethel May; McNamara, Maggie; McNamara, James B.; McNamara, Thomas B.; Brown, H. C. (Adm. Est. Margaret McNamara)	Foreclosure of mortgage	7: 257	28 Mar 1889
2116	Pacific Mutual Life Insurance Company of California	Pickett, William & Pickett, Catharine B.	To foreclose pledge	7: 258	23 Mar 1889
2117	Barnes, John J.	Barnes, Ella M. T.	Divorce	7: 259	1 Apr 1889
2118	Ashurst, John H.	Rayner, Ann & Rayner, John	Foreclosure of mortgage	7: 260	1 Apr 1889
2119	People	Martin, John	Grand larceny	7: 261	30 Mar 1889
2120	Garnier, Jean Baptiste Emile	Lancel, Anselme		7: 262	6 Apr 1889

248

Suit #	Plaintiffs	Defendants	Cause of Suit	Register of Actions Volume: page(s)	Action Date
2121	Dortmond, Henry	Petaluma, City of & Studdert, Michael (Street Commissioner of Petaluma)		7: 263	5 Apr 1889
2122	Williams, George R.	Hartman, W. D.; Hartman, Hattie, his wife; Meyer, Samuel; Doe, John; Roe, Richard; Smith, Jane	Foreclosure of mortgage	7: 264	6 Apr 1889
2123	Watriss, Martha C.	Reed, E. S.	Ejectment	7: 265; 9: 235	11 Apr 1889
2124	Baker, Clara	Baker, Theodore	Divorce	7: 266	11 Apr 1889
2125	McReynolds, Elizabeth	McReynolds, R. E. L.	Divorce	7: 267	12 Apr 1889
2126	People	Butler, James	Burglary	7: 268	11 Apr 1889
2127	People	Lopez, Bernardo	Murder	7: 269	11 Apr 1889
2128	McGown, J. E. & Clarkson, P. M. (dba McGown & Clarkson)	Santa Rosa, Common Council of the City of	Application for a writ of mandamus	7: 270	12 Apr 1889
2129	Holst, Peter		Voluntary insolvency	7: 271	12 Apr 1889
2130	Cropley, William & Cropley, H. M. (dba Cropley & Son)		Voluntary insolvency	7: 272, 295, 334, 384	16 Apr 1889
2131	Mecham, H.	Faught, Willis; Goodman, James; Tucker, M. W.	Promissory note	7: 273	17 Apr 1889
2132	Sam, Ah		Application for writ of habeas corpus	7: 274	16 Apr 1889
2133	Martin, John		Application for writ of habeas corpus	7: 275	16 Apr 1889
2134	Kendall, Homer		Application for writ of habeas corpus	7: 276	16 Apr 1889

Suit #	Plaintiffs	Defendants	Cause of Suit	Register of Actions Volume: page(s)	Action Date
2135	People	Justin, Felix & Fletcher, D. E.	Obtaining money by false pretenses	7: 277	19 Apr 1889
2136	Poppe, Charles J.		Application to be released from bond	7: 278	24 Apr 1889
2137	Kennedy, C. W.	Kennedy, George H.	To quiet title	7: 279	27 Apr 1889
2138	Cannan, S. W.	Jaffe, L.	Appeal	7: 280	1 May 1889
2139	People	Haw, Jack Wah	Murder	7: 282	10 May 1889
2140	Millikin, Belle	Millikin, Daniel	Divorce	7: 283	13 May 1889
2141	Hall, E. G.		Voluntary insolvency	7: 284	15 May 1889
2142	Pasalaqua, Frank	Marchisio, Delfino		7: 285	14 May 1889
2143	Joyce, Martin	Rodgers, Edward		7: 286	14 May 1889
2144	Tupper, G. A.	Gamble, Abram & Gamble, Mary C.	Foreclosure of mortgage	7: 287	16 May 1889
2145	Denny, Carrie	Denny, John P.	Divorce	7: 288	14 May 1889
2146	Carroll, Mary Alice	Carroll, Patrick	Divorce	7: 289, 310	16 May 1889
2147	Gounsky, Fanny	Gounsky, J.	Divorce	7: 290	17 May 1889
2148	Hamilton, James P.	Hood, George, Sr. (Adm. Est. Marie Richardson)		7: 291	23 May 1889
2149	People	Prowse, James	Murder	7: 292	25 May 1889
2150	People	Murphy, Matt & Russell, Henry	Arson	7: 293	28 May 1889
2151	Pedrini, Angelo	Brown, William	Damages	7: 294	21 May 1889
2152	Bank of Healdsburg	Kennedy, G. H.	Promissory note	7: 295	21 May 1889
2153	Marchisio, Katie	Marchisio, Delfino	Divorce	7: 296	29 May 1889
2154	Bank of Healdsburg	Barker, John; Payne, William; Carmichael, J. T.	To quiet title	7: 297	31 May 1889
2155	Nichols, Asa C.	Cropley, William; Cropley, H. M.; Colgan, E. P. (Assignee Cropley & Son); Doe, Reuben; Doe, Mary	Foreclosure of mortgage	7: 298	3 Jun 1889

Suit #	Plaintiffs	Defendants	Cause of Suit	Register of Actions Volume: page(s)	Action Date
2156	Santa Rosa, City of	Duncan, Florence B.; Duncan, S. M., Jr.; Boyce, J. F.; Boyce, Martha A.; Wheeler, Jacob; Savings Bank of Santa Rosa; Bank of Sonoma County		7 : 299	5 Jun 1889
2157	Rogers, E. A.	Sonoma, Board of Supervisors of the County of	Application for a writ of mandamus	7 : 300	5 Jun 1889
2158	Fowler, Annie C.	Cooper, F. M. & Cooper, Annie O.		7 : 301	6 Jun 1889
2159	Berringer, William	Deveraux, E. W.	Promissory note	7 : 302	7 Jun 1889
2160	Vaughn, E. K.	Miller, G. T.; Phillips, D. D.; Phillips, S. E.		7 : 303	8 Jun 1889
2161	Walsh, Michael		Voluntary insolvency	7 : 304	13 Jun 1889
2162	Lord, Bessie A.	Lord, F. F.	Divorce	7 : 305	14 Jun 1889
2163	Johnson, Margaret	Johnson, James Charles	Divorce	7 : 306	14 Jun 1889
2164	Von Geldern, Minnie Francisca Elizabeth	Von Geldern, Joseph	Divorce	7 : 307	15 Jun 1889
2165	Hansen, Sarah	Hansen, Henry	Divorce	7 : 308	17 Jun 1889
2166	Sonoma, County of	Santa Rosa, City of	Appeal	7 : 309	3 Jun 1889
2167	People	Barnes, H. L.	Burglary	7 : 310	3 Jun 1889
2168	Daly, Edward		Application for writ of habeas corpus	7 : 311	5 Jun 1889
2169	Burnham, J. W.		Application for writ of habeas corpus	7 : 312	8 Jun 1889
2170	Green, William S.	Baxter, T. P. & Green, Paul F. (dba Baxter & Green)	Attachment	7 : 313	21 Jun 1889
2171	Santa Rosa Bank	Baxter, T. P. & Green, P. F. (dba Baxter & Green)	Account	7 : 314	22 Jun 1889
2172	Bosworth, James O., Jr.; Bosworth, Clemena D.; Bosworth, Viola; Bosworth, Lucinda W.; Bosworth, Albert (minors by their guardian C. M. Bosworth); Bosworth, Fannie L.	Bosworth, Lillian V.	To quiet title	7 : 315	24 Jun 1889

251

Suit #	Plaintiffs	Defendants	Cause of Suit	Register of Actions Volume: page(s)	Action Date
2173	Johnson, Mary	Pipher, Andrew & Pipher, Philip		7: 316	26 Jun 1889
2174	Pabst, George		Voluntary insolvency	7: 317	26 Jun 1889
2175	Baxter, Thomas P. & Green, Paul F. (dba Baxter & Green)		Involuntary insolvency	7: 318, 382, 371	27 Jun 1889
2176	Williams, Harriet	Donahue, James M.	To quiet title	7: 319; 9: 249	2 Jul 1889
2177	Glenn, Robert	Watson, Charles N. & Meeker, M. C.	Foreclosure of mortgage	7: 320	9 Jul 1889
2178	McNamara, B.		Application for writ of habeas corpus	7: 321	10 Jul 1889
2179	People	Wilson, J. K. (True name Wilson, J. R.)	Attempt to commit burglary	7: 322	10 Jul 1889
2180	Cooper, Lewis S.	Adams, John & Adams, H. D. R.	Foreclosure of mortgage	7: 323	11 Jul 1889
2181	Bates, George E.	Hoen, Mary Anderson (Adm. Est. Berthold Hoen); Hoen, Mary Anderson; Hoen, Mary E.; Hoen, Bertha; Hoen, Ernest M.; Hoen, Carl A.; Hahman, Henrietta A. (Adm. Est. Feodore Gustave Hahman); Hahman, Henrietta A.; Hahman, Henry G.; Hahman, Charlotte; Hahman, Paul; Hahman, Paulina; Hahman, Clara; Hahman, Martha; Hartman, John Doe; Hartman, Mary Roe	To quiet title	7: 324	15 Jul 1889
2182	Smith, Elwood & Randolph, Jess	Marshall, Robert & Harbin, William		7: 325	13 Jul 1889
2183	Bank of Healdsburg	Hall, E. G.; Hall, R. H.; Coffman, J. T. (Assignee of E. G. Hall, an insolvent debtor)	Foreclosure of mortgage	7: 326	16 Jul 1889
2184	Davis, G. W.; Davis, E. W.; Davis, William R.	Pipher, Philip & Pipher, Andrew	Foreclosure of mortgage	7: 327	20 Jul 1889
2185	Badger, Carrie F.		Sole trader	7: 328	22 Jul 1889

Suit #	Plaintiffs	Defendants	Cause of Suit	Register of Actions Volume: page(s)	Action Date
2186	Drees, Gustav A. (As guardian of W. E. Drees & H. A. Drees, minors)	Drees, Ernest E. (Adm. Est. Johanna H. L. Drees)		7: 329	29 Jul 1889
2187	Palmer, J. M.	Humphries, Charles		7: 330	31 Jul 1889
2188	San Francisco & North Pacific Railway Company	Buckland, C. J. & Brush, J. H.	Condemnation of right of way	7: 331	1 Aug 1889
2189	San Francisco & North Pacific Railway Company	Clark, David	Condemnation of right of way	7: 332	1 Aug 1889
2190	Burris, Elizabeth & Burris, Jessie (Adm. Est. William Burris)	Gawne, John & Alexander, William		7: 333	1 Aug 1889
2191	Polifka, Kreszentia	Polifka, Charles		7: 334	2 Aug 1889
2192	Magnolia and Healdsburg Fruit Company	Guerne, George E.		7: 335, 348	8 Aug 1889
2193	Magnolia and Healdsburg Fruit Company	Cottle, J. W. & Smith, J. W.		7: 336, 350	8 Aug 1889
2194	Welch, Patrick & Welch, M. E., his wife	Tighe, Kelly	Damages	7: 337	3 Aug 1889
2195	Cronin, Patrick	Rains, Gallant	Appeal	7: 338	5 Aug 1889
2196	People	Carrillo, Frank & Donovan, Bart	Assault with intent to rob	7: 339	12 Aug 1889
2197	People	Wilson, Thomas	Murder	7: 340	12 Aug 1889
2198	People	Hatch, J. H.	Assault with a deadly weapon	7: 341	12 Aug 1889
2199	People	Clark, William	Burglary	7: 342	15 Aug 1889
2200	Young, Mary L.	Young, James B.	Promissory note	7: 343	12 Aug 1889
2201	Wiester, W. H.	Parker, John F. & Parker, Emily, his wife	Foreclosure of mortgage	7: 344	13 Aug 1889
2202	Button, I. V.	Bihler, William	Appeal	7: 345	19 Aug 1889
2203	Young, J. S.	Hotchkiss, W. J.; Guerne, George E.; Cottle, J. W.; Raabe, M.		7: 346	13 Aug 1889

Suit #	Plaintiffs	Defendants	Cause of Suit	Register of Actions Volume: page(s)	Action Date
2204	Young, Mary L.	Young, James B. & Young, John E.	Divorce	7 : 347	15 Aug 1889
2205	Brush, J. H.	Wood, Joseph D. & Wood, Ellen	Foreclosure of mortgage	7 : 348	15 Aug 1889
2206	Sonoma County Water Company	Elphick, Thomas		7 : 349	16 Aug 1889
2207	Fritch, John	Bowman, J. C.	Promissory note	7 : 350	19 Aug 1889
2208	Dorman, Jane	Dorman, James	Divorce	7 : 351	19 Aug 1889
2209	Bowles, J. M.	Bryan, E. (Mrs.) & Bryan, F. J.	Promissory note	7 : 352	23 Aug 1889
2210	Melton, William W.; Melton, James B.; Melton, Robert W.; Melton, Clymena (minors by the guardians of their persons and estates A. B. Nalley & E. H. Barnes)	Truitt, R. K.	Foreclosure of mortgage	7 : 353	24 Aug 1889
2211	Farquar, C. S.	Miller, J. H.	Promissory note	7 : 354	26 Aug 1889
2212	Kessler, August	Connor, E. P.	On judgment	7 : 355	26 Aug 1889
2213	Jones, John H.	Hoag, O. H.	To quiet title	7 : 356	26 Aug 1889
2214	Bloch, Lora A.	Bloch, George, Jr.	Divorce	7 : 357	26 Aug 1889
2215	Cohen, A. S.	Englehardt, F.	Appeal	7 : 358	21 Aug 1889
2216	Santa Rosa Bank	Langley, Jacob	Foreclosure of mortgage	7 : 359	26 Aug 1889
2217	Pearce, George	Clark, James, Sr.; Clark, W. H.; Clark, J. T.; Clark, James, Jr.	Appeal	7 : 360	2 Sep 1889
2218	Barnes, H. L.	Barnes, Sallie J.	Divorce	7 : 361	4 Sep 1889
2219	Hewitt, Emma	Hewitt, Chassuel F.	Divorce	7 : 362	7 Sep 1889
2220	Ord, Augustias	Moritz, Michel		7 : 363	6 Sep 1889
2221	Fulkerson, Rachel A.	Fulkerson, John	Divorce	7 : 364	4 Sep 1889
2222	Wickersham, I. G.	Sears, G. C. P.; Sears, Franklin; Snyder, Rachel J.	Promissory note	7 : 365	5 Sep 1889
2223	Wickersham, I. G.	Sears, G. C. P.; Sears, Franklin; Craig, Oliver W.	Promissory note	7 : 366	5 Sep 1889

Suit #	Plaintiffs	Defendants	Cause of Suit	Register of Actions Volume: page(s)	Action Date
2224	Forsyth, J. H.	Forsyth, W. B.	Promissory note	7 : 367	10 Sep 1889
2225	Santa Rosa, City of	Armstrong, Sheldon	Condemnation	7 : 368	10 Sep 1889
2226	Santa Rosa, City of	Teague, C. P.	Condemnation	7 : 369	10 Sep 1889
2227	Santa Rosa, City of	Tunly, B.	Condemnation	7 : 370	10 Sep 1889
2228	Santa Rosa, City of	Santa Rosa Packing Company	Condemnation	7 : 371	11 Sep 1889
2229	Powell, R.	Hall, E. G.; Ellis, E. G.; Coffman, J. T. (Assignee of E. G. Hall, an insolvent debtor); Big Bottom Mill Company of Guerneville; Brown, Albert; Armstrong, J. B.; Armstrong, Catharine M.; Armstrong, Lizzie	Foreclosure of mortgage	7 : 372	11 Sep 1889
2230	Leary, Minnie	Leary, Austin A.	Divorce	7 : 373	12 Sep 1889
2231	Wrightson, Francis	Knust, Charles & Knust, Sarah	Foreclosure of mortgage	7 : 374	13 Sep 1889
2232	Burris, John F.	Rehart, F. M.	To quiet title	7 : 375	16 Sep 1889
2233	Alexander, Thomas	Carmichael, J. T. (Adm. Est. Archibald Carmichael)	Foreclosure of mortgage	7 : 376	18 Sep 1889
2234	Bank of Healdsburg	Mintzer, A. E.; Swain, R. M. (Adm. Est. P. B. Mintzer); Rehart, Fannie M.; Burris, John F.; Malloy, John; Kelly, C. E.	Foreclosure of mortgage	7 : 377	18 Sep 1889
2235	Fix, J. K. & Fix, Mary R. J.		Application for writ of habeas corpus	7 : 378	16 Sep 1889
2236	Martin, F. McG.	Sonoma, County of	Appeal	7 : 379	18 Sep 1889
2237	People	Lamar, W. F.	Burglary	7 : 380	14 Sep 1889
2238	People	Johnson, George & Eldridge, William	Burglary	7 : 381	14 Sep 1889
2239	People	Taylor, Clay	Burglary	7 : 383	23 Sep 1889

Suit #	Plaintiffs	Defendants	Cause of Suit	Register of Actions Volume: page(s)	Action Date
2240	People	Taylor, Clay	Burglary	7: 383½	23 Sep 1889
2241	Gaffeny, Miles		Application for writ of habeas corpus	8: 1	25 Sep 1889
2242	Macdonald, D. F.		Application for writ of habeas corpus	8: 2	5 Oct 1889
2243	Lippitt, E. S.	Petaluma, Board of Trustees of the City of	Writ of mandate	8: 3	12 Oct 1889
2244	People	Hale, Elias	Grand larceny	8: 4	14 Oct 1889
2245	McCluskey, William	Austin, Charles & Austin, Rosie	Foreclosure of mortgage	8: 5	19 Sep 1889
2246	Carrington, C. N.	King, G. F.	Appeal	8: 6	19 Oct 1889
2247	Watson, Charles N.		Voluntary insolvency	8: 7	21 Sep 1889
2248	Ossman, Abner	Tumblin, David	Attachment	8: 8	23 Sep 1889
2249	Haskell, William B.	Lawler, Bridget	Attachment	8: 9	25 Sep 1889
2250	Praetzel, Albert		Voluntary insolvency	8: 10	25 Sep 1889
2251	Farmer, Henry Thomas & Farmer, Frances May	Fox, Sarah Angeline; Farmer, Lillie Bell; Farmer, C. C. (Trustee for Sarah Angeline Fox, Henry Thomas Farmer, Frances May Farmer & Lillie Bell Farmer, a minor)	Partition	8: 11	26 Sep 1889
2252	Bihler, William	Frunz, N.	Attachment	8: 12	30 Sep 1889
2253	Hopkins, Moses	Hoen, Mary Anderson; Hoen, Mary Anderson (Executrix Will Berthold Hoen); Hoen, Mary Elizabeth; Hoen, Bertha; Hoen, Ernest Martin; Hoen, Carl Anderson; Bell, Henry	To quiet title	8: 13	27 Sep 1889

256

Suit #	Plaintiffs	Defendants	Cause of Suit	Register of Actions Volume: page(s)	Action Date
2254	Warner, Alexander	Lancel, Anselme H.; Doe, John; Roe, Richard; Small, John; Light, Jane; Dark, Mary; Lancel, Eugene H.; Lancel, Leon A.; Stewart, J. H.	Foreclosure of mortgage	8: 14	2 Oct 1889
2255	Warner, Alexander	Lancel, Anselme H.; Lancel, Eugene H.; Lancel, Leon A.; Doe, John; Roe, Richard; Small, John; Light, Jane; Dark, Mary	Foreclosure of mortgage	8: 15	2 Oct 1889
2256	Wood, Ben S.	Richard, G. W.	Attachment	8: 16	2 Oct 1889
2257	Sanger, Casker M.	Henderson, Charles; Green, William S.; Seawell, James W.; Seawell, Alice; Seawell, George C.; Faessler, R.	Foreclosure of mortgage	8: 17	5 Oct 1889
2258	Meeker, Melvin C.	Fish, Francis L.	Foreclosure of mortgage	8: 18	26 Sep 1889
2259	Holden, E. S. & Harris, T. M.	Ford, M.	Attachment	8: 19	11 Oct 1889
2260	Connell, John	Millerick, John	Attachment	8: 20	14 Oct 1889
2261	Gillespie, Lizzie & Gillespie, William M., her husband	Kearney, Dennis H.; Kearney, Annie, his wife; De Coe, Thomas C.; Ames, Charles G.; Farmer, Charles R.; Farmer, Henry T.; Farmer, Francis May; Farmer, Rebecca W.; Fox, Sarah Angeline; Fox, John Doe; Farmer, Lillie Bell (a minor); Doe, John; Doe, Susan; Roe, Richard; Stiles, Mary; Black, John; Black, Sarah	Foreclosure of mortgage	8: 21	14 Oct 1889
2262	Lippitt, E. S.	Edwards, W. P.		8: 22	4 Oct 1889
2263	People	Nick, A. D.	Gaming	8: 23	24 Oct 1889
2264	People	Bell, Charles	Burglary	8: 24	26 Oct 1889
2265	People	Grater, Henry	Gaming	8: 25	24 Oct 1889
2266	People	Jones, C. B.	Grand larceny	8: 26	4 Nov 1889
2267	People	Burns, John Doe (alias Burns, Jud)	Assault with a deadly weapon	8: 27	24 Oct 1889
2268	Yonker, S. N.	Seegelken, E. A.	Appeal	8: 28	4 Nov 1889
2269	Clark, A. E.	Gardner, Clement	Appeal	8: 29	5 Nov 1889
2270	McDonald, Mark L.	Gleason, Patrick		8: 30	17 Oct 1889

257

Suit #	Plaintiffs	Defendants	Cause of Suit	Register of Actions Volume: page(s)	Action Date
2271	Finley, Cynthia J.	Finley, Henry M.	Divorce	8: 31	18 Oct 1889
2272	Fisher, Mollie	Fisher, Eugene	Divorce	8: 32	19 Oct 1889
2273	Hassett, J. T.	Hassett, Ella	Divorce	8: 33	22 Oct 1889
2274	Bumpus, C. H.	Graham, J. P.	Promissory note	8: 34	29 Oct 1889
2275	Chisholm, Annie C.	Chisholm, William	Divorce	8: 35	31 Oct 1889
2276	Taylor, O. A.	Graham, J. P.	Foreclosure of chattel mortgage	8: 36	2 Nov 1889
2277	Massa, Antonio	Bancheri, Bartolmeo & Botto, Giovanni	Foreclosure of mechanic's lien	8: 37	2 Nov 1889
2278	People (ex rel. E. S. Lippitt)	Edwards, W. P.		8: 38	2 Nov 1889
2279	Millerick, M. J.	Millerick, John	Promissory note	8: 39	2 Nov 1889
2280	Yandle, T. J. & Glynn, F. B. (dba Yandle & Glynn)	Graham, J. P.	Attachment	8: 40	4 Nov 1889
2281	Montfort, A. R.		Involuntary insolvency	8: 41	7 Nov 1889
2282	Drummond, E. W.		Voluntary insolvency	8: 42	7 Nov 1889
2283	Graham, J. P.		Voluntary insolvency	8: 43	7 Nov 1889
2284	Badger, H. L.		Voluntary insolvency	8: 44	11 Nov 1889
2285	Bruyere, Louis	Lancel, A.	Promissory note	8: 45	12 Nov 1889
2286	People	Masterson, John	Gaming	8: 46	24 Oct 1889
2287	Roberts, Benjamin F.	Roberts, Ella Jane	Divorce	8: 47	21 Sep 1889
2288	Hassett, J. T.	Hassett, Ella	Divorce	8: 48	13 Nov 1889
2289	Pulver, O. H.	Murphy, Wyman	Damages	8: 49	13 Nov 1889

258

Suit #	Plaintiffs	Defendants	Cause of Suit	Register of Actions Volume: page(s)	Action Date
2290	Schwan, Leonard & Schwan, Wilhelmina	Drummond, E. W. & Drummond, Harriet Elizabeth	Foreclosure of mortgage	8: 50	14 Nov 1889
2291	Pauli, John	Kendall, John & Kendall, Maria		8: 51	15 Nov 1889
2292	Holman, Francis C.	Knecht, Frederich	Foreclosure of mortgage	8: 52	19 Nov 1889
2293	Grissim, W. H.	Bishop, Mary (Adm. Est. T. C. Bishop)		8: 53	21 Nov 1889
2294	Powell, Ransom	Truitt, R. K. & Truitt, E. R.		8: 54	22 Nov 1889
2295	Savings Bank of Santa Rosa	Smith, James L.	Foreclosure of mortgage	8: 55	22 Nov 1889
2296	Müller, John	Müller, Maria	Promissory note	8: 56	26 Nov 1889
2297	Farquar, C. S.	Decker, Phoebe M.	Attachment	8: 57	26 Nov 1889
2298	Antram, Mary	Galvin, M. J. C.	Foreclosure of mortgage	8: 58	27 Nov 1889
2299	Duncans Mills Land and Lumber Company	Dollar, John M.; Fraser, William; Duncan Mills Lumber Company	Unlawful detainer	8: 59	29 Nov 1889
2300	Moody, Richard	Manning, N. E. & Manning, Kate, his wife	Foreclosure of mortgage	8: 60	3 Dec 1889
2301	Hopper, Thomas	Holmes, Henderson P. & Holmes, Rebecca M.	Foreclosure of mortgage	8: 61	5 Dec 1889
2302	Gutermute, H. S.	Furner, George	Attachment	8: 62	5 Dec 1889
2303	Donahue, James M.; Von Schroeder, Mary Ellen; Donahue, Annie	Peters, John T.; Peters, Norah; Harrison, A.	Foreclosure of mortgage	8: 63	7 Dec 1889
2304	Savings Bank of Santa Rosa	Drummond, John H.	Foreclosure of mortgage	8: 64	2 Dec 1889
2305	Curtis, Catharine	Curtis, Richard H.	Divorce	8: 65	3 Dec 1889
2306	Drummond, Harriet E.	Drummond, Erastus W.	Divorce	8: 66	10 Dec 1889
2307	Litton, Agnes D.	Donahue, James M.		8: 67	13 Dec 1889
2308	McChristian, Sarah	Faught, John H. & Keser, Louis, Jr.	Foreclosure of mortgage	8: 68	30 Nov 1889

Suit #	Plaintiffs	Defendants	Cause of Suit	Register of Actions Volume: page(s)	Action Date
2309	Genazzi, Annie A.	Genazzi, Louis	Divorce	8: 69	30 Nov 1889
2310	Coffey, Henry	Starr, Theodore C.	Writ of mandate	8: 70	14 Dec 1889
2311	Martin, F. McG.	Sonoma, Board of Supervisors of the County of	Writ of mandate	8: 71	18 Dec 1889
2312	Bank of Sonoma County	Smith, W. H. E.	Promissory note	8: 72	18 Dec 1889
2313	Green, Julia B.	Green, Thomas W.	Divorce	8: 73	18 Dec 1889
2314	Burris, John F.	Gardner, Clement	Damages	8: 74	19 Dec 1889
2315	Anderson, Mary A.	Tomblin, David	Promissory note	8: 75	19 Dec 1889
2316	Jasper, G. A. & Rees, T.		Application for writ of habeas corpus	8: 76	21 Dec 1889
2317	Andrew (an Indian)		Application for writ of habeas corpus	8: 77	24 Dec 1889
2318	People	Drummond, E. W.	Assault with intent to commit rape	8: 78	24 Dec 1889
2319	People	Drummond, E. W.	Assault with intent to commit rape	8: 79	24 Dec 1889
2320	People	Neyce, J. H.	Embezzlement	8: 80	24 Dec 1889
2321	Schierhold, H. & Wohlers, Theodore		Application for writ of prohibition	8: 81	16 Dec 1889
2322	Graham, Albert W.		Voluntary insolvency	8: 82	21 Dec 1889
2323	First Baptist Church of Healdsburg		Application to sell real estate	8: 83	23 Dec 1889

Suit #	Plaintiffs	Defendants	Cause of Suit	Register of Actions Volume: page(s)	Action Date
2324	Nichols, Ellen W. (Executrix Will Asa. C. Nichols)	Cropley, William; Cropley, H. M.; Colgan, E. P. (Assignee of William Cropley & Cropley & Son, insolvent debtors)	Foreclosure of mortgage	8 : 84	26 Dec 1889
2325	Wilgues, Lola & Wilgues, Lorenzo D.	De Forest, William F. & De Forest, Margaret	To set aside sale	8 : 85	27 Dec 1889
2326	Fogaerty, Michael		Voluntary insolvency	8 : 86	31 Dec 1889

Heritage Books by the Sonoma County Genealogical Society, Inc.:

www.ingramcontent.com/pod-product-compliance
Lightning Source LLC
Chambersburg PA
CBHW080233270326
41926CB00020B/4219